FODOR'S BED & BREAKFASTS
AND COUNTRY INNS

California's Best Bed & Breakfasts

2nd Edition

*Delightful Places to Stay and Great
Things to Do When You Get There*

Fodor's Travel Publications, Inc.
New York • Toronto • London • Sydney • Auckland

California's Best Bed & Breakfasts

Editor: Daniel Mangin
Contributors: Colleen Dunn Bates, Robert Blake, Deke Castleman, Dennis Harvey, Pamela P. Hegarty, Patrick Hoctel, Marty Olmstead, Tracy Patruno, Terry Trucco, Bobbi Zane
Creative Director: Fabrizio La Rocca
Cartographer: David Lindroth
Illustrators: Alida Beck, Karl Tanner
Cover Design: Guido Caroti
Cover Photograph: Francis Hammond

Special Sales

Contributors

Colleen Dunn Bates, who contributed to the Central Coast chapter, is the food editor for the *Los Angeles Times* syndicate. A resident of Pasadena, she was formerly the editor of the Gault Millau series of guidebooks and a contributing editor for *L.A. Style.*

Deke Castleman, who contributed to the High Sierra chapter, is the author of *Nevada Handbook* and Discover America's *Las Vegas,* and is managing editor of the *Las Vegas Advisor.* A resident of Las Vegas, he is a frequent contributor to many Fodor's guides, including *Fodor's California '95, America's Best Bed & Breakfasts,* and *Bed & Breakfasts and Country Inns: The Southwest.*

Dennis Harvey, who updated the Monterey Bay chapter and the North Coast and Redwood Country chapter, is a San Francisco–based freelance writer. He is the Bay Area correspondent for *Variety,* and has written articles on entertainment and travel for national publications such as *Details* and for the *San Francisco Chronicle* and the *San Francisco Bay Guardian.*

Pamela P. Hegarty, who lives in the San Francisco Bay Area, has written extensively on travel in northern California and is the author of *San Francisco and Beyond: 101 Affordable Excursions.* Her work has appeared in *Woman's Day, Good Housekeeping,* and other prominent publications. She wrote the San Francisco and Bay Area chapters.

Patrick Hoctel updated the San Francisco chapter. He is the assistant editor of the *Bay Area Reporter,* a weekly newspaper, and has published short fiction in *Christopher Street* and other national publications. His travel writing includes contributions to *Fodor's San Francisco '95* and *Fodor's California '95.*

Marty Olmstead, a travel writer and editor who lives in Sonoma, California, wrote the Wine Country chapter and contributed to the Bay Area chapter. She is co-author of *Hidden Florida* and writes for numerous publications about California food, wine, travel, and history.

Terry Trucco, who wrote the Gold Country chapter, grew up in northern California. Currently living in New York City, she writes on a variety of subjects, including travel, design, and beauty, for the *New York Times,* the *Wall Street Journal, Travel & Leisure,* and other publications.

Bobbi Zane, who wrote six California chapters, lives in southern California and is the publisher of *Yellow Brick Road,* a monthly newsletter devoted to bed-and-breakfast travel in the western United States. A contributor to *Fodor's California '95* and *Fodor's Los Angeles '95,* her byline has also appeared in the *Orange County Register* and the *Los Angeles Times.*

Contents

Foreword v
Introduction vi

Southern Counties *1*
Including San Diego and Palm Springs

The San Bernardino Mountains *17*
From Lake Arrowhead to Big Bear Lake

Los Angeles *27*
With Orange County

Central Coast *47*
From Santa Barbara to San Simeon

Monterey Bay *71*
Including Santa Cruz and Carmel

San Francisco *91*
From North Beach to the Sunset District

Bay Area *113*
Marin, East Bay, and the Peninsula

Wine Country *129*
Napa, Sonoma, Southern Mendocino Counties

North Coast and Redwood Country *149*
Including Mendocino and Eureka

Sacramento and the Central Valley *165*
Including the Sierra Foothills

Gold Country *177*
Along Highway 49

High Sierra *195*
Including Yosemite, Lake Tahoe, and Western Nevada

Directory 1: Alphabetical *214*

Directory 2: Geographical *217*

Maps
The Bay Area ix, Northern California x–xi,
Southern California xii–xiii

Foreword

While every care has been taken to ensure the accuracy of the information in this guide, the passage of time will always bring change, and consequently, the publisher cannot accept responsibility for errors that may occur.

All prices and listings are based on information supplied to us at press time. Details may change, however, and the prudent traveler will avoid inconvenience by calling ahead.

Fodor's wants to hear about your travel experiences, both pleasant and unpleasant. When an inn or B&B fails to live up to its billing, let us know and we will investigate the complaint and revise our entries where the facts warrant it.

Send your letters to the editors of Fodor's Travel Publications, 201 E. 50th St., New York, NY 10022.

Introduction

You'll find bed-and-breakfasts in big houses with turrets and little houses with decks, in mansions by the water and cabins in the forest, not to mention structures of many sizes and shapes in between. B&Bs are run by people who were once lawyers and writers, homemakers and artists, nurses and architects, singers and businesspeople. Some B&Bs are just a room or two in a hospitable local's home; others are more like small inns. So there's an element of serendipity to every B&B stay.

But while that's part of the pleasure of the experience, it's also an excellent reason to plan your travels with a good B&B guide. The one you hold in your hands serves the purpose neatly.

To create it, we've hand-picked a team of professional writers who are also confirmed B&B lovers: people who adore the many manifestations of the Victorian era; who go wild over wicker and brass beds, four-posters and fireplaces; and who know a well-run operation when they see it and are only too eager to communicate their knowledge to you. We've instructed them to inspect the premises and check out every corner of the premier bed-and-breakfasts and inns in the areas they cover, and to report critically on only the best in every price range.

They've returned from their travels with comprehensive reports on the pleasure of B&B travel, which may well become your pleasure as you read their reports in the pages that follow. These are establishments that promise a unique experience, a distinctive sense of time and place. All are destinations in themselves, not just places to rest your head at night, but an integral part of a weekend escape. You'll learn what's good, what's bad, and what could be better; what our writers liked and what you might not like.

At the same time, Fodor's reviewers tell you what's up in the area and what you should and shouldn't miss—everything from historic sites and parks to antiques shops, boutiques, and the area's niftiest restaurants and nightspots. We also include names and addresses of B&B reservation services, just in case you're inspired to seek out additional properties on your own. Reviews are organized by region.

In the italicized service information that ends every review, a second address in parentheses is a mailing address. A double room is for two people, regardless of the size or type of its beds. Unless otherwise noted, rooms don't have phones or TVs. Note that even the most stunning homes, farmhouses and mansions alike, may not provide a private bathroom for each individual. Rates are for two, excluding tax, in the high season and include breakfast unless otherwise noted; ask about special packages and midweek or off-season discounts.

What we call a restaurant serves meals other than breakfast and is usually open to the general public. At inns listed as operating on the Modified American Plan (MAP), rates include two meals, generally breakfast and dinner.

Where applicable, we note seasonal and other restrictions. Although we abhor discrimination, we have conveyed information about innkeepers' restrictive practices so that you will be aware of the prevailing attitudes. Such discriminatory practices are most often applied to parents traveling with small children, who may not, in any case, feel comfortable having their offspring toddle amid breakable bric-a-brac and near precipitous stairways.

When traveling the B&B way, always call ahead; and if you have mobility problems or are traveling with children, if you prefer a private bath or a certain type of bed, or if you have specific dietary needs or any other concerns, discuss them with the innkeeper. At the same time, if you're traveling to an inn because of a specific feature, make sure that it will be

*available when you get there and not closed for renovation.
The same goes if you're making a detour to take advantage of
specific sights or attractions.*

*It's a sad commentary on other B&B guides today that we feel
obliged to tell you that our writers did, in fact, visit every
property in person, and that it is they, not the innkeepers, who
wrote the reviews. No one paid a fee or promised to sell or
promote the book in order to be included in it. (In fact, one of
the most challenging parts of the work of a Fodor's writer is to
persuade innkeepers and B&B owners that he or she wants
nothing more than a tour of the premises and answers to a few
questions!) Fodor's has no stake in anything but the truth. If a
room is dark, with peeling wallpaper, we don't call it quaint or
atmospheric—we call it run-down and then steer you to a
more appealing section of the property.*

*So trust us, the way you'd trust a knowledgeable, well-traveled
friend. Let us hear from you about your travels, whether you
found that the B&Bs you visited surpassed their descriptions
or the other way around. And have a wonderful trip!*

*Karen Cure
Editorial Director*

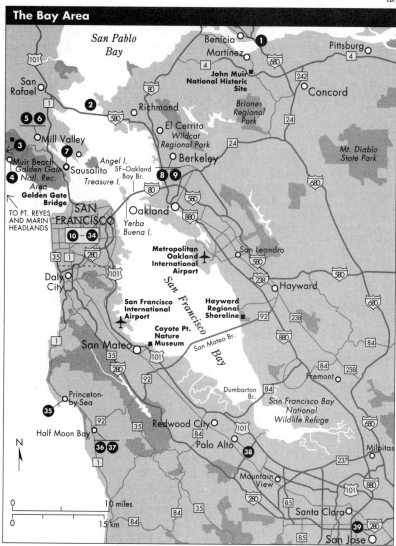

The Bay Area

The Alamo Square Inn, **34**

Albion House Inn, **10**

Archbishops Mansion, **11**

Bancroft Hotel, **8**

The Bed and Breakfast Inn, **12**

Bock's Bed and Breakfast, **13**

Casa del Mar, **3**

Casa Madrona Hotel, **7**

Chateau Tivoli, **14**

Cowper Inn, **38**

East Brother Light Station, **2**

Golden Gate Hotel, **15**

Gramma's Inn, **9**

The Hensley House, **39**

Hotel Griffon, **16**

Hotel Triton, **17**

Inn at the Opera, **18**

Inn San Francisco, **19**

Inn at Union Square, **20**

Jackson Court, **21**

James Court Hotel, **22**

The Mansions Hotel, **23**

The Mill Rose Inn, **37**

Mill Valley Inn, **5**

The Monte Cristo, **24**

Mountain Home Inn, **6**

Old Thyme Inn, **36**

The Pelican Inn, **4**

Petite Auberge, **25**

Pillar Point Inn, **35**

The Queen Anne, **26**

Savoy Hotel, **27**

The Sherman House, **28**

Spencer House, **29**

Union Gardens, **1**

Union Street Inn, **30**

Victorian Inn on the Park, **31**

Washington Square Inn, **32**

White Swan Inn, **33**

Abigail's, **31**
The Alpenhaus, **27**
Amber House, **32**
Applewood, **54**
Auberge du Soleil, **68**
Beltane Ranch, **60**
Blackthorne Inn, **65**
The Boonville
Hotel, **45**
Brannan Cottage
Inn, **35**
Busch and Herringlake
Country Inn, **10**
The Cain House, **85**
Camellia Inn, **50**
Camino Hotel, **72**
Campbell Ranch
Inn, **48**
Carter House, **1**
The Chichester–
McKee House, **24**
City Hotel, **78**
Clover Valley Mill
House, **12**
The Coloma Country
Inn, **23**
Combellack-Blair
House, **25**
Cooper House, **80**
The Court Street
Inn, **76**
Cross Roads Inn, **58**
Deer Run Ranch, **17**
El Dorado Hotel, **62**
Dunbar House,
1880, **77**
"An Elegant Victorian
Mansion", **2**
Fallon Hotel, **79**
The Feather Bed, **6**
Flume's End, **14**
The Foxes Bed and
Breakfast Inn, **74**
The Gaige House, **61**
Genoa House Inn, **29**
Gingerbread
Mansion, **3**
Gols Hill Hotel, **18**
Grandmère's, **15**
Grey Gables, **75**
Grey Whale Inn, **38**
Groveland Hotel, **83**
Harbor House, **43**
Harkey House, **21**
Hartley House, **33**
Harvest Inn, **57**
Haus Bavaria, **19**
The Headlands Inn, **39**
Healdsburg Inn
on the Plaza, **51**
The Heirloom, **70**
High Country Inn, **11**

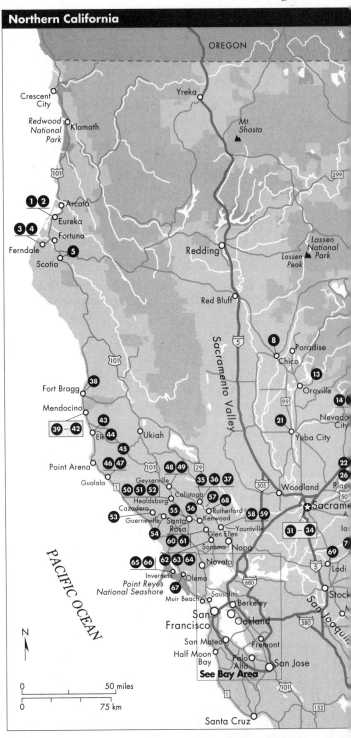

Northern California

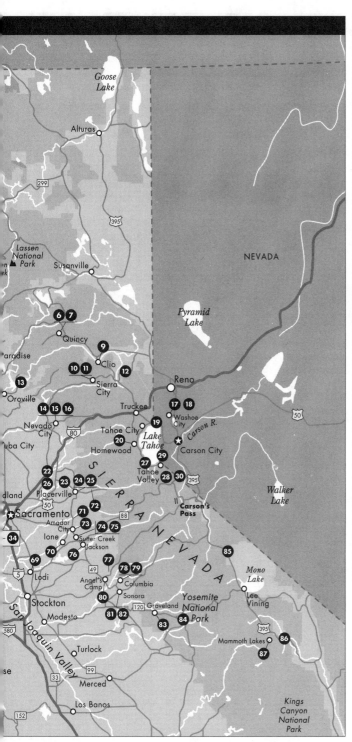

Highland Ranch, **44**

Hope-Merrill
House, **49**

Imperial Hotel, **73**

Indian Creek, **71**

Johnson's Country
Inn, **8**

Joshua Grindle Inn, **40**

Kenwood Inn, **56**

Lake Oroville
Bed and Breakfast, **13**

Larkmead, **36**

Madrona Manor, **52**

Maison Fleurie, **59**

Nenzel Mansion, **30**

New England
Ranch, **7**

Power's
Mansion Inn, **22**

Quail Mountain, **37**

Rachel's Inn, **41**

Rainbow Tarns, **86**

Red Castle Inn, **16**

Rockwood Lodge, **20**

Roundstone Farm, **67**

The Ryan House, **81**

St. Orres, **46**

Scotia Inn, **5**

Serenity, **82**

The Shaw House
Inn, **4**

Sonoma Hotel, **63**

Sorenson's, **28**

The Stanford Inn by
the Sea, **42**

The Sterling Hotel, **34**

Ten Inverness Way, **66**

Thistle Dew Inn, **64**

Timberhill Ranch, **53**

Victorian Manor, **22**

Vintners Inn, **55**

The Whale Watch Inn
by the Sea, **47**

White Horse Inn, **87**

White Sulphur
Springs, **9**

Wine & Roses Country
Inn, **69**

The Yosemite
Peregrine, **84**

Anaheim Country
Inn, **63**
Apple Lane Inn, **6**
Apples Bed and
Breakfast Inn, **69**
Babbling Brook Inn, **9**
Ballard Inn, **34**
Bath Street Inn, **35**
Bayberry Inn, **36**
Bayview Hotel, **7**
The Beach House, **25**
Bed and Breakfast Inn
at La Jolla, **92**
Bella Maggiore Inn, **53**
Blue Lantern Inn, **78**
Blue Quail Inn, **37**
Blue Spruce Inn, **4**
The Blue Whale
Inn, **26**
Brookside Farm, **87**
Carriage House, **79**
The Carriage
House, **65**
Casa Tropicana, **83**
Centrella, **11**
Chalfant House, **2**
Channel Road Inn, **56**
Chateau Du Lac, **66**
The Chesire Cat, **38**
Christmas House, **64**
Cliff Crest Bed and
Breakfast Inn, **10**
The Cottage, **94**
Country Rose Inn, **1**
Eagle Inn, **39**
Eagle's Neat, **70**
Eiler's Inn, **80**
El Encanto, **40**
Garden Street Inn, **31**
Gatehouse Inn, **16**
Glenborough Inn, **41**
Gold Mountain
Manor, **71**
Gosby House, **12**
Green Gables Inn, **13**
Happy Landing
Inn, **19**
Heritage Park Bed &
Breakfast Inn, **95**
Ingleside Inn, **74**
Inn at Depot Hill, **5**
The Inn at
Fawnskin, **68**
Inn at
Laguna Beach, **81**
Inn at Rancho
Santa Fe, **9**
Inn 657, **59**
Inn at
Summer Hill, **51**
Inn on Mt. Ada, **84**
J. Patrick House, **27**
The Jabberwock, **17**

Southern California

PACIFIC OCEAN

San Jose

Santa
Cruz
Capitola
Aptos
Castroville
Salinas
Pacific Grove
Monterey Carmel
Big Sur

San Simeon
Cambria
San Luis Obispo

Santa Maria
Los Alamos
Lompoc Solvang Santa
Barbara
Summerland
Santa Barbara Channel Oxn
Vent

San Miguel

Santa Rosa Santa Cruz

CHANNEL ISLANDS

San Nicolas

Merced
Chowchilla
Los Banos Madera
Fresno

Sierra
National
Forest

SAN JOAQUIN VALLEY

Soledad

Coolinga

Tulare
Lake Bed

McKittrick

Teja
Pa

Visali

N

0   50 miles
0   75 km

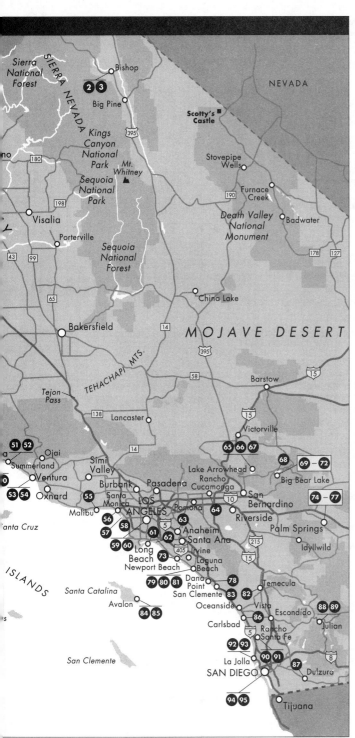

Julian Hotel, **88**

Korakia Pensione, **75**

Loma Vista Bed and Breakfast, **82**

Lord Mayor's Inn, **61**

Malibu Beach Inn, **55**

Mangels House, **8**

Mansion Inn, **58**

Martine Inn, **14**

The Matlick House, **3**

La Mer, **54**

Los Olivos Grand Hotel, **33**

Montecito Inn, **49**

Olallieberry Inn, **28**

Old Monterey Inn, **18**

Old Turner Inn, **85**

Old Yacht Club Inn, **42**

The Olive House, **43**

Orchard Hill Country Inn, **89**

The Parsonage, **44**

Pelican Cove Inn, **86**

Pickford House, **29**

Portofino Beach Hotel, **73**

Post Ranch Inn, **24**

Rancho Valencia Resort, **91**

Romantique Lakeview Lodge, **67**

Salisbury House, **60**

San Ysidro Ranch, **50**

Sandpiper Inn, **20**

Scripps Inn, **93**

Sea View Inn, **21**

Seal Beach Inn and Gardens, **62**

Seven Gables Inn, **15**

Simpson House Inn, **45**

Squibb House, **30**

Stonehouse Inn, **22**

Stonepine, **23**

Summerland Inn, **52**

Switzerland Haus, **72**

Tiffany Inn, **46**

Tres Palmas, **76**

Union Hotel/ Victorian Mansion, **32**

The Upham, **47**

Venice Beach House, **57**

Villa Rosa, **48**

Villa Royale, **77**

Special Features at a Glance

Name of Property	Accessible for Disabled	Antiques	On the Water	Good Value	Car Not Necessary	Full Meal Service	Historic Building	Romantic Hideaway	
SOUTHERN COUNTIES									
Bed and Breakfast Inn at La Jolla	✓	✓					✓		
Brookside Farm		✓		✓		✓		✓	
The Cottage		✓		✓					
Heritage Park Bed & Breakfast Inn	✓	✓			✓		✓		
Ingleside Inn		✓				✓	✓	✓	
Inn at Rancho Santa Fe	✓	✓				✓	✓	✓	
Julian Hotel		✓					✓		
Korakia Pensione		✓					✓		
Loma Vista Bed and Breakfast									
Orchard Hill Country Inn	✓								
Pelican Cove Inn	✓								
Rancho Valencia Resort	✓					✓		✓	
Scripps Inn	✓		✓	✓					
Tres Palmas Bed and Breakfast	✓	✓							
Villa Royale	✓	✓				✓		✓	
SAN BERNARDINO MOUNTAINS									
Apples Bed & Breakfast Inn	✓							✓	
The Carriage House		✓						✓	
Chateau Du Lac		✓						✓	
Eagle's Nest		✓		✓					
Gold Mountain Manor		✓					✓		
The Inn at Fawnskin									
The Romantique Lakeview Lodge		✓					✓		
Switzerland Haus								✓	

Luxurious	Pets Allowed	No Smoking Indoors	Good Place for Families	Beach Nearby	Cross-Country Ski Trails	Golf Within 5 Miles	Fitness Facilities	Near Wineries	Good Biking Terrain	Skiing	Tennis	Swimming on Premises	Conference Facilities	Hiking Nearby
		✓		✓		✓			✓					
		✓												✓
		✓												
		✓			✓	✓								
✓			✓			✓						✓		
✓	✓		✓	✓		✓	✓					✓	✓	
									✓				✓	✓
		✓				✓						✓		
		✓				✓		✓	✓					
		✓							✓				✓	✓
		✓		✓		✓								
✓			✓	✓		✓	✓		✓		✓	✓	✓	
	✓		✓	✓		✓			✓					
		✓				✓			✓			✓		✓
✓						✓			✓			✓		✓
		✓			✓	✓			✓	✓				✓
		✓		✓	✓				✓					✓
✓		✓		✓	✓				✓					✓
	✓		✓		✓	✓			✓	✓				✓
		✓			✓	✓			✓	✓				✓
		✓			✓				✓	✓				✓
		✓			✓				✓					✓
		✓			✓	✓			✓	✓				✓

Special Features at a Glance

Name of Property	Accessible for Disabled	Antiques	On the Water	Good Value	Car Not Necessary	Full Meal Service	Historic Building	Romantic Hideaway
LOS ANGELES/ORANGE COUNTY								
Anaheim Country Inn		✓					✓	
Blue Lantern Inn	✓		✓					✓
Carriage House		✓						
Casa Tropicana			✓			✓		✓
Channel Road Inn	✓	✓					✓	
Christmas House	✓	✓					✓	✓
Eiler's Inn					✓			
Inn at Laguna Beach	✓		✓		✓			
Inn at 657				✓				
Inn on Mt. Ada		✓			✓	✓	✓	✓
Lord Mayor's Inn		✓			✓		✓	
Malibu Beach Inn	✓		✓			✓		✓
Mansion Inn	✓				✓			
Old Turner Inn					✓		✓	✓
Portofino Beach Hotel		✓	✓				✓	✓
Salisbury House				✓			✓	
Seal Beach Inn and Gardens		✓					✓	✓
Venice Beach House		✓		✓			✓	
CENTRAL COAST								
Ballard Inn	✓							✓
Bath Street Inn		✓			✓		✓	
Bayberry Inn		✓			✓			✓
The Beach House			✓					
Bella Maggiore Inn	✓	✓		✓	✓		✓	

Luxurious	Pets Allowed	No Smoking Indoors	Good Place for Families	Beach Nearby	Cross-Country Ski Trails	Golf Within 5 Miles	Fitness Facilities	Near Wineries	Good Biking Terrain	Skiing	Tennis	Swimming on Premises	Conference Facilities	Hiking Nearby
		✓												
✓	✓	✓		✓		✓	✓		✓				✓	✓
	✓			✓										
		✓		✓					✓					
		✓	✓	✓					✓					✓
✓		✓				✓								
				✓		✓								
			✓	✓								✓	✓	
		✓												
✓		✓		✓		✓			✓				✓	✓
		✓		✓										
✓				✓			✓							
			✓	✓		✓			✓					
		✓		✓		✓			✓					✓
				✓		✓			✓					
		✓												
✓		✓		✓								✓	✓	
		✓		✓										
✓		✓						✓	✓					✓
		✓		✓		✓			✓					✓
	✓	✓		✓		✓			✓					✓
		✓	✓	✓					✓					✓
				✓		✓								

Special Features at a Glance

Name of Property	Accessible for Disabled	Antiques	On the Water	Good Value	Car Not Necessary	Full Meal Service	Historic Building	Romantic Hideaway	
Blue Quail Inn		✓		✓	✓			✓	
The Blue Whale Inn			✓					✓	
The Cheshire Cat		✓			✓			✓	
The Eagle Inn				✓	✓				
El Encanto	✓					✓	✓	✓	
Garden Street Inn	✓	✓					✓	✓	
Glenborough Inn		✓			✓		✓	✓	
Inn at Summer Hill	✓							✓	
J. Patrick House	✓	✓						✓	
La Mer		✓							
Los Olivos Grand Hotel	✓	✓			✓	✓		✓	
Montecito Inn	✓			✓	✓	✓	✓		
Olallieberry Inn	✓	✓		✓			✓	✓	
Old Yacht Club Inn		✓		✓			✓	✓	
The Olive House		✓					✓	✓	
The Parsonage		✓					✓	✓	
Pickford House	✓	✓		✓					
San Ysidro Ranch	✓				✓	✓	✓	✓	
Simpson House Inn	✓	✓					✓	✓	
The Squibb House		✓		✓			✓		
Summerland Inn				✓					
Tiffany Inn		✓			✓		✓	✓	
Union Hotel/Victorian Mansion		✓					✓	✓	
The Upham	✓			✓	✓		✓		
Villa Rosa					✓			✓	

	Luxurious	Pets Allowed	No Smoking Indoors	Good Place for Families	Beach Nearby	Cross-Country Ski Trails	Golf Within 5 Miles	Fitness Facilities	Near Wineries	Good Biking Terrain	Skiing	Tennis	Swimming on Premises	Conference Facilities	Hiking Nearby
			✓	✓	✓		✓			✓					
	✓		✓		✓					✓					✓
			✓		✓		✓			✓				✓	
				✓	✓		✓			✓					✓
	✓			✓	✓		✓			✓		✓	✓	✓	
			✓				✓								
			✓		✓		✓			✓					✓
	✓		✓		✓		✓								
			✓		✓										✓
			✓		✓										
	✓								✓	✓			✓	✓	✓
				✓	✓		✓	✓		✓			✓	✓	✓
			✓		✓					✓					✓
			✓		✓		✓	✓		✓					✓
			✓		✓				✓	✓					✓
			✓		✓		✓			✓					✓
				✓	✓					✓					
	✓	✓		✓	✓		✓			✓		✓	✓		✓
	✓		✓		✓		✓			✓					✓
			✓		✓					✓					✓
			✓		✓		✓			✓					
			✓		✓		✓			✓					✓
	✓				✓					✓					✓
					✓		✓			✓				✓	✓
					✓		✓		✓	✓			✓	✓	✓

Special Features at a Glance

Name of Property	Accessible for Disabled	Antiques	On the Water	Good Value	Car Not Necessary	Full Meal Service	Historic Building	Romantic Hideaway	
MONTEREY BAY									
Apple Lane Inn		✓		✓			✓		
Babbling Brook Inn	✓						✓		
Bayview Hotel		✓					✓		
Blue Spruce Inn	✓								
The Centrella	✓						✓		
Cliff Crest Bed and Breakfast Inn		✓							
Country Rose Inn		✓						✓	
Gatehouse Inn	✓	✓	✓				✓		
Gosby House		✓							
Green Gables Inn		✓	✓						
Happy Landing Inn			✓						
Inn at Depot Hill		✓		✓			✓	✓	
The Jabberwock		✓		✓	✓				
Mangels House		✓		✓			✓		
Martine Inn	✓	✓	✓				✓		
Old Monterey Inn		✓						✓	
Post Ranch Inn	✓		✓			✓		✓	
Sandpiper Inn		✓							
Sea View Inn									
Seven Gables Inn		✓	✓				✓		
Stonehouse Inn							✓		
Stonepine		✓				✓		✓	
SAN FRANCISCO									
The Alamo Square Inn					✓		✓	✓	

Luxurious	Pets Allowed	No Smoking Indoors	Good Place for Families	Beach Nearby	Cross-Country Ski Trails	Golf Within 5 Miles	Fitness Facilities	Near Wineries	Good Biking Terrain	Skiing	Tennis	Swimming on Premises	Conference Facilities	Hiking Nearby
	✓	✓	✓	✓		✓	✓	✓	✓					✓
		✓	✓	✓		✓		✓	✓					
		✓	✓			✓		✓	✓					✓
		✓	✓			✓		✓	✓					
		✓	✓			✓		✓						
		✓		✓		✓		✓	✓					
		✓				✓		✓						
		✓		✓		✓			✓					
		✓		✓		✓			✓				✓	
		✓		✓		✓			✓					
		✓		✓		✓								
✓		✓		✓		✓			✓					
		✓		✓		✓			✓				✓	
		✓		✓		✓			✓					✓
✓				✓		✓			✓				✓	
✓		✓		✓		✓			✓				✓	
✓		✓		✓								✓	✓	✓
			✓			✓			✓					
		✓		✓		✓			✓					
		✓		✓		✓			✓					
		✓		✓		✓			✓					
✓						✓	✓		✓		✓	✓		✓
		✓	✓			✓							✓	

Special Features at a Glance

Name of Property	Accessible for Disabled	Antiques	On the Water	Good Value	Car Not Necessary	Full Meal Service	Historic Building	Romantic Hideaway	
Albion House Inn		✓		✓	✓		✓	✓	
Archbishops Mansion		✓		✓	✓		✓	✓	
The Bed and Breakfast Inn					✓			✓	
Bock's Bed and Breakfast				✓	✓			✓	
Chateau Tivoli		✓			✓		✓	✓	
Golden Gate Hotel		✓		✓	✓		✓		
Hotel Griffon	✓		✓	✓		✓	✓	✓	
Hotel Triton	✓			✓		✓		✓	
Inn at the Opera	✓	✓				✓	✓	✓	
Inn San Francisco		✓			✓		✓	✓	
Inn at Union Square	✓	✓		✓	✓		✓	✓	
Jackson Court		✓		✓			✓	✓	
James Court Hotel				✓	✓				
The Mansions Hotel		✓		✓	✓	✓	✓	✓	
The Monte Cristo		✓		✓			✓	✓	
Petite Auberge		✓		✓	✓		✓	✓	
The Queen Anne	✓	✓		✓			✓	✓	
Savoy Hotel	✓			✓	✓	✓		✓	
The Sherman House		✓				✓	✓	✓	
Spencer House		✓		✓	✓		✓	✓	
Union Street Inn		✓			✓		✓	✓	
Victorian Inn on the Park		✓		✓	✓		✓	✓	
Washington Square Inn		✓		✓	✓			✓	
White Swan Inn		✓		✓	✓		✓	✓	

	Luxurious	Pets Allowed	No Smoking Indoors	Good Place for Families	Beach Nearby	Cross-Country Ski Trails	Golf Within 5 Miles	Fitness Facilities	Near Wineries	Good Biking Terrain	Skiing	Tennis	Swimming on Premises	Conference Facilities	Hiking Nearby
		✓	✓	✓											
	✓		✓				✓							✓	
			✓							✓					
			✓												✓
	✓	✓	✓	✓			✓								
		✓		✓											
	✓	✓						✓						✓	
	✓		✓	✓										✓	
	✓	✓		✓						✓				✓	
		✓		✓											
	✓		✓	✓											
	✓		✓							✓				✓	
		✓													
	✓	✓		✓										✓	
			✓												
	✓			✓											
	✓		✓	✓						✓				✓	
	✓		✓	✓										✓	
	✓		✓							✓				✓	
	✓		✓				✓			✓					✓
			✓	✓											
	✓		✓				✓			✓					✓
	✓		✓	✓											
	✓													✓	

Special Features at a Glance

Name of Property	Accessible for Disabled	Antiques	On the Water	Good Value	Car Not Necessary	Full Meal Service	Historic Building	Romantic Hideaway	
BAY AREA									
Bancroft Hotel					✓		✓		
Blackthorne Inn								✓	
Casa del Mar				✓					
Casa Madrona Hotel			✓		✓	✓		✓	
Cowper Inn							✓		
East Brother Light Station			✓		✓	✓	✓		
Gramma's Inn							✓		
The Hensley House		✓					✓		
The Mill Rose Inn								✓	
Mill Valley Inn	✓			✓					
Mountain Home Inn					✓			✓	
Old Thyme Inn							✓		
The Pelican Inn		✓				✓		✓	
Pillar Point Inn	✓		✓	✓				✓	
Roundstone Farm		✓							
Ten Inverness Way				✓					
Union Gardens		✓	✓				✓		
WINE COUNTRY									
Auberge du Soleil	✓					✓		✓	
Beltane Ranch		✓		✓			✓		
The Boonville Hotel				✓		✓	✓		
Brannan Cottage Inn					✓		✓	✓	
Camellia Inn	✓	✓			✓		✓	✓	
Campbell Ranch Inn	✓								

	Luxurious	Pets Allowed	No Smoking Indoors	Good Place for Families	Beach Nearby	Cross-Country Ski Trails	Golf Within 5 Miles	Fitness Facilities	Near Wineries	Good Biking Terrain	Skiing	Tennis	Swimming on Premises	Conference Facilities	Hiking Nearby
			✓											✓	
			✓		✓					✓					✓
			✓		✓					✓					✓
	✓													✓	✓
			✓											✓	
					✓										
			✓												
			✓											✓	
			✓		✓								✓	✓	
			✓							✓					✓
										✓				✓	
			✓				✓	✓							✓
					✓					✓				✓	
			✓		✓		✓								
			✓		✓									✓	✓
			✓		✓					✓					✓
	✓			✓			✓	✓	✓	✓		✓	✓	✓	✓
			✓				✓		✓	✓	✓				✓
				✓					✓	✓					✓
			✓						✓	✓					✓
	✓								✓	✓					✓
			✓		✓				✓	✓					✓

Special Features at a Glance

Name of Property	Accessible for Disabled	Antiques	On the Water	Good Value	Car Not Necessary	Full Meal Service	Historic Building	Romantic Hideaway	
Cross Roads Inn									
El Dorado Hotel	✓				✓	✓	✓		
The Gaige House	✓							✓	
Harvest Inn	✓			✓					
Healdsburg Inn on the Plaza		✓			✓		✓		
Highland Ranch				✓		✓			
Hope-Merrill House	✓	✓					✓		
Kenwood Inn								✓	
Larkmead		✓							
Madrona Manor	✓	✓		✓		✓	✓	✓	
Maison Fleurie		✓			✓		✓		
Quail Mountain				✓					
Sonoma Hotel		✓				✓	✓		
Thistle Dew Inn	✓	✓							
Vintners Inn	✓			✓		✓		✓	
NORTH COAST AND REDWOOD COUNTRY									
Applewood	✓					✓	✓	✓	
Carter House	✓	✓						✓	
"An Elegant Victorian Mansion"		✓					✓		
Gingerbread Mansion		✓							
Grey Whale Inn	✓			✓			✓		
Harbor House		✓	✓			✓	✓	✓	
The Headlands Inn	✓	✓							
Joshua Grindle Inn		✓					✓		
Rachel's Inn	✓							✓	

Luxurious	Pets Allowed	No Smoking Indoors	Good Place for Families	Beach Nearby	Cross-Country Ski Trails	Golf Within 5 Miles	Fitness Facilities	Near Wineries	Good Biking Terrain	Skiing	Tennis	Swimming on Premises	Conference Facilities	Hiking Nearby
		✓						✓	✓					✓
								✓	✓					✓
		✓						✓	✓		✓	✓		✓
			✓					✓	✓			✓		
		✓						✓						✓
			✓					✓			✓	✓	✓	✓
		✓	✓					✓	✓			✓		✓
✓		✓						✓	✓			✓		✓
								✓	✓					✓
	✓	✓	✓					✓	✓			✓		✓
		✓						✓	✓			✓		✓
		✓	✓					✓				✓		✓
								✓	✓					✓
		✓						✓	✓					✓
			✓					✓	✓				✓	✓
✓		✓										✓		✓
✓		✓				✓							✓	
		✓				✓								
✓		✓		✓										
		✓	✓										✓	
		✓		✓										✓
		✓				✓								
		✓	✓			✓			✓					✓
✓				✓		✓								✓

Special Features at a Glance

Name of Property	Accessible for Disabled	Antiques	On the Water	Good Value	Car Not Necessary	Full Meal Service	Historic Building	Romantic Hideaway	
Scotia Inn						✓			
The Shaw House Inn		✓					✓		
St. Orres				✓		✓		✓	
The Stanford Inn by the Sea	✓	✓	✓		✓			✓	
Timberhill Ranch	✓					✓		✓	
The Whale Watch Inn by the Sea			✓					✓	
SACRAMENTO AND THE CENTRAL VALLEY									
Abigail's		✓					✓	✓	
Amber House		✓					✓	✓	
Harkey House		✓					✓		
Hartley House		✓					✓	✓	
Johnson's Country Inn	✓	✓						✓	
Lake Oroville Bed & Breakfast	✓							✓	
The Sterling Hotel						✓	✓	✓	
Victorian Manor		✓		✓			✓		
Wine & Roses Country Inn	✓	✓				✓	✓	✓	
GOLD COUNTRY									
Camino Hotel		✓		✓			✓		
The Chichester–McKee House		✓		✓			✓		
City Hotel		✓		✓		✓	✓		
The Coloma Country Inn	✓	✓					✓	✓	
Combellack-Blair House		✓					✓		
Cooper House		✓					✓		
The Court Street Inn		✓					✓		
Dunbar House, 1880		✓					✓	✓	

	Luxurious	Pets Allowed	No Smoking Indoors	Good Place for Families	Beach Nearby	Cross-Country Ski Trails	Golf Within 5 Miles	Fitness Facilities	Near Wineries	Good Biking Terrain	Skiing	Tennis	Swimming on Premises	Conference Facilities	Hiking Nearby
			✓											✓	
	✓		✓				✓			✓					✓
	✓		✓		✓		✓								✓
	✓	✓	✓		✓		✓	✓		✓			✓		✓
	✓		✓							✓		✓	✓	✓	✓
	✓		✓		✓					✓					✓
			✓				✓			✓				✓	
	✓		✓				✓			✓				✓	
			✓												
			✓				✓			✓				✓	
			✓				✓							✓	
			✓							✓					✓
			✓				✓			✓				✓	
			✓				✓			✓					✓
	✓		✓	✓			✓			✓		✓		✓	
			✓				✓		✓	✓					✓
			✓				✓		✓						✓
			✓	✓			✓		✓	✓					✓
			✓						✓	✓					✓
			✓						✓						✓
			✓	✓					✓	✓	✓				✓
			✓						✓	✓					✓
			✓			✓	✓		✓	✓					✓

Special Features at a Glance

Name of Property	Accessible for Disabled	Antiques	On the Water	Good Value	Car Not Necessary	Full Meal Service	Historic Building	Romantic Hideaway	
Fallon Hotel	✓	✓		✓			✓		
Flume's End	✓	✓					✓		
The Foxes Bed and Breakfast Inn		✓					✓	✓	
Grandmère's		✓					✓		
Grey Gables	✓	✓		✓			✓	✓	
Groveland Hotel	✓	✓		✓		✓	✓	✓	
The Heirloom	✓	✓		✓			✓		
Imperial Hotel		✓				✓	✓		
Indian Creek		✓					✓		
Power's Mansion Inn		✓					✓		
Red Castle Inn		✓					✓	✓	
The Ryan House	✓	✓		✓			✓	✓	
Serenity, A Bed & Breakfast Inn	✓			✓					
HIGH SIERRA									
The Alpenhaus		✓				✓	✓		
Busch and Heringlake Country Inn		✓				✓	✓		
The Cain House							✓		
Chalfant House		✓		✓			✓		
Clover Valley Mill House		✓					✓	✓	
Deer Run Ranch								✓	
The Feather Bed		✓		✓			✓	✓	
Genoa House Inn							✓		
Gold Hill Hotel		✓		✓		✓	✓		
Haus Bavaria		✓							
High Country Inn		✓						✓	

Luxurious	Pets Allowed	No Smoking Indoors	Good Place for Families	Beach Nearby	Cross-Country Ski Trails	Golf Within 5 Miles	Fitness Facilities	Near Wineries	Good Biking Terrain	Skiing	Tennis	Swimming on Premises	Conference Facilities	Hiking Nearby
		✓	✓			✓		✓	✓					✓
		✓				✓		✓	✓					✓
✓		✓						✓	✓					✓
✓		✓				✓			✓					✓
		✓						✓	✓					✓
	✓	✓				✓							✓	✓
		✓				✓		✓	✓					✓
		✓				✓		✓	✓					✓
		✓						✓	✓			✓		✓
✓		✓						✓	✓					✓
✓		✓				✓		✓	✓		✓			✓
		✓				✓		✓	✓		✓			✓
		✓						✓	✓					✓
		✓	✓	✓	✓	✓			✓	✓		✓		✓
✓		✓			✓				✓	✓				✓
✓		✓			✓									✓
		✓			✓	✓			✓		✓			✓
		✓			✓				✓					✓
		✓	✓	✓	✓				✓	✓		✓		✓
		✓			✓				✓					✓
		✓						✓	✓					✓
	✓			✓									✓	✓
		✓		✓	✓	✓	✓		✓	✓	✓			✓
		✓			✓		✓		✓			✓		✓

Special Features at a Glance

Name of Property	Accessible for Disabled	Antiques	On the Water	Good Value	Car Not Necessary	Full Meal Service	Historic Building	Romantic Hideaway	
The Matlick House		✓		✓			✓		
Nenzel Mansion							✓		
New England Ranch		✓					✓	✓	
Rainbow Tarns		✓		✓			✓	✓	
Rockwood Lodge		✓						✓	
Sorensen's						✓	✓	✓	
White Horse Inn		✓							
White Sulphur Springs		✓					✓		
The Yosemite Peregrine								✓	

Luxurious	Pets Allowed	No Smoking Indoors	Good Place for Families	Beach Nearby	Cross-Country Ski Trails	Golf Within 5 Miles	Fitness Facilities	Near Wineries	Good Biking Terrain	Skiing	Tennis	Swimming on Premises	Conference Facilities	Hiking Nearby
		✓			✓	✓			✓		✓			✓
		✓	✓			✓		✓	✓					
		✓			✓	✓			✓		✓			✓
			✓		✓				✓	✓				✓
✓		✓		✓	✓			✓	✓					✓
	✓		✓		✓				✓	✓			✓	✓
✓		✓	✓		✓	✓	✓		✓	✓	✓	✓		✓
		✓	✓		✓	✓			✓	✓		✓		✓
		✓			✓					✓				✓

Southern Counties

Southern Counties
Including San Diego and Palm Springs

*"From the desert to the sea . . ." is the signature of longtime
southern California TV newsman Jerry Dunphy. These are
the natural boundaries of the vast area known as the Southern
Counties: San Diego, Riverside, Imperial. Each has its own
charms.*

*San Diego hugs the sea, stretching inland 4,255 square miles
over mile-high mountains to the desert at sea level. Beyond is
vast Riverside, the desert resorts of Palm Springs and Palm
Desert, and the date-growing areas surrounding Indio. To the
north are a dozen wineries in the historic Temecula countryside and a pair of mountains more than 10,000 feet high, San
Jacinto and San Gorgonio. Imperial, ranging along the
Mexican border, is the source of most of the tomatoes, lettuce,
and grapefruit consumed by Americans.*

*The Southern Counties also contain the oldest and newest
communities in California. San Diego is the birthplace of
California; Portuguese explorer Juan Rodríguez Cabrillo
landed here and claimed the area for Spain in 1542. The
burgeoning suburban communities of Riverside County
represent the youngest and fastest-growing in the state.*

*History and geography aside, this is a land of recreation.
Hiking on wooded mountain trails. Sailing the deep-green
Pacific or blue inland lakes. Playing golf at one of dozens of
championship courses. Tennis. Bicycling. Ballooning. Wine
tasting. Discovering the lushness of a flower-carpeted desert
in spring. Delving into history at southern California's only
gold-rush town. Encountering wild animals at the San Diego
Zoo and Wild Animal Park. Cavorting with the whales at
Sea World. Exploring the vast 1,400-acre Balboa Park.
Watching thoroughbred racing from the grandstand or
elegant clubhouse at Del Mar. Basking on a long white
beach.*

*Culture abounds here, too. San Diego's Old Globe Theatre is
world-famous for its performances of classics, contemporary
drama, experimental works, and its summer Shakespeare
Festival. The San Diego Opera draws audiences from all over
southern California. Art galleries flourish in seaside La Jolla.
Balboa Park's art, anthropological, natural history, and other
museums lure Sunday-afternoon visitors.*

*While this is an area of many splendid resorts, the Southern
Counties also offer the intimacy, individuality, and personal
contact that only bed-and-breakfast lodging can provide.*

Places to Go, Sights to See

Balboa Park (tel. 619/239–0512). In addition to the *San Diego Zoo (see below)*,
the 1,074-acre urban park contains 13 museums, including the *San Diego
Museum of Art* (tel. 619/232–7931), *Reuben H. Fleet Space Theater and Science
Center* (tel. 619/238–1233), *Museum of Man* (tel. 619/239–2001), *Museum of
Photographic Art* (tel. 619/239–5262), and *Centro Cultural de la Raza* (tel.
619/235–6135). The *Simon Edison Centre for the Performing Arts* houses three
stages, including the famed *Old Globe Theatre* (tel. 619/239–2255), the oldest
professional theater in California. On weekends the park fairly sings with fun as
street performers, mimes, and musicians work the crowd on the Prado.

Cabrillo National Monument (tel. 619/557–5450), atop the tip of Point Loma,
commemorates Juan Rodríguez Cabrillo's 1542 exploration of San Diego, offering
exhibits, films, and lectures at the visitor center about the monument, tidal pools,
and gray whales migrating offshore. Descriptive signs line the cliffside walks
leading to a promontory that affords stunning views over the bay as far south as
Mexico. You can explore the old Point Loma lighthouse, replaced in 1891 by one
closer to shore.

The Desert. *Indian Canyons* (S. Palm Canyon Dr., tel. 619/325–5673), ancestral
home of the Agua Caliente Indians, begins 5 miles south of downtown Palm
Springs. Inside this Indian-owned sanctuary, visitors can see relics of ancient
American history while wandering through landscapes of palms and wildflowers, towering rockfaces, and dense growths of sycamores, willows, and mesquite.
Joshua Tree National Park (north of I–10 via Hwy. 62, Twentynine Palms, tel.
619/367–7511), about a one-hour drive from Palm Springs, is a colorful preserve
illustrating desert life and history, with hiking trails, picnic areas, and natural-
ist-led walks. This meeting place of the Mojave and Colorado deserts includes
such sights as Hidden Valley, a legendary cattle rustlers' hideout, the Oasis of
Mara, and Key's View, an outstanding scenic point commanding a superb sweep
of valley, mountain, and desert. The southern part of the park is especially
beautiful in spring, when wildflowers bloom. *Living Desert Reserve* (17–900
Portola Ave., tel. 619/346–5694) in Palm Desert is a 1,200-acre wildlife park and
botanical garden with bighorn sheep, coyotes, birds of prey, reptiles, and other

desert wildlife roaming in natural settings. *Palm Springs Aerial Tramway* (1 Tramway Rd., tel. 619/325–1391) is a 2½-mile gondola ride from the desert to an observation area at the 8,516-foot level of Mt. San Jacinto, where there are 54 hiking trails, camping and picnic areas, and a restaurant and lounge. *The Desert Museum* (101 Museum Dr., tel. 619/325–7186) in Palm Springs offers art exhibitions, often western in flavor, and natural history and science sections illuminating aspects of the surrounding desert. The *McCallum Theater* (73-000 Fred Waring Dr., tel. 619/346–ARTS) in Palm Desert features top-name popular entertainers.

The *Fabulous Palm Springs Follies* (128 S. Palm Canyon Dr., tel. 619/327–0225), a glitzy vaudeville show starring high-stepping showgirls, comedians, singers and dancers (all over 50 years old), is the hottest ticket in the desert. Performances run from November through May at Palm Springs's historic Plaza Theater, the 1930s radio home of Jack Benny and Bob Hope.

Gaslamp Quarter National Historic District. The 16-block area in downtown San Diego, centered around 4th and 5th avenues from Broadway to Market Street, contains most of the city's Victorian commercial architecture, now housing antiques shops, cafés and restaurants, lively nightspots, and the San Diego Repertory Theater. Walking tours of the district are conducted on Saturdays at 11 and 11:30 AM starting at the Gaslamp Quarter Association headquarters (410 Island Ave., tel. 619/233–5227). Also located in the area is the Center City East Arts Association (600–1300 G St.), a large concentration of galleries, art studios, boutiques, and coffeehouses.

Hot-Air Ballooning. *Sunrise Balloons* (tel. 800/548–9912) offers 45- to 60-minute balloon flights in the Palm Springs and Temecula areas, with packages that include picnics and ground transportation.

Julian (tel. 619/765–1857). East of San Diego and reached by Highway 78–79, this is the site of the only gold rush to take place in southern California. The historic mountain town, now known for its apples, has a gold mine that can be visited, *Eagle Mine* (tel. 619/765–0036); an old-fashioned soda fountain in an 1880s drugstore; a historical museum in an old brewery (tel. 619/765–0227); antiques shops; and restaurants, many of which serve a mean apple pie.

Mission Bay, a 4,600-acre aquatic playground, is the largest of its kind in the world and is devoted to boating, waterskiing, swimming, board sailing, and other forms of recreation, such as cycling and kite flying. There are 27 miles of bayfront beaches with six designated swimming areas and numerous picnic grounds. *Giant Dipper,* a 65-year-old wooden roller coaster at Belmont Park—an abandoned amusement park turned shopping and dining center—has been restored and is running again. *Sea World* (1720 S. Shores Rd., tel. 619/226–3901) is a 150-acre, ocean-oriented amusement park featuring trained, performing killer whales, seals, and dolphins. The Penguin Encounter has a moving sidewalk passing by a glass-enclosed arctic environment, where hundreds of emperor penguins slide over glaciers into icy waters.

Old Town State Historic Park (tel. 619/220–5422), just north of downtown San Diego at Juan Street, near the intersection of I–5 and I–8, was the center of San Diego when it was incorporated in 1850. The historic buildings, clustered around

California Plaza, include original and reproduction adobe and log houses in a subdued Mexican colonial style. Bazaar del Mundo is a shopping and dining enclave built to resemble a colonial Mexican square.

San Diego Zoo (Balboa Park, tel. 619/234–3153) is recognized as one of the world's best zoos. More than 3,900 animals of 800 species reside in 100 acres of expertly crafted habitats, including the African Rain Forest, Gorilla Tropics, Sun Bear River, and Tiger River. The zoo is also an enormous botanical garden, with one of the world's largest collections of subtropical plants.

San Diego Wild Animal Park (15500 San Pasqual Valley Rd., Escondido, tel. 619/747–8702) is a 1,800-acre wildlife preserve containing more than 2,500 wild animals that roam free over hillsides resembling their native habitats in Asia and Africa.

Scripps Institution of Oceanography (8602 La Jolla Shores Dr., La Jolla, tel. 619/534–6933) has a fine aquarium filled with saltwater fish, and an outdoor tidalpool exhibit with live starfish, anemones, and other shoreline creatures.

Temecula, 60 miles northeast of San Diego off Highway 15, has an Old Town with a number of historic buildings dating from the 1890s, when Temecula was a frontier cow town. Most of the action is on Front Street, where you'll find an everchanging array of antiques and gift shops. A favorite local restaurant is the *Baily Wine Country Cafe* (27644 Ynez Rd., tel. 909/676–9567), which is operated by the Baily Winery. Twelve wineries can be found scattered along Rancho California Road, about 5 miles from Old Town. Tours and tastings are offered on weekends. Most prominent is *Callaway Vineyard and Winery* (32720 Rancho California Rd., tel. 909/676–4001), which offers a calendar of tastings, seminars, picnics, chefs' dinners, and festivals. Another popular spot is the *Thornton Winery* (32575 Rancho California Rd., tel. 909/699–0099), which has a champagne bar, gift shop, and the Café Champagne (tel. 909/699–0088).

Beaches

The long beaches of San Diego are one of the county's principal attractions. The turquoise Pacific invites swimming, surfing, and sunbathing while whales, seals, and dolphins frolic. **Imperial Beach,** a classic southern California beach, is the site of the U.S. Open Sandcastle Competition every July. With the famous Hotel Del Coronado as a backdrop, the **Coronado Beach** is one of the largest in the county and is surprisingly uncrowded on most days. **Sunset Cliffs,** beneath the jagged cliffs on the west side of Point Loma peninsula, is one of the more secluded beaches in the area, popular primarily with surfers and locals. It's not Atlantic City, but the boardwalk stretching along **Mission Beach** is a magnet for strollers, roller skaters, and bicyclists. The south end attracts surfers, swimmers, and volleyball players. **La Jolla Cove** is one of the prettiest spots in the world: A beautifully palm-tree-lined park sits atop cliffs formed by the incessant pounding of the waves. The beach below the cove is almost nonexistent at high tide, but the cove is still a must-see. One of the most overcrowded beaches in the county, **La Jolla Shores** lures bathers with a wide sandy beach, relatively calm surf, and a concrete boardwalk paralleling the beach. Admission to **Mission Bay's** 27 miles of bayfront beaches and 17 miles of ocean frontage is free.

Restaurants

San Diego's gastronomic reputation rests primarily on its seafood. At **Cafe Pacifica** (tel. 619/291–6666), the approach to fish is moderately nouvelle, with light, interesting sauces and imaginative garnishes. With its extravagant view of La Jolla Cove, **Top O' the Cove** (tel. 619/454–7779) is more or less synonymous with romance, but it also boasts competently prepared luxury fare—beef, fowl, veal, and seafood—dressed with creamy, well-seasoned sauces. Also in La Jolla, **Cindy Black's** (tel. 619/456–6299) has attained a national reputation for southern French fare. Dining options in the desert continue to improve as the one-time winter resort becomes a year-round home for the well heeled. Noteworthy establishments along El Paseo in Palm Desert include the clubby **Daily Grill** (tel. 619/779–9911), the bistro-like **Café des Artistes** (tel. 619/346–0669), and **Palomino** (tel. 619/773–9091), popular for grilled seafood and pizza. **Las Casuelas Original** (tel. 619/325–3213) is a longtime favorite among natives when it comes to great margaritas and average Mexican dishes. It gets very, very crowded during the winter months. Hearty eaters will enjoy **Di Amico's Steak House** (tel. 619/325–9191), an early California-style restaurant featuring such dishes as prime Eastern corn-fed beef, liver steak vaquero, and son-of-a-gun stew.

Tourist Information

Julian Chamber of Commerce (Box 413, Julian, CA 92036, tel. 619/765–1857); **Palm Springs Desert Resorts Convention and Visitors Bureau** (69930 Hwy. 111, Suite 201, Rancho Mirage, CA 92270, tel. 619/770–9000); **San Diego Convention and Visitors Bureau** (401 B St., Suite 1400, San Diego, CA 92101–4237, tel. 619/232–3101); **Temecula Valley Chamber of Commerce** (27450 Ynez Rd., Suite 104, Temecula, CA 92591, tel. 909/676–5090).

Reservation and Referral Services

Bed and Breakfast Guild of San Diego (tel. 619/523–1300); **Bed and Breakfast International** (Box 282910, San Francisco, CA 94128–2910, tel. 415/696–1690); **Eye Openers B&B Reservations** (Box 694, Altadena, CA 91003, tel. 213/684–4428 or 818/797–2055, fax 818/798–3640).

Brookside Farm

Edd and Sally Guishard have created a mountain retreat out of an old dairy farm in the tiny hamlet of Dulzura, a 30-minute drive from downtown San Diego. Set on 4 tree-shaded acres bisected by the seasonal brook for which the inn is named, the farm is surrounded by colorful gardens planted with geraniums, poppies, roses, and sweet peas.

Rooms, scattered throughout the property—in the main house, built in 1928, in the old stone dairy barn, and in two cottages—have farm motifs. The Delft-blue Room With a View actually has two views: a tree-top scene from the deck outside and a crackling fire in a see-through fireplace visible from the bathtub or the bed. Pink Jennie's Room has a separate step-up sitting area behind a white spooled fence and Sally's childhood doll collection. The bright-green Sun Porch room in the main house has wooden car-siding walls, wraparound windows, and a small garden patio; you can hear doves cooing and a fountain gurgling nearby. One of two very private cottages, the Hunter's Cabin, hangs right over the brook. Originally the pump house, it is decorated in an Old West style and has a wood-burning stove standing in front of an iron bed and a screened-porch entry.

While no longer a commercial farm, Brookside still has animals—chickens and geese, a pair of Nubian goats, and a pig—and gardens planted with corn, tomatoes, berries, lettuce, zucchini, and herbs. These ingredients are used in the excellent four-course dinners prepared by Edd, a professional chef, on weekends. Featured entrées might be chicken mirabella, poulet Louis in tarragon sauce, or grilled chicken with rosemary. Accompanied by soup, salad and dessert, meals are a bargain at $15 per person.

While Edd enjoys cooking, Sally likes to party. You're likely to find yourself part of a celebration: tacky-crafts party, honeymoon in June, tricycle-race weekend. Guests tend to return time and again. "We have a sort of extended family here," Edd says. "Brookside Farm is everybody's second home."

Address: *1373 Marron Valley Rd., Dulzura, CA 91917, tel. 619/468-3043.*
Accommodations: *8 double rooms with baths, 2 suites.*
Amenities: *Fireplace in 6 rooms, refrigerator in 4 rooms, library, guest refrigerator and phone; outdoor hot tub, badminton, horseshoes, croquet.*
Rates: *$65–$115; full breakfast, dinner ($15) Fri.–Sat. AE, MC, V.*
Restrictions: *No smoking indoors, no pets; 2-night minimum on weekends.*

Heritage Park
Bed & Breakfast Inn

This turreted Victorian in a historic park is the ideal headquarters for touring San Diego's Old Town, a shopping-restaurant complex across the street. It's also convenient for exploring San Diego's other attractions via the Old Town Trolley, which stops at the zoo, Seaport Village, Coronado, Balboa Park, and Horton Plaza.

A beautiful 1889 Queen Anne, the inn has a wraparound veranda decorated with spindlework, a variety of chimneys, stained-glass windows, and very ornate millwork on its banisters and wainscoting. Furnishings include an unusual double Eastlake panel bed with carved sunflowers, four-poster canopy beds, an antique fainting couch, and antique quilts.

Rooms range from smallish to ample; most are bright and cheery. Those upstairs have views of the park and Mission Bay beyond. One of the most popular rooms is the Turret, which has a sitting room in the inn's two-story tower that offers city and park views. From Queen Anne, a spacious room on the second floor, you can gaze out to the water through a squared bay window. Downstairs, the Garden Room, which looks out on the sunny Victorian garden, is a guest favorite.

When they purchased the inn in early 1992, longtime San Diegans Charles and Nancy Helsper brought a new vitality to the Heritage Park and developed a number of packages to entertain guests. Five-course, catered candlelight dinners are now served in the dining room. The Helspers will also make arrangements for picnics at the waterfront Sunday pops concerts, balloon excursions, and Sunday-morning breakfasts at Tiffany's, with a ride in the antique Bentley that Queen Elizabeth II rode to her coronation.

Breakfast is served in a formal dining room with burgundy flowered wallpaper. Nancy, formerly director of catering at a San Diego resort hotel, puts out her best antique Spode china and stemware and offers a varied menu that includes entrées such as banana walnut pancakes and eggs Benedict.

Address: *2470 Heritage Park Row, San Diego, CA 92110, tel. 619/299–6832 or 800/995–2470, fax 619/299–9465.*
Accommodations: *6 double rooms with baths, 2 doubles share bath, 1 suite in adjacent house.*
Amenities: *Fireplace in 3 rooms, robes, Jacuzzi in suite, old-time movies shown at night; off-street parking.*
Rates: *$85–$200; full breakfast, afternoon refreshments. MC, V.*
Restrictions: *No smoking indoors, no pets; 2-night minimum on weekends in July and Aug.*

Inn at Rancho Santa Fe

One of California's most elegant hideaways, this family-operated inn dates to 1924, when architect Lillian Rice designed what was known as the Inn at La Morada. Originally used by the Santa Fe Railroad to house prospective purchasers of land the company was developing northeast of San Diego, the inn became a gathering place in the 1930s for movie stars such as Errol Flynn, Bette Davis, and Jimmy Stewart. A celebrity staying here today would enjoy the same pampering and tranquillity that attracted earlier stars.

Steve Royce, a former pitcher with the New York Giants, purchased the inn in 1958; the family has operated it ever since. Duncan Royce Hadden, a grandson, is the current innkeeper. Family memorabilia decorates much of the inn. Team photos of Steve Royce taken in 1914 line corridors; embroidery and needlepoint canvases done by Duncan's grandmother adorn guest-room walls; and Chinese paintings collected by family members hang in the living room.

Accommodations are located in the original structure and in a series of red-tile-roofed cottages scattered around 20 acres of manicured, eucalyptus-shaded grounds. Those in the main building tend to be smallish, while newer rooms in the cottages are very spacious, some with large living rooms and private bricked and flower-decked patios. Decor is traditional, but colors tend to be bright: reds, greens, blues.

Over the years the inn's dining rooms have become popular gathering places for Rancho Santa Fe's wealthy residents, who enjoy Sunday brunch in the Garden Room or the book-filled Library. The fare is as traditional as the inn itself.

Just a few miles away at the beach at Del Mar, the inn maintains a cottage for guest use. The inn also owns box seats at the famed Del Mar racetrack and makes seats available to guests during the summer thoroughbred season.

Address: *5951 Linia del Cielo, Box 869, Rancho Santa Fe, CA 92067, tel. 619/756–1131 or 800/654–2928, fax 619/759–1604.*
Accommodations: *78 double rooms with baths, 11 cottage suites.*
Amenities: *TV, phone, air-conditioning, refrigerator in rooms, fireplace in 45 rooms, wet bar in 30 rooms, Jacuzzi in 7 suites, fitness facilities, 4 dining rooms, room service during meal hours; swimming pool, 3 tennis courts, croquet.*
Rates: *$80–$180, suites $480. AE, DC, MC, V.*
Restrictions: *2-night minimum on selected holiday weekends.*

Loma Vista
Bed and Breakfast

The first bed-and-breakfast accommodations in California were the 21 missions built during the 18th century by the Spanish padres, providing lodging and food along El Camino Real. The missions are also the inspiration for the design—and the hospitality—of the Loma Vista Bed and Breakfast.

The inn, which sits like a terra-cotta crown atop a hill in the Temecula wine country, about an hour's drive north of San Diego, is the creation of Betty Ryan, who designed it from the ground up. The look is more like a hacienda than a mission. Carefully tended rose gardens border red-tiled patios. A fountain gurgles. Hummingbirds poke their long beaks into the hearts of fragrant flowers.

Inside, the inn is cool and inviting, with ceiling beams and other oak details. Objects collected from years of world travel, from African brasswork to Thai silk-screen hangings, are displayed throughout the house. Large picture windows in the common rooms reveal gardens and vineyard-covered hillsides. The views from the bedrooms upstairs are more dramatic, unfolding in a broad panorama of citrus groves, distant mountains, and even Mt. Palomar observatory.

The guest rooms are named for varietal wines, but the connection ceases there. Zinfandel is swathed in green and peach, with Colonial reproductions that include a handsome Chippendale-style secretary bookcase with bonnet top. Chardonnay is furnished in oak and has a Laura Ashley look. Art deco describes Champagne, with a black lacquer bed, tubular steel chairs, and photographs of Marilyn Monroe and Fred Astaire on the walls. Each room is stocked with fresh fruit and sherry. Weeping wisteria frames the edges of balconies of four rooms.

Whatever room you select, the setting is lovely. Don't miss the chance to spend some time sitting on the veranda sipping local wine, enjoying the fresh, cooling breezes, colorful gardens, or setting sun.

Champagne at breakfast, served family-style in the inn's large dining room, makes it a festive meal. Betty has a large repertoire of southwestern favorites, such as *huevos rancheros*.

Address: *33350 La Serena Way, Temecula, CA 92591, tel. 909/676–7047.*
Accommodations: *6 double rooms with baths.*
Amenities: *Air-conditioning, TV in living room; outdoor hot tub, fire pit.*
Rates: *$95–$125; full breakfast, afternoon refreshments. D, MC, V.*
Restrictions: *No smoking indoors, no pets; 2-night minimum on weekends.*

Rancho Valencia Resort

Secluded hideaways are especially rare in sprawling southern California, which partially accounts for the popularity of Rancho Valencia, a striking collection of Mediterranean-style casitas. The tennis resort, surrounded by horse ranches and millionaire homes—including one owned by former Clinton administration Secretary of the Treasury Lloyd Bentsen—attracts well-heeled patrons who demand luxury and top-notch service.

There are 20 pink-stuccoed, red-roofed casitas scattered among the gardens, each containing two uncommonly large and private guest accommodations. All suites, they have sunken sitting-dining areas or separate bedrooms, terra-cotta-tile floors, sand-colored walls, hand-painted decorator tiles, adobe fireplaces, and open-beam ceilings. Spacious bathrooms have tiled countertops, walk-in closets, and separate dressing areas. Outside each suite is a private flower-filled patio with dining table and chairs and chaise longues.

As beautiful as the suites are, the grounds—lush gardens of crimson bougainvillea, hibiscus, palm and citrus trees—astound even more; look up at sunset and a squadron of hot-air balloons drifting over a nearby hillside completes the already-mesmerizing picture.

Rancho Valencia has 18 tennis courts, a staff of eight pros, group and individual instruction, and tennis workout programs for men and women. Golf privi-

leges are available at four area courses. A professional conditioning program provides personal training, fitness assessment, bicycle touring, and nutritional counseling. Those interested in less strenuous activities can take advantage of the resort's walking-hiking program; complimentary conducted walks take place daily. Spa services are also available.

The inn now contains a first-rate restaurant that is earning raves from guests and locals for setting, service, and cuisine. The dinner menu, which changes quarterly, features contemporary cuisine, such as sautéed sea scallops with sweet-pepper coulis and duck foie gras with turnip confit. Vegetables come from nearby Chino Farms, where Alice Waters and other famed California chefs buy their vegetables.

Address: *5921 Valencia Circle, Box 9126, Rancho Santa Fe, CA 92067, tel. 619/756–1123 or 800/548–3664, fax 619/756–0165.*
Accommodations: *43 suites.*
Amenities: *Air-conditioning, 2 TVs with VCRs, phones, fireplace, stocked minibar, safe, coffeemaker, robes, hair dryer in rooms; newspaper, fresh-squeezed orange juice, and cut rose delivered each morning; 24-hour room service, 2 pools, 2 Jacuzzis, children's programs, gift shop, guest laundry, conference facilities.*
Rates: *$315–$450 ($710–$825 full casita); breakfast not included. AE, DC, MC, V.*
Restrictions: *No pets.*

Bed and Breakfast Inn at La Jolla

We should build our houses, simple, plain and as substantial as a boulder, then leave the ornamentation to nature." This was the philosophy of Irving Gill, who in 1913 designed the Bed and Breakfast Inn at La Jolla, a simple white stucco box with an occasional arched window or doorway. Additional natural "ornamentation"—helped along by famous horticulturist Kate Sessions—takes the form of a crimson-bougainvillea—filled garden with fountain and Japanese pine.

Set in a quiet neighborhood near the town's commercial district, the inn consists of the original house and a sympathetic, well-designed addition in the rear. Each room is individually decorated, with furnishings ranging from rattan-and-white-iron bedsteads to American-country pine; unfortunately, some are beginning to reflect the wear and tear of ten years of use. The most spacious accommodations are the Holiday Room and the Irving Gill Penthouse, a duplex with its own deck.

Address: *7753 Draper Ave., La Jolla, CA 92037, tel. 619/456–2066, fax 619/454–9055.*
Accommodations: *14 double rooms with baths, 1 double shares public bath, 1 suite.*
Amenities: *Robes in rooms, hair dryer in several rooms, fireplace in 3 rooms, refrigerator in 8 rooms, TV in suite and sitting room; off-street parking.*
Rates: *$85–$225; Continental breakfast, afternoon refreshments. MC, V.*
Restrictions: *No smoking, no pets; 2-night minimum on weekends.*

The Cottage

Two accommodations are available in this garden-graced, tree-shaded 1913 homestead, located in a quiet neighborhood containing an eclectic mix of small businesses, lovely old homes and bungalows, and some of the best inexpensive restaurants in San Diego. The cottage, a small house located behind Carol and Bob Emrick's home, contains a bedroom, living room, and kitchen-dining room; furnishings include an antique pump organ, a 1920s Austrian sideboard full of books, and a wood stove. A smallish room done in white and green florals is available in the main house. It has a private garden entrance, an antique sideboard filled with books, and a lift-top desk.

Guests have the use of the inn's antiques-filled parlor and dining room, which reflect the Emricks' interest in music: The rooms contain old opera posters—"from Puccini's garage," according to Carol—a player piano, and a player organ.

Address: *3829 Albatross St., San Diego, CA 92103, tel. 619/299–1564, fax 619/299–6558.*
Accommodations: *1 double room with bath, 1 cottage suite.*
Amenities: *Wood stove and phone in cottage, TV and refrigerator in both rooms.*
Rates: *$55–$75; Continental breakfast. AE, MC, V.*
Restrictions: *No smoking indoors, no pets; 2-night minimum.*

Ingleside Inn

Garbo slept here—so did Elizabeth Taylor, Marlon Brando, and diva Lily Pons. Ingleside Inn has been a Palm Springs hideaway for celebrities, Hollywood and otherwise, since the 1930s. The reasons become obvious when you step inside this unpretentious hacienda-style inn. Located on a quiet street just a few blocks from Palm Canyon Drive, the inn is a tranquil and private enclave surrounded by verdant gardens and a high adobe wall. Individually and elegantly decorated villas and cottages are scattered around the property. All rooms have whirlpool tubs and steam showers. Some are furnished with valuable antiques; the suite occupied by Pons for 13 years features her Louis XV bedroom set. Ingleside is noted for an old-Hollywood ambience; those seeking spiffy, up-to-date digs may find the look a bit dull.

Address: *2000 W. Ramon Rd., Palm Springs, CA 92264, tel. 619/325–0046 or 800/772–6655, fax 619/325–0710.*
Accommodations: *24 double rooms with baths, 5 double suites.*
Amenities: *Air-conditioning, TV with VCR, phone, stocked refrigerator, whirlpool bath, and steam shower in rooms, fireplace in 13 rooms, restaurant, lounge, meeting facilities, room service; outdoor pool and whirlpool tub, limousine pickup at local airport.*
Rates: *$95–$205, suites $235–$385; Continental breakfast. AE, D, MC, V.*
Restrictions: *2-night minimum on weekends Oct.–May.*

Julian Hotel

When Steve and Gig Ballinger moved to Julian in 1976 to take over the Julian Hotel, they had a major undertaking ahead of them: restoring one of the oldest continuously operating hotels in southern California to its former glory. Set at the top of the mountains east of San Diego, Julian was the site of a major gold rush during the 1870s.

The hotel was founded in 1897 by a freed slave, Albert Robinson, and his wife, Margaret. Rooms were small then; they have not been enlarged. Beds are of brass, iron and brass, or wood with applied decoration. The bathrooms are called "Necessary Rooms," in deference to Victorian modesty; three have claw-foot tubs.

The Victorian theme starts in the hotel's lobby, furnished with a settee, black leather armchairs with carved lion heads, and a Kayton tiger-oak piano dating from 1910. In cool weather a fire crackles in the wood stove. Guests can also relax in a wicker-filled sun room or in the parlor, which has a stove.

Address: *2032 Main St., Box 1856, Julian, CA 92036, tel. 619/765–0201 or 800/734–5854.*
Accommodations: *3 double rooms with baths, 12 doubles and 1 single share 4 baths, 1 suite.*
Amenities: *Private veranda off 1 room, fireplace and dressing room in suite.*
Rates: *$76–$94, suite $145; full breakfast, afternoon tea. AE, MC, V.*
Restrictions: *No smoking, no pets; 2-night minimum on weekends.*

Korakia Pensione

A striking property located on a quiet back street in Palm Springs, this Moroccan-style retreat has catered to artists since 1924, when a Scottish painter named Gordon Coutts built it to replicate a villa in Tangier. A contrast to the surrounding single-story ranch houses, Korakia Pensione is a walled, white fortress with a red-tiled entry courtyard and keyhole entrance. Over the decades artists—the most famous of whom was Winston Churchill—have found inspiration from the vistas framed by the villa's arched windows.

Before architectural preservationist Doug Smith converted the two-story stucco villa into a bed and breakfast, the building had been carved up for apartments. As a result, guest accommodations have private entrances and sometimes peculiar kitchen and dining room configurations. Room furnishings include antiques, Oriental rugs, and handmade beds. The large, second-floor Artist's Studio—popular perhaps because Churchill stayed here—has a view of the San Jacinto mountains.

Address: *257 S. Patencio Rd., Palm Springs, CA 92262, tel. 619/864-6411.*
Accommodations: *4 double rooms with baths, 7 suites.*
Amenities: *Air-conditioning, kitchen in 8 rooms, refrigerator in 3 rooms, balcony or patio off 5 rooms, fireplace in 5 rooms, guest kitchen, TV available; swimming pool, barbecues.*
Rates: *$89–$155; full breakfast, dinner available. No credit cards.*
Restrictions: *No smoking indoors, no pets; 2-night minimum on weekends.*

Orchard Hill Country Inn

O rchard Hill, a luxury inn opened in 1994, sets a new standard in historic Julian, renowned for its rusticity. To create their inn, owners Darrell and Pat Straube reconstructed three Craftsman cottages from the foundation up. Each cottage contains three beautifully appointed guest rooms surrounded by a broad veranda with big green wicker chairs. The rooms have whirlpool tubs, see-through fireplaces visible from both bedroom and bathroom, wet bars, and window seats. Pat, an interior designer, has also incorporated down-filled love seats, blue toile fabric wall coverings, and pine antique furniture into the decor.

One of the nicest accommodations is the large and very private McIntosh. It's decorated with green plaid wallpaper and contains a bathroom accessible to guests with disabilities. The Black Gilflower is also a charmer, with pillow-ticking-style wallpaper and an oversized Jacuzzi in the bathroom. Orchard Hill's unusually large bathrooms also have closets, an unexpected luxury at a bed and breakfast inn.

Address: *Washington St., Box 425, Julian, CA 92036, tel. 619/765-1700.*
Accommodations: *9 double rooms with baths.*
Amenities: *Private entrance, fireplace, wet bar, TV with VCR, coffee service in rooms, whirlpool tub in 4 rooms, 1 room with private patio; gardens, horseshoe court.*
Rates: *$130–$138; full breakfast, afternoon refreshments. AE, MC, V.*
Restrictions: *No smoking indoors, no pets; 2-night minimum on weekends.*

Pelican Cove Inn

The beachfront town of Carlsbad has long been a popular summer destination for southern Californians seeking sand and sun. Those are the lures of Pelican Cove Inn, which is located just two short blocks from the beach. Kris and Nancy Nayudu, who came to the area from Juneau, Alaska, preside over this contemporary, vaguely Cape Cod–style inn.

Guest rooms, all with private outside entrances, are furnished with a mix of antiques, period reproductions, and modern pieces. The most striking is the La Jolla Room, where tall, arched bay windows, two-story cathedral ceiling, and an elegant champagne color scheme can best be appreciated from the turn-of-the-century French fainting couch. Nancy serves a full, buffet-style breakfast, consisting of French

toast or cottage cheese pancakes, in the parlor; guests usually take a tray outside to the garden gazebo, sun deck, or wraparound porches. Beach chairs, towels, and picnic baskets waiting to be filled are provided for those heading for the surf.

Address: *320 Walnut Ave., Carlsbad, CA 92008, tel. 619/434–5995.*
Accommodations: *8 double rooms with baths.*
Amenities: *TV and fireplace in rooms, whirlpool tub in 2 rooms; railroad station pickup.*
Rates: *$85–$175; full breakfast, afternoon refreshments. AE, MC, V.*
Restrictions: *No pets; 2-night minimum on weekends.*

Scripps Inn

This comfortable, reasonably priced inn offers spacious, attractively decorated rooms and a stunning seaside location. Resembling a classic three-level motel, it was built in 1937 to provide accommodations for families and patients at the adjacent Scripps Clinic.

Rooms are oddly configured with large closets, tiny bathrooms, and irregular alcoves. The simple furnishings include overstuffed chairs, sofas covered in wine-colored plaids, and stenciled white chests, dressers, and tables. Some rooms have Shaker accent pieces. If you want a sweeping view of La Jolla Cove, request one of the front rooms; number 14, for example, has windows on three sides.

Innkeepers Larry and Bell Blesi present breakfast buffet-style in the inn's cramped lobby. Guests can carry trays to their rooms or to the beach across the street.

Address: *555 Coast Blvd. S, La Jolla, CA 92037, tel. 619/454–3391, fax 619/459–6758.*
Accommodations: *9 double rooms with baths, 4 suites.*
Amenities: *TV, phone, refrigerator, safe, hair dryer in rooms, fireplace in 2 rooms, kitchenette in 5 rooms; off-street parking.*
Rates: *$110–$165; Continental breakfast. AE, DC, MC, V.*
Restrictions: *2-night minimum on weekends.*

Tres Palmas Bed and Breakfast

The first bed and breakfast to open in posh Palm Desert provides an affordable glimpse into the lifestyle that lures thousands of wealthy vacationers to this resort town each winter. Located on a residential street just a block from El Paseo shops and galleries, this is a typical sand-colored, stucco desert home with red-tiled roof and deep covered porches. Landscaped gardens include a gurgling fountain, succulents, and cactus. An azure swimming pool dominates the back yard.

The house itself is spacious and bright, its design highlighted by enormous windows, high open-beamed ceilings, whitewashed wood, and textured peach tile floors. Southwestern decor in common areas and guest rooms includes fine old Navajo rugs from the collection of innkeepers Terry and Karen Bennett. Rooms are functional rather than luxurious. A lodgepole pine bed is the centerpiece of the Coyote. Kokpelli has a pencil-point bed, a Navajo rug on the wall, and French doors leading to a small private patio.

Address: *73135 Tumbleweed La., Box 2115, Palm Desert, CA 92261, tel. 619/773-9858.*
Accommodations: *4 double rooms with baths.*
Amenities: *Air-conditioning, TV in rooms, guest phone; swimming pool, outdoor hot tub, wet bar.*
Rates: *$90–$140; Continental breakfast, afternoon refreshments. MC, V.*
Restrictions: *No smoking, no pets; 2-night minimum on weekends.*

Villa Royale

A European-style country inn in the desert, Villa Royale in Palm Springs is a walled, flower-filled oasis with pilasters, glazed terra-cotta walls, marble and tile floors, open-beam ceilings, French doors, canopied and painted beds, heavy carved-wood furnishings, and delicate flowered upholstery. All are set beneath the red-tiled roofs of eight buildings on 3½ acres of grounds.

Rooms surround a series of three gardens of bougainvillea, where guests lounge around one of two swimming pools or the outdoor hot tub. The inn has a noted garden restaurant, the Europa, which serves dinner during the winter season. The Villa Royale's reputation had slipped in recent years, but it's back in the hands of original owner Bob Lee, who has reintroduced high standards for service and facilities.

Address: *1620 Indian Trail, Palm Springs, CA 92264, tel. 619/327-2314 or 800/245-2314, fax 619/322-3794.*
Accommodations: *23 double rooms with baths, 10 housekeeping suites, 3 double housekeeping suites.*
Amenities: *Air-conditioning, TV and phone in rooms, fireplace in 16 rooms, whirlpool tub in 8 rooms, kitchen in 10 double rooms, restaurant, cocktail lounge, massage and facials available, room service during restaurant hours; 2 swimming pools, hot tub.*
Rates: *$75–$165, suites $165–$225; Continental breakfast. AE, MC, V.*
Restrictions: *No pets; 2-night minimum on weekends, 3-night minimum on holidays.*

The San Bernardino Mountains

The San Bernardino Mountains
From Lake Arrowhead to Big Bear Lake

Not for every Los Angeleno the sunny life of sea and surf. Thousands instead opt to spend their leisure time in the mountains, shedding the smog and fast track for lakeside walks and lift lines. When time doesn't permit the long trek to Lake Tahoe or Mammoth, southern Californians head up to the nearby San Bernardino Mountains, usually to Big Bear Lake, Lake Arrowhead, or such tiny neighboring hamlets as Fawnskin, Arrowbear, and Running Springs.

Set within the more than 600,000 acres of the San Bernardino National Forest (home to some of the tallest peaks in southern California), these towns are perched above San Bernardino, a small, smoggy city about 60 miles east of Pasadena and 50 miles west of Palm Springs. If you're not fighting the Friday-night crowds, the drive can be pleasant, up Highway 330 to Highway 18, dubbed the Rim of the World because of its dramatic views of the urban valley below.

If the snow is good, winters draw skiers and lovers of other cold-weather sports. Summers bring visitors for waterskiing on the lakes, fishing, and hiking. But off-season visitors won't be disappointed. On closer inspection, the somewhat barren-looking spring hills prove to be filled with wildflowers, and the creeks flow with the runoff of melting snow, and the dogwood trees bloom in April and May. Autumn brings an Octoberfest and cold, crisp nights—perfect for sitting around a fireplace.

Since it's closest to urban areas (only about a half hour up the mountain from San Bernardino), Lake Arrowhead is the preferred site for quick visits. The "cabins"—often four-bedroom luxury homes—surrounding crystalline Lake Arrowhead have been hideaways for L.A.'s famous, well-to-do, and socially connected since the 1910s. Arrowhead isn't for everyone: It can be almost impossible for visitors to use the lake (with the exception of an hour-long boat tour), since most

*of it is fronted by private property, and the ski areas aren't
conveniently close.*

*The Big Bear area, about 20 miles farther east on Highway 18
from Arrowhead, is considerably more eclectic, home of
charming inn and tacky motel alike. With plenty of public
beaches, docks, and waterfront walking areas, huge Big Bear
Lake is also more easily accessible to visitors than Lake
Arrowhead. Three distinct communities—Big Bear Lake, Big
Bear City, and Fawnskin—grew up around the lake. Big Bear
Lake is a weekend base for skiers bound for Snow Summit, a
good-size, often crowded but well-run ski area a few miles to
the south; Bear Mountain is a few minutes from town. In
summer, visitors head for the local golf course, public
swimming beach, or lake, where boat rentals are available.
Year-round, the less athletic wander the rustic boutiques in
town or stop in for a beer and burger at one of the local joints;
Big Bear Lake is down-home and inelegant, a place to shed
big-city pretensions. On the North Shore, where Fawnskin is
located, there are picnic parks and campgrounds right at the
water's edge. Big Bear City is a bit off the lake, a quiet
community where year-rounders congregate.*

*Although the San Bernardino Mountains have long been one
of L.A.'s favorite nearby resorts, the mountain communities
have only recently joined the bed-and-breakfast bandwagon.
Before the late '80s, overnight visitors to the area had to choose
among sparsely furnished cabins, impersonal condos servic-
ing mostly skiers, and an abundance of shabby post–World
War II–era motels. If these mountains have come lately to the
idea of bed-and-breakfast inns, they have come with
enthusiasm. Innkeepers seeking a new life for themselves have
discovered beautiful properties ranging from the rustic '20s-
era hunting lodges to contemporary wood-and-glass-and light
flooded aeries.*

Places to Go, Sights to See

Alpine Slide at Magic Mountain (Big Bear Blvd. before town, between Forest and Lakeview, tel. 909/866–4626). In the summer, attractions include a waterslide and a chair lift to a summit from which one descends on a cart via a "slic-trac"; in winter there's a snow-play area.

Bear Mountain Golf Course (43101 Goldmine Dr., Big Bear Lake, tel. 909/585–8002). Balls seem to sail farther than normal at this nine-hole course at elevation 7,000 feet.

Blue Jay Ice Castle (27307 Hwy. 189, tel. 909/336–2111). Many Olympic hopefuls practice at this open-air skating rink set amid a forest of pines. Lessons and public skating are available.

Boat Rentals (Pine Knot Marina, at the foot of Big Bear Village, tel. 909/866–BOAT). Pontoons, canoes, sailboats, speedboats, rowboats, and fishing gear can be rented, and waterskiing and windsurfing lessons are available.

Boat Tours. The *Arrowhead Queen* (tel. 909/336–6992), moored on the waterfront at Lake Arrowhead Village, leaves hourly from 10 AM to 5 PM; offering a look at the area's luxurious private homes, it's great for real-estate enthusiasts. In Big Bear, the *Sierra* and *Queen* operate from Pine Knot Landing (tel. 909/866–3218), afternoons during the week, all day on weekends.

Gold Fever Trail. At the Forest Service Ranger Station in North Shore (tel. 909/866–3437) you can pick up a free map for a self-guided tour through Holcomb Valley; it'll take you past an old log saloon, mill, gold-digging areas, cabins, mines, and grave sites.

Heap's Peak Arboretum (Hwy. 18 between Skyforest and Running Springs, no phone). An interpretive nature trail, perhaps the best in the area, goes for 7/10 of a mile along easy terrain through a variety of landscapes–bracken fern, vanilla-smelling Jeffrey Pine, and beautiful blooming dogwood.

Lake Arrowhead Children's Museum (lower Lake Arrowhead Village, end of the peninsula, tel. 909/336–1332). Terrific for very small children, this museum has hands-on nature and science exhibits, a toddler area, and a puppet theater.

Moonridge Wild Animal Park (Moonridge Dr. at the end of Bear Mountain Golf Course, tel. 909/585–5156). This unique, tiny facility houses and cares for wild animals of the area—coyotes, bears, eagles, foxes, and deer, among others—that have been hurt, illegally kept as pets, or otherwise rendered unable to fend for themselves in the wild. Open daily May–Oct.

Mountain biking. Some of the best riding terrain in southern California is found in the Big Bear Valley. In summer bikers can take their equipment to the mountaintop via the Snow Summit chair lift and ride over 60 miles of roads and trails. *Mountain Bike Center* (880 Summit Blvd., Big Bear Lake, tel. 909/866–4565) rents equipment and arranges guided tours.

Rim of the World Scenic Byway (Hwy. 18 between Big Bear and Cajon Pass, tel. 909/383–5588). On a clear winter day this is one of the most spectacular drives in southern California. Carved out of the mountainside at the 5,000-foot level, the drive offers sweeping views of the San Bernardino Valley below.

Ski Resorts. Big Bear boasts two downhill ski areas that draw thousands of experts and snow bunnies from the city each weekend in winter. *Snow Summit* (tel. 909/866–5766) has 12 runs, a family snow park, a snowboarding area and a freestyle area for experts; runs are lit for night skiing Wednesday and Friday through Sunday. *Bear Mountain* (tel. 909/585–2519) has 35 ski trails, the longest 2 miles; the resort is open daily from 8 AM to 4 PM. Cross-country skiers head to *Bluff Lake Nordic Ski Center* (tel. 909/866–1669).

Restaurants

Don't expect L.A.-quality restaurants in the San Bernardino Mountains; eateries here are rustic and casual, and there isn't a bit of California cuisine for miles around. In Arrowhead, many fast-food and casual restaurants can be found in the Village area. It says a lot about Arrowhead Village that the best lake views are offered by the local McDonald's. **The Chef's Inn and Tavern** (tel. 909/336–4487) serves good Continental and American cuisine in an 1840 building in Cedar Glen; **Antler's Inn** (tel. 909/337–4020), in another converted historic building (established 1925) in Twin Peaks, is fine for steak and barbecue. A good, family-owned Italian restaurant is **Paoli's Country Kitchen** (tel. 909/866–2020), which has locations in Arrowhead and Big Bear Lake. In Big Bear Lake, the casual patio of **Boo Bear's Den** (tel. 909/866–2932), right in the village, is often bustling; the **Blue Whale Lakeside** (tel. 909/866–5771) rewards early evening diners with sunset views; out by the ski area, **La Montana** (tel. 909/866–2606) offers decent Mexican food and margaritas. In Fawnskin, the **Longhorn Cafe and Grill** (tel. 909/866–3136) uses homemade ingredients for hearty mountain meals.

Tourist Information

Big Bear Chamber of Commerce (630 Bartlett St., tel. 909/866–7000) has recorded tourism information; **Lake Arrowhead Chamber of Commerce** (Vineyard Bank Building, at entrance to Lake Arrowhead Village, tel. 909/337–3715).

Apples Bed & Breakfast Inn

With its pink facade and ornate design, this new inn stands out among Big Bear's predominantly rustic architecture. In designing and building Apples, Jim and Barbara McLean integrated contemporary comforts and Victorian-accents. Their inn, set amid an acre of pine trees, feels remote and peaceful despite its location on the busy road to the ski lifts.

Colorful floral wallpapers and linens adorn the rooms, named for historic apples. Each room has either a king-size four-poster or canopied bed; some have dressing areas separate from the bathroom. Apple-scented soaps and bath gels, down comforters, and satin-covered hangers in the closets are among the extra touches that make a stay here special.

The second-floor Royal Gala room is bright and appealing, with a forest view, bay windows, and sunny yellow wallpaper. Two rooms on the first floor have contrasting atmospheres. Jonathan, done in shades of hunter green and pink, has a cozy feel; it's dominated by a king-size, roll-top panel bed. The best four rooms are in the recently completed turret. Somewhat larger, they have separate sitting areas and double Jacuzzis in the bathrooms.

Common areas include a gathering room in the center of the inn, which contains an enormous, playpen-style sofa and a large reading loft. The dining room has a table long enough to seat 20 people. French doors are everywhere, leading to the broad veranda out front, shady gardens, several decks, and a hot tub out back.

Barbara, a fine cook, ran a catering business before moving to Big Bear. A typical four-course breakfast might include cold strawberry pineapple soup, thick and crunchy French toast, herb scrambled eggs, and apple cider syrup.

In the short time since it opened in 1993, Apples has become a hideaway for celebrities. Autographed pictures of Robert Wagner, Stephanie Powers, Mike Connors, and Lucinda Crosby already grace the dining room walls.

Address: *42430 Moonridge Rd., Box 7172, Big Bear Lake, CA 92315, tel. 909/866–0903, fax 909/866–6524.*
Accommodations: *12 double rooms with baths, 1 wheelchair-accessible room.*
Amenities: *Fireplace and TV with VCR in rooms, Jacuzzi in 4 rooms, grand piano in gathering room; hot tub and sports court in garden, ski and mountain bike storage, transportation to ski areas.*
Rates: *$135–$185; full breakfast, afternoon refreshments, after-dinner dessert, snacks available. AE, D, MC, V.*
Restrictions: *No smoking indoors, no pets; 2-night minimum on weekends, 2-person-per-room maximum.*

Chateau Du Lac

Dramatic architecture and sweeping lake and mountain views are the primary draws at this contemporary inn, perched on a hillside above Lake Arrowhead. Chateau Du Lac is an exceptionally bright space with more than 100 windows, some two stories tall. The three-level house, which wraps around an atrium containing an ancient oak tree, has numerous places to relax or curl up with a good book: on the decks surrounding the house, in a hammock strung across the gazebo, in the library, or up in the secluded tower music room.

As seen from the second-floor Lakeview room, which extends across the front of the house, Lake Arrowhead shimmers like a bowl of clear-blue water rimmed by green trees. The view commands attention from all points, including the Jacuzzi strategically positioned in the large master bathroom. Two other spacious rooms on this level have quirky nooks and crannies set into gables; both provide a cool, dark alternative to the brightness elsewhere in the house.

Owners Oscar and Jody Wilson moved to the mountains from the Los Angeles area, where he had a long career on the technical side of the entertainment industry and she operated a catering business. Their breakfast buffet is one of the day's highlights. In fine weather, which is most of the time, the Wilsons place several tables on the deck so their guests can enjoy the view. If it's cool, Jody stokes up a fire to warm the dining room. Taking afternoon tea is another pleasure at Chateau Du Lac. Jody normally keeps things informal, but from time to time lucky guests get a chance to experience an English high tea.

Although the main appeal of this inn is the chance to bask in the lovely surroundings, there are nearby hiking and nature trails and good picnic sites, as well. The innkeepers direct casual hikers and joggers to a pine-shaded, abandoned road in Willow Creek, about a mile from the house. Just a few yards from the inn, serious hikers can find trails to Little Bear and Hook Creek.

Address: *911 Hospital Rd., Box 1098, Lake Arrowhead, CA 92352, tel. 909/337–6488, fax 909/337–6746.*
Accommodations: *2 double rooms with baths, 2 doubles share bath, 2 suites.*
Amenities: *TV and phone in rooms, fireplace in 2 rooms, Jacuzzi in suites and 1 room, private balcony off 2 rooms, library with games and TV with VCR; gazebo.*
Rates: *$95–$215; full breakfast, afternoon tea. AE, D, MC, V.*
Restrictions: *No smoking indoors, no pets; 2-night minimum on summer weekends.*

The Carriage House

Those seeking a romantic weekend with tranquil walks along a beautiful shore should consider this New England–style, gray clapboard house in a residential Lake Arrowhead neighborhood. Lee and Johan Karstens built this house as a weekend home; they so enjoyed the process that they built another place for themselves next door in 1988 and turned this one into a B&B.

The Carriage House was designed to take advantage of fabulous views of pine trees. The summer parlor backs onto a sunny breakfast deck, and the winter parlor has a large fireplace. The accommodations have lake views framed by pine trees; one room has a private balcony. Furnishings are a tasteful combination of antiques, whitewashed pine, and vintage finds: hand-stenciled wardrobes, lace-trimmed window seats, and needlepoint chair covers. Other features of the inn are a lakeside path, a garden hammock and gazebo, and a talking parrot who whistles the theme from *Andy Griffith.*

Address: *472 Emerald Dr., Box 982, Lake Arrowhead, CA 92352, tel. 909/336–1400.*
Accommodations: *3 double rooms with baths.*
Amenities: *TV with VCR in rooms.*
Rates: *$95–$120; full breakfast, afternoon refreshments, after-dinner dessert. D, MC, V.*
Restrictions: *No smoking indoors, no pets; 2-night minimum on weekends, 3-night minimum on some holidays.*

Eagle's Nest

The more than 50 bald eagles that make the Big Bear area their winter home inspired the name of this eclectic dwelling. Guests at Jack Draper and Jim Joyce's establishment can choose between the convivial bed-and-breakfast atmosphere of the lodge or more secluded cottages.

The lodge has five guest rooms done in Western motifs echoing movies such as *Rio Bravo* and *Cat Ballou.* Antique dressers with log-front doors lend a rustic air, as do heirloom family quilts and stained-glass and bay windows. The country feel continues in the living room, where big, overstuffed sofas flank a stone fireplace.

Designed as romantic retreats, the tree-shaded cottages out back are furnished in contemporary Southwest decor. Some have a convenient mini-kitchen and private entrance.

Address: *41675 Big Bear Blvd., Box 1003, Big Bear Lake, CA 92315, tel. 909/866–6465.*
Accommodations: *5 double rooms with baths in main house, 7 cottages.*
Amenities: *Phone and cable TV in all cottages, whirlpool tub in 4 cottages, mini-kitchen in 3 cottages, guest phone in main house.*
Rates: *$85–$110; full breakfast. MC, V.*
Restrictions: *Smoking in cottages only; 2-night minimum on weekends.*

Gold Mountain Manor

So picturesque that it's been used as a backdrop for Ralph Lauren and Eddie Bauer ads, Gold Mountain Manor is the largest surviving building by famous '20s builder Guy Maltby. Close to skiing, the manor was a summer retreat for a wealthy Angeleno, as evidenced by such luxurious details as bird's-eye maple floors, beamed ceilings, and a wine cellar. Truth be told, the house offers more character than comfort, although common rooms are spacious and there's a proper front porch.

The nicest room is the pine-paneled Presidential Suite, in its own wing with a massive river-rock fireplace. The most romantic is the Honeymoon Room, which has a canopy bed, wicker furniture, and a brick fireplace. The more masculine Clark Gable Room is done in forest green with a potbellied stove (reputed to be from Gable's old cabin).

Address: *1117 Anita Dr., Box 2027, Big Bear City, CA 92314, tel. 909/585–6997.*
Accommodations: *1 double room with bath, 1 double with half-bath, 4 doubles share 2 baths, 1 double suite.*
Amenities: *TV and robes in rooms, Jacuzzi in 1 room, fireplace or wood-burning stove in 6 rooms and suite, self-serve coffee and tea in kitchen, billiard table, player piano; gardens.*
Rates: *$75–$180; full breakfast, afternoon hors d'oeuvres. MC, V.*
Restrictions: *No smoking indoors, no pets; 2-night minimum on weekends.*

The Inn at Fawnskin

This inn is one of the few noncamping accommodations on the north shore of Big Bear Lake, whose many charms include walks and woods and access to good boating. A shaded, two-story contemporary log cabin, the Inn at Fawnskin was built with wood brought here from Wyoming.

Of the four rooms, the second-floor Master Suite, with its own rock fireplace and superlative lake view from the balcony, appeals to couples seeking a romantic getaway. Three common lounging areas include one with a sofa, concert grand piano, and fireplace, and another with a regulation-size billiards table and big-screen TV with VCR. In the third, guests gather at the fireside table to eat a hearty breakfast—fresh breads and "Egg McFawnskin" or Belgian waffles.

Groups can book the inn for a murder mystery weekend, a tradition started by the previous innkeeper. Winter ski packages that include transportation to Bear Mountain and discount lift tickets are also available.

Address: *880 Canyon Rd., Box 378, Fawnskin, CA 92333, tel. 909/866–3200.*
Accommodations: *1 double room with bath, 2 doubles share bath, 1 suite.*
Amenities: *Robes in rooms; TV, fireplace, and balcony in suite, library; basketball court, secure ski and bike storage.*
Rates: *$85–$185; full breakfast, afternoon refreshments. MC, V.*
Restrictions: *No smoking indoors, no pets; 2-night minimum on weekends.*

The Romantique Lakeview Lodge

Located a short distance from Lake Arrowhead Village, this cozy retreat on a tree-shaded hillside is a logical choice for those who want to be near shops and restaurants. Full or partial lake views from most rooms, something not available at most area inns, are another bonus.

The lodge, which was built in the 1920s, consists of a puzzle of rooms located on three levels accessed by steep staircases and connected by walkways. The building is surrounded by gardens and gray stone patios. Rooms are decorated in an effusive Victorian style with floral wallpapers and bedspreads, brass beds, and crystal chandeliers. Third-floor rooms, set into the gambrel roof, have the best lake views. Like most others at this lodge, their ambience is somewhat dark. Bathrooms are nicely equipped, though some are cramped. Breakfast is served on a couple of tables in a tiny guest kitchen off the lobby.

Address: *28051 Hwy. 189, Box 128, Lake Arrowhead, 92352, tel. 909/337-6633 or 800/358-5253.*
Accommodations: *7 double rooms with baths, 2 suites.*
Amenities: *TV with VCR in rooms, fireplace in 7 rooms, tape library, guest phone; off-street parking.*
Rates: *$65–$225; Continental breakfast. AE, MC, V.*
Restrictions: *No smoking indoors, no pets; 2-night minimum July through Dec.*

Switzerland Haus

It's hard to imagine a more appropriate design for a bed and breakfast inn located just 200 yards from the ski slopes than this cozy Swiss chalet complete with colorful flower boxes, stenciling with alpine motifs on the walls, and a welcoming winter fire. Linda Ford, who used to manage the nearby Knickerbocker Mansion, now applies her many talents and good cheer and to Switzerland Haus.

The best accommodation is the huge Summit Room that takes up the back of the chalet; warm and woody, it has open-beam ceilings and pine-paneled walls, a bear rug on the floor, and a long balcony with a view of the slopes. Other rooms have half-canopied beds, handmade quilts, and private decks.

The inn's common areas are as comfortable as the individual rooms. There's a sitting area in front of the fireplace, a big open kitchen where one is likely to encounter Linda whipping up some delicious cookies, a dining area with great mountain views, and a flower-filled garden out back.

Address: *41829 Switzerland Dr., Big Bear Lake, CA 92315, tel. 909/866-3729.*
Accommodations: *5 double rooms with baths.*
Amenities: *TV in rooms; gas fireplace, refrigerator, microwave, CD player in 1 room; secured ski storage and boot warmers; guest phone; adjacent to Ski Summit.*
Rates: *$125–$175; full breakfast, afternoon refreshments. MC, V.*
Restrictions: *No smoking indoors, no pets; 2-night minimum on weekends.*

Los Angeles

Los Angeles
With Orange County

Set off from the rest of the continent by mountains and desert, and from the rest of the world by an ocean, this incredible corner of creation has evolved its own identity, which conjures envy, fascination, ridicule, and scorn—often all at once.

Los Angeles is a city of ephemera, of transience, and above all, of illusion. Nothing here is quite real, and that's the reality of it all. The lure that "anything can happen"—and it often does—is what keeps thousands moving to this promised land each year and millions more vacationing here. They come not just from the East or Midwest, but from the Far East, Down Under, Europe, and South America. It's this influx of cultures that's been the lifeblood of Los Angeles since its Hispanic beginning.

The first immigrants were the Spanish padres who, following a dream to save souls in California, founded their Pueblo de la Reina de Los Angeles in 1781. Oil and oranges helped the town shed its image as a dusty outpost, but the golden key to success came on the silver screen: the movies.

In 1913, the same sunshine that draws today's visitors and new residents drew Cecil B. DeMille and Jesse Lasky, who were searching for a new place to make movies outside of New York City. The silent-film era made Hollywood's name synonymous with fantasy, glamour, and, as the first citizens would snicker in disgust, with sin. Outrageous partying, extravagant homes, eccentric clothing, and money, money, money have been symbols of life in Los Angeles ever since. Even the more conservative oil, aerospace, computer, banking, and import-export industries on the booming Pacific Rim have enjoyed the prosperity that often leads to excess. But even without piles of money, many people have found Los Angeles conducive to their colorful lifestyles, be they spiritually, socially, or sexually unusual.

No city embraces the romance of the automobile as does Los Angeles. Cars announce the wealth, politics, and taste of their drivers. Vanity license plates condense the meaning of one's life into seven letters (MUZKBIZ). Sun roofs, ski racks, and cardboard windshield visors sell better here than anywhere else. You are what you drive—a thought worth remembering when you rent a car. Yes, Lamborghinis are available—even by the hour.

The distance between places in Los Angeles explains the ethnic enclaves that do not merge, regardless of the melting-pot appearance of the city. The tensions between racial and ethnic groups learning to share Los Angeles have been well publicized. More notable for visitors, however, is the rich cultural and culinary diversity this mix of peoples creates.

You can laze on a beach or soak up some of the world's greatest art collections. You can tour the movie studios and stars' homes or take the kids to Disneyland, Magic Mountain, or Knott's Berry Farm. You can shop luxurious Beverly Hills' Rodeo Drive or browse for novelties on boutique-lined Melrose Avenue. The possibilities are endless—rent a boat to Catalina Island, watch the floats in Pasadena's Rose Parade, or dine on tacos, sushi, goat cheese pizza, or just plain hamburgers, hot dogs, and chili. You can experience the best in theater, music, and dance; world-class spectator sports; and a great outdoors that beckons nearly 365 days a year.

As for the bed and breakfast scene, it's a decidedly mixed bag. The city proper has few B&Bs—far fewer than, say, smaller San Francisco—and they tend to be more functional than luxurious. Outlying areas such as Catalina Island and Laguna Beach have a greater range of accommodations.

Places to Go, Sights to See

Catalina Island, the island of song and legend, lies a bit more than 20 miles across the sea from Los Angeles. The island is known for the clear-blue waters surrounding it, warm sunny beaches, and the crescent-shaped harbor of Avalon. Inland there's hiking and mountain-bike riding over virtually unspoiled mountains and canyons, coves, and beaches. You reach the island via a two-hour cruise. Contact *Catalina Express* (tel. 310/519–1212) for departure schedules from San Pedro and Long Beach.

Disneyland (Harbor Blvd. exit, I–5, tel. 714/999–4565), Walt Disney's land of fantasy, is even grander than it was when it opened in Anaheim in 1955. New rides, adventures, and attractions are added every year. From Fantasyland to Tomorrowland, Disneyland has many different shops, restaurants, and entertainment areas, but lines for rides can be long; to reduce the wait, plan to arrive early or late, midweek or off-season. A highlight for many visitors is the Electrical Parade and fireworks display presented on summer evenings.

Ethnic Los Angeles. As a major port of entry to the United States, Los Angeles boasts more ethnic diversity than any other city in the country. While every aspect of life here is colored by the culture brought by the newcomers—Hispanics from various Latin American countries, Filipinos, Japanese, Chinese, Vietnamese, Koreans—some communities are more accessible than others. Olvera Street, in the heart of downtown Los Angeles, boasts a colorful Mexican marketplace, restaurants, and several historic buildings—including Old Plaza Church, Old Plaza Firehouse, and Avila Adobe. Little Tokyo, between 1st and San Pedro streets, is the cultural and commercial center for the Japanese community, with restaurants, sushi bars, shops, and Buddhist temples. Koreatown, Chinatown, Monterey Park (another Chinese community), Fairfax (the Jewish neighborhood), and East Los Angeles (one of the Latino neighborhoods) all have a wide variety of ethnic restaurants, shops, and cultural events.

Griffith Park. The largest city park in the United States (tel. 213/665–5188) straddles the mountains between Hollywood and the San Fernando Valley. It's a favorite of locals for many reasons: Hiking and horseback riding trails that crisscross the hills; hilly roadways that make great—and sometimes thrilling—bikeways; the mythical reach for the brass ring from horses on the 1926 merry-go-round. There are picnic areas, golf courses, an outdoor transportation museum at Travel Town, a world-class zoo, and the Observatory and Planetarium. The *Gene Autry Western Heritage Museum* (tel. 213/667–2000), located near the zoo, celebrates the American West with an outstanding collection of movie, radio, and television memorabilia.

Hollywood. It may not be the glitter town it once was, but even the name still evokes a bygone era of glamour and legendary movie stars. The corner of Hollywood and Vine *does* exist. The Walk of Fame lines both sides of Hollywood Boulevard from Gower to Sycamore and on Vine from Yucca to Sunset; the walk glitters with terrazzo and brass stars engraved with the names of more than 1,800 entertainment personalities. *Mann's Chinese Theater* (6925 Hollywood Blvd.), originally Grauman's, is where you'll find the names, foot, hand, hoof, or leg prints of famous stars eternalized in concrete in the entryway. To see how movies are made, there are two opportunities: *Paramount Pictures* (860 N. Gower St., Los Angeles, tel. 213/956–1777) offers two-hour weekday guided tours of production facilities and has a limited number of free tickets to shows being produced there. *Warner Bros. Studios* (4000 Warner Blvd., Burbank, tel. 818/954–1744) offers personalized VIP tours during the week, permitting visitors to watch live shooting wherever possible.

Horse Racing. Thoroughbred horse racing takes place at two local tracks: *Santa Anita* (tel. 818/574–7223) and *Hollywood Park* (tel. 310/419–1500).

Knott's Berry Farm (8039 Beach Blvd., tel. 714/220–5200), in Buena Park, is one of the West's most popular attractions, with more than 165 rides, shops, and shows. Don't miss Mrs. Knott's Chicken Dinner Restaurant—it's as popular now as it was during the 1930s, when Walter Knott built the original "ghost town" to entertain diners waiting for a table.

Melrose Avenue between Highland Avenue and Doheny Drive is the best street for people-watching in Los Angeles. The hippest of the hip hang out here in one-of-a-kind boutiques, chic restaurants, theaters, and exclusive clubs.

Rodeo Drive is the famed Beverly Hills shopping street. You'll find international stores such as Chanel, Gucci, Giorgio, and Alfred Dunhill, among many other luxury boutiques.

South Coast Plaza and Crystal Court (Bristol and Sunflower Sts., Costa Mesa, tel. 714/241–2500) in Orange County, has one of the largest concentrations of upscale retail stores in the world.

Universal Studios Hollywood (100 Universal Pl., Universal City, tel. 818/622–3801) is a vast entertainment complex comprising the world's largest television and movie studio backlot; themed rides that take you inside movies such as *Back to the Future*, *Jaws*, and *E.T.*; and the glittery City Walk with shops, restaurants, and entertainment.

Museums

George C. Page Museum of La Brea Discoveries (5801 Wilshire Blvd., Los Angeles, tel. 213/936–2230) contains fossils and bones recovered from the La Brea Tar Pits, the world's richest source of Ice Age mammal and bird fossils. The glass-enclosed Paleontological Laboratory permits observation of the ongoing cleaning, identification, and cataloguing of fossils excavated from the nearby asphalt deposits.

Hollyhock House (4800 Hollywood Blvd., Hollywood, tel. 213/662–7272), built in 1921, was the first of a number of houses that Frank Lloyd Wright designed in the Los Angeles area. Now owned by the city (as is Barnsdall Park, where it is located), it has been restored and furnished with originals and reproductions of Wright's furniture.

Huntington Library, Art Collections, and Botanical Gardens (1151 Oxford Rd., San Marino, tel. 818/405–2100) displays 18th- and 19th-century British art, including Gainsborough's *Blue Boy*. The library exhibits rare books, prints, and manuscripts. There are more than 14,000 varieties of plants on the beautiful grounds.

J. Paul Getty Museum (17985 Pacific Coast Hwy., Malibu, tel. 310/458–2003) is a re-creation of a 1st-century Roman villa, with formal gardens, major collections of Greek and Roman antiquities, paintings ranging from the 13th century to the late-19th century, and decorative arts. Admission is free, but parking reservations are required—or you can obtain a pass on the local Santa Monica–Malibu bus.

Los Angeles County Museum of Art (5905 Wilshire Blvd., Los Angeles, tel. 213/857–6000) is a complex of five buildings on the site of the La Brea Tar Pits that houses fine collections of paintings, sculpture, textiles, costumes, and decorative arts. Of particular interest to movie fans is the classic film series presented in the Leo S. Bing Theater.

Museum of Contemporary Art (250 S. Grand Ave., Los Angeles, tel. 213/626–6222) is a unique below-ground-level museum, designed by Arata Isozaki, featuring modern art from 1940 to the present.

Norton Simon Museum of Art (411 W. Colorado Blvd., Pasadena, tel. 818/449–6840) houses many famous Old Master artworks, including paintings by Rembrandt, Rubens, Raphael, and Goya. Highlights of the modern art collection include bronze ballet dancers and horses by Degas and works by Cézanne, Toulouse-Lautrec, Renoir, and Van Gogh.

Southwest Museum (234 Museum Dr., Los Angeles, tel. 213/221–2163) contains extensive collections of Native American art and artifacts housed in a 1914 Mission Revival building. Exhibits include Navajo blankets, an incredible array of baskets, and a full-size Blackfoot tepee.

Performing Arts

Hollywood Bowl (2301 N. Highland Ave., Los Angeles, tel. 213/850–2000), a 17,680-seat amphitheater, offers a summer season of outdoor concerts ranging from pop and jazz to classical. Elegant picnics are part of the experience here; bring your own or purchase one when you get here.

Music Center of Los Angeles (135 N. Grand Ave., Los Angeles, tel. 213/972–7211) is a three-theater complex. The large Dorothy Chandler Pavilion presents classical concerts, ballet, and opera; resident companies include the Los Angeles Philharmonic Orchestra, the Los Angeles Music Center Opera, and the Los Angeles Master Chorale. The Mark Taper Forum, an intimate theater, features regional productions, some of which land on Broadway. The Ahmanson Theater stages large musical productions.

Orange County Performing Arts Center (600 Town Center Dr., Costa Mesa, tel. 714/556–ARTS) presents musical theater, opera, dance, and classical and jazz concerts.

Restaurants

El Cholo (tel. 213/734–2773), one of the oldest eateries in Los Angeles, is known for its margaritas and green tamales. Blue collar workers dine with the blue suits at the counter of Mayor Richard Riordan's down-home **Original Pantry Café** (tel. 213/972–9279), located near the Convention Center. **McCormick & Schmick's** (tel. 213/629–1929), LA's edition of the famed Seattle seafood house, is another popular downtown spot. **Tokyo Kaikan** (tel. 213/489–1333) is a longtime Little Tokyo favorite. **Ocean Seafood** (tel. 213/687–3088) is one of Chinatown's best. LA's movers and shakers conduct power breakfasts at the venerable, clubby **Pacific Dining Car** (213/483–6000), renowned for some of the best beef in town.

In Hollywood, **Yamashiro** (tel. 213/466–5125), perched on a hillside above all the action, is popular with tourists. On a clear night, the view and tranquil gardens are stunning, though the food doesn't always match the surroundings. Santa Monica's **Gladstone's 4 Fish** (tel. 310/573–0212) and **The Reel Inn** (tel. 310/395–5538) are cheap and informal—but quite good—for seafood. You need reservations at Gladstone's; just join the line at the Reel Inn. **Granita** (tel. 310/456–0488) in Malibu, a Wolfgang Puck creation, attracts the rich and famous with its eclectic Pacific Rim and Mediterranean dishes and stunning decor. Although its Tinseltown owners (including director Tony Bill) recently hired a French chef, Venice Beach's **72 Market St.** (tel. 310/392–8720) is known for its meatloaf, chili, and stargazing. **C&O Trattoria** (tel. 310/823–9491), located near the Mansion Inn, serves huge portions of salad, pasta, and seafood, and fabulous garlic yeast rolls indoors and outdoors.

In Orange County, contemporary Italian cuisine is the fare at **Thee White House** (tel. 714/772–1381), an old mansion consisting of several cozy dining rooms. **Luciana's** (tel. 714/661–6500), an intimate, romantic spot in Dana Point, also serves Italian. Dinner here is sometimes included in midweek packages offered by the Blue Lantern Inn.

You can get everything from fast food to gourmet fare at Laguna Beach. **The Beach House** (714/494–9707) serves up prodigious seafood portions and an ocean view, while Southwest cuisine is the specialty of lively **Kachina** (tel. 714/497–5546). Euro-Chinese dishes and the work of local artists are the lures at **Five Feet** (tel. 714/497–4955). Trendy restaurants abound in Newport Beach, but the waterfront **Crab Cooker** (714/673–0100), housed in a walk-up shanty, is popular for its mesquite-grilled seafood, clam chowder, and cole slaw. **Randall's** (tel. 714/556–0770) in Santa Ana combines live jazz and good food with a lakeside view.

Tourist Information

Orange County Visitor and Convention Bureau (800 W. Katella Ave., Box 4270, Anaheim, CA 92802, tel. 714/999–8999); **Long Beach Area Convention and Visitors Council** (1 World Trade Center, Suite 300, Long Beach, CA 90831, tel. 310/436–3645 or 800/452–7829, fax 310/435–5653); **Los Angeles Convention and Visitors Bureau** (633 W. 5th St., Suite 6000, Los Angeles, CA 90071, tel. 213/624–7300 or 800/689–8822, fax 213/624–9746).

Reservation Services

Bed & Breakfast International (Box 282910, San Francisco, CA 94128–2910, tel. 415/696–1690, fax 415/696–1699); **Eye Openers** (Box 694, Altadena, CA 91003, tel. 213/684–4428 or 818/797–2055).

Los Angeles

Blue Lantern Inn

The Blue Lantern Inn hasn't been open long, but it already has quite a following. This Cape Cod–style hotel is perched on a bluff above the Dana Point Marina in southern Orange County. One of the only inns around, it offers sweeping marina and ocean views from almost every room. You can watch as the more than 2,000 small boats move in and out of their slips, or keep an eye on the children as they explore a replica of the tall ship *Pilgrim,* immortalized by Richard Henry Dana in his book *Two Years Before the Mast.*

The Blue Lantern is operated by Four Sisters, which owns a number of inns and small hotels, mostly in northern California. Each guest room contains an unusually spacious bathroom; most have double sinks, showers, and whirlpool baths. The decor is contemporary; light mauve with accents in soft green and cream is a favorite color scheme. There's a tall mahogany four-poster bed in the Tower Suite; other rooms have brass, sleigh, or rattan beds. Wicker side chairs, small boudoir chairs, and Queen Anne–style desks can be found in nearly every room, as well as armoires that conceal TV sets, and refrigerators stocked with complimentary soft drinks.

The lobby is set up with tables for two and four for the buffet-style breakfast. French doors lead to an outdoor sitting area, where many guests take coffee and the morning paper. The library, which contains a small collection of

books you might actually want to read, is where guests gather in the afternoons for wine and hors d'oeuvres.

Although visitors might be tempted to spend an entire weekend enjoying the beauty and comfort of the inn, the marina complex offers a number of activities. Bicycles are available for exploring the many trails that crisscross the surrounding hills. The innkeepers will make arrangements for sail- or powerboat charters or whale-watching excursions in season. They will also prepare a picnic basket for guests to enjoy at one of the two parks within walking distance of the inn. In addition, guests can visit the mission and the chic boutiques, art galleries, and antiques stores at San Juan Capistrano, just a 10-minute drive away.

Address: *34343 St. of the Blue Lantern, Dana Point, CA 92629, tel. 714/661–1304, 800/950–1236, fax 714/496–1483.*
Accommodations: *29 double rooms with baths.*
Amenities: *Robes, whirlpool tub, refrigerator, TV, and phone in rooms; fitness center, conference facilities, picnic baskets available, bicycles.*
Rates: *$135–$350; full breakfast, afternoon refreshments. AE, MC, V.*
Restrictions: *No smoking, no pets.*

Casa Tropicana

Rick Anderson, a young building contractor, had a dream: to turn the somewhat seedy oceanfront of San Clemente into a showplace. The centerpiece would be his unique bed-and-breakfast inn. Casa Tropicana, the inn and restaurant he created and opened in 1990, has a young, beach-bum-casual ambience—the kind of place where guests are more likely to be parking their boogie boards than their BMWs.

The five-story, whitewashed Mediterranean-style inn sits on a narrow hillside across the street from the historic San Clemente pier. On a clear day, the view from some rooms goes all the way to Catalina Island. Right across the street is a prime surfing beach where most of the year surfers can be seen riding the breakers to shore. The Tropicana Grill occupies the ground floor, and guest rooms are located on the upper floors. Each level has its own deck overlooking the ocean.

Every room offers the fulfillment of a different tropical fantasy. Out of Africa holds a step-up four-poster bed topped with faux mosquito netting; guests can soak in the double whirlpool tub while watching TV or enjoying the view through a peek-a-boo window. Other rooms are equally fantastic. Coral Reef has a bed with a peach rattan-clamshell headboard. Emerald Forest is cool and green with vines hanging from the ceiling. The Penthouse has a three-sided fireplace and a deck with outdoor Jacuzzi. Only the rooms facing the ocean have a view or much outside light; if you tend to be claustrophobic, take one of these.

The laid-back atmosphere carries through to the Tropicana Grill, whose bar is tucked under a thatched roof. The reasonably priced menu offers Cabo swordfish tacos, chicken fajita salad, and Ragin' Cajun garlic ribs. Room service is available to guests from the restaurant beginning at 7:30 in the morning. Guests can select breakfast from the restaurant menu and have it delivered to their rooms or outdoor deck. On Sundays brunch is served to guests in the grill.

Address: *610 Avenida Victoria, San Clemente, CA 92672, tel. 714/492–1234.*
Accommodations: *7 double rooms with baths, 3 housekeeping suites.*
Amenities: *TV, refrigerator, and phone in rooms, double whirlpool tub in 8 rooms, fireplace in 9 rooms, restaurant, room service, evening entertainment weekends.*
Rates: *$120–$220, suites $240, penthouse $350; full breakfast, complimentary champagne. AE, MC, V.*
Restrictions: *No smoking indoors, no pets; 2-night minimum on weekends.*

Channel Road Inn

O riginally the home of Thomas McCall, a pioneering Santa Monica businessman, this house was moved from a hilltop site to its current location tucked in a hillside of Santa Monica Canyon, one block from the beach. With the help of the local historical society, innkeeper Susan Zolla saved the Colonial Revival building from demolition and turned it into a gracious inn.

The house is sheathed in blue shingles, a rarity in Los Angeles and for a Colonial Revival house. The architectural details are pure Craftsman. Windows are very large and abundant to take advantage of cool ocean breezes and bright sunlight. The honey-colored woodwork in the living room is unusually elegant, with moldings and baseboards carefully milled. Other woodwork has been painted white, which Susan says is historically accurate.

The decor covers a variety of styles, with a common thread of wicker throughout, including the dining room, library, and several of the guest rooms. Beds are the focal point: four-poster beds, pencil-post canopy beds, or sleigh beds. Special attention has been paid to the needs of guests, particularly business travelers who require phones or writing surfaces. Not all rooms, however, have comfortable chairs for extended sitting.

Several rooms have access to balconies or decks with views of the flowering

hillside and a glimpse of the ocean. There's an attractive garden sitting area for people who want to relax at the inn. Robes and oversize towels are provided for beach goers or spa users.

The broad white-sand beach is just across Pacific Coast Highway; it's bordered on one side by a 30-mile-long bicycle path that stretches north to Malibu and south to Venice Beach. The Venice portion of the path is a colorful carnival on weekends as crazily clad street musicians beat out tunes, vendors sell everything from food to art, and skaters zip by. The J. Paul Getty Museum, with its lovely gardens and superb collection specializing in ancient and French 18th-century art, is only a five-minute drive away.

Address: *219 Channel Rd., Santa Monica, CA 90402, tel. 310/459–1920, fax 310/454–9920.*
Accommodations: *12 double rooms with baths, 2 suites.*
Amenities: *Cable TV and phone in rooms, refrigerator in 4 rooms, VCR in 8 rooms; outdoor hot tub, bicycles, off-street parking.*
Rates: *$95–$180, suites $175–$200; full breakfast, afternoon refreshments. AE, MC, V.*
Restrictions: *No smoking indoors, no pets.*

Christmas House

Built by wealthy ranchers in 1904, this late Queen Anne mansion was known locally as the Christmas House because of the many lavish holiday parties thrown here. Indeed, when Jay and Janice Ilsley opened the inn in 1985, they held to custom and had a Christmas party of their own. Holiday celebrations have been a tradition at the inn ever since.

Set amid an acre of grapefruit and tangerine trees, this inviting house has turrets, gables, stained-glass windows, sweeping verandas, seven working fireplaces, dark wood wainscoting, and a grand staircase leading to the second floor. Colors are cool deep greens and burgundies. Among the inn's fine group of antiques are a 150-year-old brass bed and a family collection of framed handkerchiefs.

Guest rooms are located on the first and second floors of the main house and in a carriage house behind. Accommodations in the latter are unique: Decorated with an English floral theme, Elizabeth has a private rose garden entry, a black iron bed and green wicker furnishings; French doors lead to a romantic tropical plant-filled grotto containing a massive outdoor shower. The adjacent Carriage Room has a more masculine feel, with its fireplace, burgundy sofa, and dark antiques, including a sleigh bed. This room has a private garden with a whirlpool tub set into a gazebo.

In the main house, one ground-floor room has a private courtyard with its own hot tub. In the front of the mansion, the Celebration Suite, a huge double room with bed chamber and parlor divided by an enormous pocket door, is a popular choice of honeymooners. It has fireplaces in the corners of both rooms; a dining table set up in front of the fireplace, where breakfast is served; and a lace-draped antique canopy bed.

Convenient to the companies of the nearby city of Ontario and to Ontario International Airport, the Christmas House has become a favorite address of business travelers, but it continues to attract leisure visitors, too. Festivities include a monthly murder-mystery weekend and a follow-the-actors production of *A Christmas Carol* during the holidays.

Address: *9240 Archibald Ave., Rancho Cucamonga, CA 91730, tel. 909/980–6450.*
Accommodations: *3 double rooms with baths, 2 doubles share bath, 1 suite.*
Amenities: *Air-conditioning, robes, fireplace in 3 rooms, TV with VCR in 1 room, hot tub in 2 rooms, TVs available, guest phone, library, gift shop, tea room.*
Rates: *$70–$170; full breakfast, afternoon refreshments. AE, D, MC, V.*
Restrictions: *No smoking indoors, no pets.*

Inn on Mt. Ada

Chewing-gum magnate William Wrigley, Jr., built this impressive Georgian Colonial mansion in 1921 as his Catalina Island summer home. Occupying a five-acre hilltop site, it has a stunning view of Avalon Harbor, the coastline, and the mountains beyond from nearly every room.

Though the home is grand, Wrigley furnished it as a less-formal (for his times) retreat for his family and guests, who included U.S. presidents Calvin Coolidge and Herbert Hoover and the Duke of Windsor. But you don't have to be royalty to enjoy the millionaire's mansion that Susie Griffin and Marlene McAdam transformed into an inn in 1986. From the moment they pick you up at the boat terminal you'll feel pampered here: a guided tour of Avalon on the way to the inn, an invitation to lunch even before you check into your room, instruction in use of the golf cart provided each guest for island transportation. You'll be tempted to collapse into a chair on the expansive veranda and admire the view of jewel-like Avalon harbor. Or you may want to select a book or magazine from the inn's library, spy on the town through the telescope that's set up in the solarium window, or sample the cookies that are always out.

Furnishings are comfortable rather than elegant: overstuffed sofas and wingback chairs in the living room, natural wicker in the downstairs den. The rooms range from spacious to small, but all offer a sea view and they come with little touches such as a ladies dressing table in Ada Wrigley's suite. Not surprisingly, the standout room is Wrigley's own suite, which occupies a second-floor corner; it has a large living room that opens onto a very private deck.

Guests staying in the east-facing rooms have a beautiful early morning view of the sun rising over the Los Angeles basin—illuminating the San Gabriel Mountains, the sprawling city, and the ocean below.

Meals at the Inn on Mt. Ada include a full breakfast, three-course dinner, buffet-style lunch, evening wine and hors d'oeuvres, and beverages.

Address: *398 Wrigley Rd., Box 2560, Avalon, CA 90704, tel. 310/510–2030, fax 310/510–2237.*
Accommodations: *4 double rooms with baths, 2 suites.*
Amenities: *Fireplace in 4 rooms, robes, TV and VCR available, guest phone, conference facilities; golf cart for island transportation.*
Rates: *$320–$460, suites $490–$590; all meals included. MC, V.*
Restrictions: *No smoking indoors, no pets; 2-night minimum on weekends and holidays.*

Lord Mayor's Inn

I n 1987, Reuben and Laura Brasser, anticipating retirement, were ready to chuck their ranch house and move into something smaller. Instead the couple discovered a historic house that needed to be rescued.

Thus was born Lord Mayor's Inn, located in the heart of Long Beach and within walking distance of the convention center, Terrace Theater, World Trade Center, and most offices. Built in 1904 by Charles Windham, the first mayor of Long Beach, the house is a classic example of Edwardian architecture—a streamlined evolution of fussy Victorian. Although it's big and boxy, with bay windows, deep porches, and generous amounts of woodwork throughout, the ornaments are straight-lined and angled rather than curved.

Reuben, formerly a music teacher, says he learned to tell Victorian from Edwardian during the renovation, which took three years. Reuben was meticulous in his attention to detail: light fixtures, brass hardware, windows, even the old sliding barn doors on the original tack house. He preserved the unusual hand-hewn Vermont granite fireplace, though a 1933 earthquake rendered its chimney unusable.

The five spacious guest rooms, all on the second floor, open onto a small sitting parlor. They contain an impressive collection of antiques, one of the most notable of which is a carved bed with

Hawaiian motif in which Andy Warhol is said to have slept. The Eastlake Room contains an early folding chair dating to 1870 and a fainting couch. A pair of carved 18th-century mahogany twin beds from Austria with opposing crowns on the headboards grace Margarita's Room.

Common rooms downstairs are unusually cozy. Original wainscoting and built-in cabinets in the living room, dining room, and foyer are gleaming golden oak. Furnishings are comfortably Victorian: a sofa, cherry-wood breakfront, Stickley chairs in the foyer. The library is modern, however, with Danish lounge chairs set in front of the guest TV.

Gregarious hosts, Reuben and Laura are longtime Long Beach residents with roots deep in the community. Thus they can be particularly helpful to guests wanting to explore Shoreline Village or cruise to Catalina.

Address: *435 Cedar Ave., Long Beach, CA 90802, tel. 310/436–0324, fax 310/436–0324.*
Accommodations: *5 double rooms with baths.*
Amenities: *Phone in rooms, TV in library, computer available, gift shop; off-street parking.*
Rates: *$85–$105; full breakfast, afternoon refreshments. AE, MC, V.*
Restrictions: *Smoking on porches and balconies only; no pets.*

Malibu Beach Inn

The Malibu Beach is one of the few southern California inns situated right on the shore. Its location, ocean views, and high level of service and amenities draw the occasional famous guest. This inn is the creation of Skip and Lu Miser, local developers who previously owned a restaurant and small motel on the property. When a storm in 1983 destroyed the restaurant, Skip decided he liked being an innkeeper better than being a restaurateur and opted to construct new lodgings instead of an eatery.

The pink-stucco, Mediterranean-style inn has what is coming to be called the "Malibu look": red-tiled roof, terra-cotta floors, soft pink and blue accents on hand-painted tiles in the lobby and bathrooms. All the rooms have an ocean theme, with images of sea horses, scallop shells, and sea snails stenciled on warm, white walls. Rattan headboards and dresser modules were specially made in the Philippines for the inn. All rooms have private balconies, workspaces, sofa beds, and bathrooms with separate dressing areas. A deep-tiled deck extending the length of the building on the ocean side is an ideal spot to sit and watch the surfers work the waves off Malibu Point, to enjoy breakfast and the morning sun—or wine and the evening sunset.

You can serve yourself from the huge bowls of fruit and baskets of muffins and croissants set up for breakfast in the inn's lobby, or you can have your breakfast brought to your room. The innkeeper has also made arrangements with Alice's Restaurant, located on the Malibu Pier just a few steps away, to cater lunch and dinner for guests.

The inn is convenient to such Malibu attractions as the J. Paul Getty Museum; guests can also explore historic Malibu pier or shop with the rich and famous at the Malibu Colony Plaza. Outdoor activities include hikes in the hills at nearby Malibu Creek State Park or snorkeling, sailboarding, and jetskiing at the beach.

Address: *22878 Pacific Coast Hwy., Malibu, CA 90265, tel. 310/456–6444 or 800/255–1007, fax 310/456–1499.*
Accommodations: *44 double rooms with baths, 3 suites.*
Amenities: *Air-conditioning; TV with VCR, phone, refrigerator, honor bar, wet bar, coffeemaker, hair dryer in rooms; robes, hot tub in 3 rooms; fireplace in 43 rooms; room service 7:30 AM–9 PM, beach towels and lounge chairs, picnic baskets, gift shop, off-street parking.*
Rates: *$150–$275; Continental breakfast. AE, DC, MC, V.*
Restrictions: *No pets; 2-night minimum on weekends, 3-night minimum on holidays.*

Seal Beach Inn and Gardens

Marjorie Bettenhausen has a romantic spirit. It's what drove her to purchase a 70-year-old hotel that had once been headquarters for rumrunners in Seal Beach—a 1920s-era seaside resort just south of Long Beach—and turn it into an antiques-filled, flower-decked bed-and-breakfast inn. Opened in 1977, it's one of the first B&Bs in southern California.

Marjorie's romantic spirit also took her to Europe, where she became enchanted with the "exquisite furnishings, lush gardens, and striking colors of the inns along the Mediterranean coast of France." She brought back the antique treasures you'll find at the inn: a 2,000-pound iron fountain from Paris; a red phone booth from Britain; Mediterranean tile murals; flower-filled Napoleonic jardinieres; stately 1920s streetlights; and classic wood-inlaid beds—including one from John Barrymore's estate.

The delightful French Mediterranean–style inn that Marjorie created includes one- and two-story buildings adorned by ornate white iron balustrades, geranium-filled window boxes, and classic blue awnings surrounding a courtyard. Another building faces a quiet residential street.

The most lavish rooms are those in the main buildings that look out onto the courtyard. Most are suites with kitchens as well as sitting rooms; furnishings include four-poster beds, stained-glass windows, and floral wallpapers and bedspreads. The recently completed Honeysuckle Suite, with windows on four sides, sunset view, large private deck, and a triangular 2-person Jacuzzi, is the most dramatic. There are also a few attractively decorated small rooms designed for budget-minded travelers.

The inn's gorgeous gardens are colorful all year. Boxes and planters lining walkways and courtyards display showy roses, shy impatiens, golden marigolds, crimson bougainvillea.

In fine weather guests enjoy breakfast and afternoon refreshments at tables set up around the pool. When it's cool they can retreat to the cozy library or breakfast room, where tables are set up in front of the fireplace. A number of packages are offered to guests, including a chocolate-lovers package, and a gondola getaway cruise through the canals of nearby Naples.

Address: *212 5th St., Seal Beach, CA 90740, tel. 310/493–2416 or 800/443–3292, fax 310/799–0483.*
Accommodations: *9 double rooms with baths, 14 housekeeping suites.*
Amenities: *TV, phone, robes, and refrigerator in rooms, fireplace in 3 rooms, Jacuzzi in 3 rooms; beach towels, picnic baskets, library, gift shop, swimming pool.*
Rates: *$118–$255; full breakfast, afternoon refreshments. AE, DC, MC, V.*
Restrictions: *No smoking indoors, no pets.*

Anaheim Country Inn

This 1910 "Princess" Anne, located on a quiet residential street, is convenient to Disneyland and the Anaheim Convention Center. It's the only inn in Anaheim, offering an intimate alternative to the hotels in the area.

The architecture of the Princess Anne is less ornate than that of the earlier Queen Anne, so the innkeepers have kept the decor very simple. Furnishings are country style, with some oak pieces dating from the turn of the century. A spool bed, an old-fashioned sewing machine, a brass bed, and Oriental rugs on the floors help sustain the comfortable country atmosphere. Unfortunately, little upgrading has been done since the inn was opened in 1983; it's gotten a bit careworn over the years. The rooms upstairs connect with each other, so combinations are possible for families or couples traveling together. The inn is surrounded by a spacious garden, planted with roses and other flowers.

Address: *856 S. Walnut, Anaheim, CA 92802, tel. 714/778–0150 or 800/755–7801.*
Accommodations: *6 double rooms with baths, 2 doubles share bath.*
Amenities: *Air-conditioning in 1 room, phone available in 3 rooms; croquet, parking.*
Rates: *$55–$80; full breakfast. AE, D, MC, V.*
Restrictions: *No smoking indoors, no pets.*

Carriage House

Like many other bed-and-breakfast inns, the Carriage House was something else first—in this case, an apartment building. When innkeepers Dee, Vernon, and Tom Taylor rescued the 1920s-era, two-story clapboard structure, located on a quiet side street a few blocks from the heart of Laguna, they converted the former parking area into a brick-floored tropical courtyard garden, installing a canopy of banana and carrotwood trees, a fish pond, bowers of hibiscus and geraniums, and an aviary.

The bright rooms reflect the building's apartment-house past: All are unusually spacious suites, with fully equipped kitchens and dining and sitting areas. Furnishings and decorative items come from the Taylor family: a silk quilt cover in a log-cabin pattern, an antique pump organ. Dee serves breakfast at a long, lace-covered table in what she calls Grandma Bean's Dining Room, but on nice days guests usually head out to the flower-filled courtyard.

Address: *1322 Catalina St., Laguna Beach, CA 92651, tel. 714/494–8945.*
Accommodations: *1 suite, 5 double housekeeping suites.*
Amenities: *TV in rooms; beach towels, parking.*
Rates: *$95–$150; Continental breakfast. No credit cards.*
Restrictions: *No pets; 2-night minimum on weekends, 3-night minimum on holidays.*

Eiler's Inn

Henk Wirtz and his family came to the United States from Germany more than 15 years ago expressly to open one of the first bed-and-breakfast inns in southern California, in the artsy town of Laguna Beach. He chose a building that had a checkered life dating from the 1930s, when families visiting the beach used its small rooms as headquarters for the day. Later, during the '60s and '70s, it became a rooming house for hippies—including Timothy Leary.

Henk made a lot of changes, creating a very proper European-style inn, complete with lace curtains and a flower-filled courtyard where breakfast, prepared by long-time resident innkeeper Jonna Iversen, is served. The rooms, surrounding the courtyard on two levels, are small, simply furnished and decorated, usually with a double bed and a chair or two; there's an occasional carved armoire or dresser. The bathrooms are small and functional.

Henk came, he said, for the same reasons that guests continue to come—because of the town's lovely beachside setting and nourishing atmosphere.

Address: *741 S. Coast Hwy., Laguna Beach, CA 92651, tel. 714/494-3004.*
Accommodations: *11 double rooms with bath, 1 housekeeping suite.*
Amenities: *TV, fireplace in suite; deck with ocean view, guest phone, TV in library.*
Rates: *$100–$175; Continental breakfast, afternoon refreshments. AE, MC, V.*
Restrictions: *No pets; 2-night minimum on weekends.*

Inn at Laguna Beach

This luxurious, Mediterranean-style inn perched on a bluff offers direct access to Main Beach. Rooms front either ocean or village; the latter, although right on the highway, are surprisingly quiet. Many rooms are spacious, containing sitting areas and flower-fringed balconies. The decor is contemporary, with walls painted in desert colors. The inn offers wheelchair-accessible rooms, TDDY telephones, close-captioned TV sets, and a security system designed to alert hearing- and vision-impaired guests in an emergency.

Convenient for those wishing to explore the Laguna Beach art scene, the inn is near the art museum and many of Laguna's galleries; in summer, there's a shuttle to the Laguna Art Festival grounds.

Address: *211 N. Coast Hwy., Laguna Beach, CA 92651, tel. 714/497-9722 or 800/544-4479, fax 714/497-9972.*
Accommodations: *70 double rooms with baths.*
Amenities: *Air-conditioning, TV with VCR, phone, refrigerator, honor bar, robes, hair dryer in rooms, microwave in 30 rooms, video rentals, conference facilities; swimming pool, Jacuzzi, off-street parking.*
Rates: *$99–$299; Continental breakfast. AE, MC, V.*
Restrictions: *No pets; 2-night minimum weekends in July and Aug., 3-night minimum on holidays.*

Inn at 657

Innkeeper Patsy Carter describes
her colorful downtown Los Angeles
neighborhood as "a polyglot place
with men in Armani suits and men in
rags, ladies who appear in the society
pages and those who sleep in them."
The former trial lawyer says she loves
the area and enjoys turning her guests
onto its diverse charms.

Set inconspicuously on a side street,
the inn, a 1930s apartment house,
offers a selection of expansive suites
designed to appeal to visitors to
nearby University of Southern California and Mt. St. Mary's College downtown campus. Spacious living rooms
are furnished with an eclectic blend of
sofas and easy chairs. Big dining-room
tables make it easy to spread out legal
briefs or lecture notes, and one can
prepare a simple dinner for colleagues
in the stocked kitchen. The inn has
plenty of quiet places: gardens all
around, a fern grotto out back, and a
big dining room where Patsy serves
monstrous breakfasts.

Address: *657 W. 23rd St., Los Angeles,
CA 90007, tel. 213/741–2200 or 800/
347–7512, fax 213/741–2200.*
Accommodations: *2 suites, 4 housekeeping suites.*
Amenities: *Air-conditioning, TV with
VCR, phone, coffeemaker in rooms,
video library; gardens with outdoor
spa, off-street parking, USC tram stop.*
Rates: *$95–$150; full breakfast. No
credit cards.*
Restrictions: *No smoking indoors, no
pets.*

Mansion Inn

This inn, offering economical
accommodations in pricey Marina
del Rey, is popular with visitors
from Europe, who take advantage of
its proximity to the largest small-boat
marina on the West Coast, the nonstop
festival at Venice Beach, and shopping
and dining at nearby Santa Monica.
Some rooms are quite small; larger
rooms have sofa beds and dining
tables, and suites have loft bedrooms.
Most rooms are on the dark side, but
the best are those facing the interior
courtyard. Simple furnishings throughout include pine beds and armoires;
colors are soft blues and mauves.

Breakfast is served in a small café
adjoining the interior courtyard.
Guests tend to sit out on the patio,
flooded with light at midday, to enjoy
the gurgling fountain, mountains of
greenery, and bowers of flowers that
fill the area.

Address: *327 Washington Blvd.,
Marina del Rey, CA 90291, tel.
310/821–2557 or 800/828–0688, fax
310/827–0289.*
Accommodations: *38 double rooms
with baths, 5 suites.*
Amenities: *Air-conditioning, TV,
phone, refrigerator, hair dryer in
rooms, free movies nightly; off-street
parking.*
Rates: *$79–$125, children under 12
free; Continental breakfast. AE, D,
DC, MC, V.*
Restrictions: *No pets.*

Old Turner Inn

A casual, beach-house feel permeates the blue-and-white clapboard Old Turner Inn, built as a family home in 1927 on a still-quiet residential street just a block from Avalon's oceanfront. Windows all across the front on the first and second floors suggest that these spaces once were sleeping porches. Now, the downstairs area contains a cheery dining room, while upstairs are sunny sitting rooms adjacent to the inn's two suites.

The Old Turner Inn's decor is a pleasant mélange of antiques and comfortable contemporary furnishings: Victorian-style white wicker chairs, mirrored armoires, and iron and brass beds in the guest rooms contrast with Scandinavian love seats, a glass-topped coffee table, and baby grand piano in the living room. Rooms are large, bright, and sunny. Four have wood-burning fireplaces and handmade quilts and are decorated in soft, romantic colors: apricot, cream, light green.

Address: *232 Catalina Ave., Box 97, Avalon, CA 90704, tel. 310/510-2236.*
Accommodations: *3 double rooms with baths, 2 suites.*
Amenities: *Fireplace in 4 rooms.*
Rates: *$125–$175 (summer); Continental breakfast, afternoon refreshments. D, MC, V.*
Restrictions: *No smoking indoors, no pets; 2-night minimum most weekends, 3-night minimum some holidays.*

Portofino Beach Hotel

T his Old World–style inn, just a few steps from the surf in a busy section of Newport Beach, is a good spot from which to watch the teenagers on skateboards, lovers strolling, and dory fishermen hawking their catch. The hotel's restaurant, Renato, is popular for its good northern Italian fare.

The decor in the common areas has an Italian accent: bouffant balloon curtains, faux-marble columns, lace antimacassars, brocade-covered wingback chairs, curved-back settees, and etched-glass windows. Guest rooms are located on the second floor of the main hotel and in a wing in back; most have some ocean view, but Portofino suites have the best vistas. Antique furnishings in the rooms include brass beds, carved headboards, and French side chairs; many of the appealing marble bathrooms have skylights, and some have step-down double whirlpool tubs.

Address: *2306 W. Oceanfront, Newport Beach, CA 92663, tel. 714/673-7030, fax 714/723-4370.*
Accommodations: *15 double rooms with baths.*
Amenities: *Air-conditioning, TV, phone in rooms, whirlpool tub in 11 rooms, private sun deck off 3 rooms; restaurant, room service during dinner hour, lounge, off-street parking.*
Rates: *$100–$235; Continental breakfast. AE, DC, MC, V.*
Restrictions: *No pets; 2-night minimum on weekends.*

Salisbury House

For their new home, located in the historic West Adams district of Los Angeles, Jay and Sue German chose a 1901 Craftsman with some Victorian touches: a curved bay window in the dining room and an abundance of leaded and stained-glass windows. There are lots of dark-stained firwood moldings, a built-in china closet in the dining room, polished oak floors, and wainscoting.

All the guest rooms are quite large and comfortable. There is a white iron bed in the Blue Room and a brass bed and braided rugs in the Attic Suite, which is finished with redwood siding. It also has a claw-foot tub positioned so that the bather can look out over the bird-filled trees. The inn's common areas include a living room, where a fire crackles most of the year, and a striking formal dining room, where Sue serves an imaginative breakfast featuring zucchini pancakes or potato frittatas. A self-described foodie, she says that the local Chinese, Korean, Mexican, Vietnamese, and Italian restaurants inspire her in the kitchen.

Address: *2273 W. 20th St., Los Angeles, CA 90018, tel. 213/737-7817 or 800/373-1778.*
Accommodations: *2 double rooms with baths, 2 doubles share bath, 1 suite.*
Amenities: *Phone, TV with VCR, and air-conditioning in attic room, refrigerator in 4 rooms; guest phone, TVs available.*
Rates: *$75–$100; full breakfast, afternoon refreshments. AE, MC, V.*
Restrictions: *No smoking indoors, no pets.*

Venice Beach House

This rambling 1911 Craftsman-style house is located just a few steps from famed Venice beach, with its surf, sand, and continuous waterside carnival. Once the home of evangelist Aimee Semple McPherson, it's long been a hideaway for beach-loving Angelenos and visiting Europeans, and shows the wear and tear of many guests.

The grey shingle-clad house is surrounded by colorful gardens. Inside there's an attractive parlor with expansive curved bay window and gleaming oak floors topped by Oriental rugs. Guest rooms on the first and second floors are bright and airy, especially those across the front of the house that capture the ocean breeze. The Pier Suite, filling a second-floor corner, has a partial ocean view, a fireplace, and separate sitting area; furnishings are traditional, rather than beachy.

Address: *15 30th Ave., Venice, CA 90291, tel. 310/823-1966, fax 310/823-1842.*
Accommodations: *3 double rooms with baths, 4 doubles share 2 baths, 2 suites.*
Amenities: *TV and phone in rooms, Jacuzzi in 1 room, fireplace in 1 suite; catered meals available, massage available, off-street parking.*
Rates: *$80–$150; Continental breakfast, afternoon refreshments. AE, MC, V.*
Restrictions: *No smoking indoors, no pets.*

Central Coast

Central Coast
From Santa Barbara to San Simeon

The drive along California's Central Coast is one of the most rewarding in the state and is the scenic California that most visitors have come to see. Except for a few smallish cities— Ventura and Santa Barbara in the south and San Luis Obispo in the north—this is a rural excursion of nearly 200 miles of rolling, golden, oak-studded hills and wave-washed beaches.

Highway 101, one of the state's great north–south thorough- fares, is also one of its most historic. The route that follows El Camino Real (Kings Road) was forged by the Spanish padres to lead from one mission to another and is now marked by a series of roadside bells.

Starting in the south, the highway passes through Ventura, gateway to the Channel Islands National Park. It hugs the coast as it moves north toward Santa Barbara. With its Spanish-style architecture, fine restaurants, and collection of outstanding bed-and-breakfast inns, Santa Barbara has become a popular destination for work-weary Angelenos. Santa Barbara strives to preserve its Mediterranean ambience, as a walk among the red-tile-roofed shops along State Street reveals.

From Santa Barbara the highway leads north along the coast, skirting a number of lovely beaches at El Capitan, Refugio, and Gaviota. Moving inland at San Marcos, it passes through the lovely Santa Ynez Valley, where wine tasting and bike riding on tranquil country lanes are two popular pursuits. This is also the home of ultratouristy Solvang, which has a Danish theme and an array of bakeries and gift shops.

The highway touches the coast again at a place locals call the Five Cities. Here visitors can explore miles of wide, hard- packed beaches and fluffy white sand dunes; these beach communities are popular with clam diggers, skin divers, and anglers.

San Luis Obispo, just a few miles up the coast, offers a number of surprises. A laid-back university town, it's the home of California Polytechnic University and has an attractive old-fashioned downtown that reveals its Spanish heritage. Like the area north of Santa Barbara, this is wine country.

Cambria, a few miles north along the coast, is the gateway to Hearst Castle and has long been a stopover for visitors to La Cuesta Encantada. It has also developed as an artists' colony, with many local artists specializing in creating luminous glass objects. Cambria also boasts a number of bed-and-breakfast inns as well as a collection of good restaurants.

No trip to the Central Coast would be complete without a visit to William Randolph Hearst's mansion on the hill at San Simeon. With money from his vast publishing empire, Hearst devoted more than 30 years to building the Italian-Spanish-Moorish-French-style castle with its acres of paintings, sculptures, and other European artwork; gardens; marble swimming pools; lavish dining room; and guest houses that are almost as opulent.

Places to Go, Sights to See

Channel Islands National Park (1901 Spinnaker Dr., Ventura 93001, tel. 805/658–5730) consists of five islands and a visitor center at Ventura Harbor. *Island Packers* (tel. 805/642–1393) offers day-long boat trips to the islands.

Hearst Castle (San Simeon State Park, 750 Hearst Castle Rd., San Simeon 93452, tel. 805/927–2020; for tour reservations, tel. 800/444–4445) is operated by the California Park Service. Half- and three-hour tours are available year-round; the garden tour is offered April through October.

Missions. *La Purisima Mission* (2295 Purisima Rd., Lompoc 93436, tel. 805/733–3713) is the state's most completely restored mission. There's a self-guided tour of this remote setting, which vividly evokes the secular and religious activities of early settlers. Occasionally, costumed docents demonstrate crafts, including weaving and bread and candle making. *Mission Santa Barbara* (Laguna and Los Olivos Sts., Santa Barbara 93105, tel. 805/682–4149) is known as the Queen of the

Missions for its Spanish Renaissance architecture, serene gardens, quiet court-yard, and exhibits of embroidered vestments and illuminated manuscripts.

Santa Barbara County Courthouse (Anacapa and Anapamu Sts., Santa Barbara 93101, tel. 805/962–6464) is a Spanish-Moorish palace with murals, painted ceilings, massive doors, balconies, and Tunisian tiles.

Santa Barbara Wine Country (Santa Barbara County Vintner's Association, Box 1558, Santa Ynez 93460–1558, tel. 805/688–0881) encompasses several valleys, most notably the Santa Maria and the Santa Ynez. More than 30 wineries are found along Highways 154 and 176. Many offer tours and tastings; some have picnic facilities.

Restaurants

Ian's (tel. 805/927–8649) in Cambria offers elegant dining and an eclectic menu featuring light California cuisine. **Robin's** (tel. 805/927–5007) down the street has a laid-back feel but serves savvy variations on Southeast Asian, Indian, Italian, and vegetarian dishes. Santa Barbara's **La Super-Rica Taco** (tel. 805/963–4940) is an unsigned corner taco stand where the line always stretches out the door. Also in Santa Barbara, **Citronelle** (tel. 805/963–0111) combines a great ocean view with outstanding California cuisine. **Oysters** (tel. 805/962–9888), an easy walk from the inns near State Street, serves fresh seafood in a casual setting. **Pane E Vino** (tel. 805/969–9274) in Montecito is popular for its sophisticated Italian cuisine. Santa Ynez wine country locals love the modern American fare at the **Ballard Store & Wine Bar** (tel. 805/688–5319). History buffs frequent **Mattei's Tavern** (tel. 805/688–4820), a stop along the old stagecoach route. Capture the spirit of San Luis Obispo and the vibrant taste of locally grown food at **Big Sky** (tel. 805/545–5401), a lively breakfast and lunch spot.

Tourist Information

Cambria Chamber of Commerce (767 Main St., Cambria 93428, tel. 805/927–3624); **San Luis Obispo County Visitors and Convention Bureau** (1041 Chorro St., Suite E, San Luis Obispo 93401, tel. 800/634–1414); **Santa Barbara Conference and Visitors Bureau** (510A State St., Santa Barbara 93101, tel. 800/927–4688); **Santa Barbara County Vintners' Association** (Box 1558, Santa Ynez 93460, tel. 800/218–0881).

Reservation Service

Santa Barbara Bed & Breakfast Innkeepers Guild (Box 90734, Santa Barbara 93190, tel. 800/776–9176).

Blue Quail Inn

There aren't a lot of luxuries at the Blue Quail—no hot tub, no VCRs, only one fireplace—but it doesn't need these extras to be one of Santa Barbara's better bed-and-breakfasts. Born into a B&B family, owner Jeanise Suding Eaton clearly learned early on how to create a welcoming inn. She sold the Blue Quail in 1994, but its new partners—Jack Greenwald, who ran a five-star restaurant in Scotland, and Christine Dunstan of the nearby Cheshire Cat—are maintaining the service and style that generated so much repeat business for Jeanise.

The antithesis of Santa Barbara's typical grand Victorian B&B, this collection of five little shingled bungalows is low-key and quiet, with an overall decor that will appeal more to lovers of American-country style than of Victorian formality. The main cottage houses a homey, carpeted living room; a dining room with hardwood floors, tan striped wallpaper, country-pine antiques, and an inviting window seat; a tiled country kitchen, where someone friendly is often baking something cinnamony; and two of the more modest guest rooms.

In the rear of the property is the inn's best quarters, the Wood Thrush cottage. There are luxurious white-on-white French linens on the king-size bed, pickled-pine shutters at the windows, and large, comfortable wicker armchairs in the living room. Those who prefer a Ralph Lauren look should try the Cardinal Suite, with its

veranda, wicker bed, botanical prints, and rich fabrics in paisleys and stripes. American-country fans will love the smaller Mockingbird, with its cheerful yellow floral fabrics and yellow, blue, and white quilt on the wall.

Outside, the cool gardens are thick with ferns and fragrant with jasmine; in fair weather (almost always), breakfast is served on the patio. The many good restaurants, shops, and sights of State Street are a comfortable stroll or quick bike ride away; beach goers will probably want to drive.

Families take note: This is one of the very few Santa Barbara B&Bs that happily welcome young children, as long as they stay in one of the more private suites.

Address: *1908 Bath St., Santa Barbara, CA 93101, tel. 805/687–2300 or 800/676–1622.*
Accommodations: *5 double rooms with baths, 4 suites.*
Amenities: *Fireplace in 1 suite, TV in main house; bicycles.*
Rates: *$85–$95, suites $125–$165; full breakfast, afternoon and evening wine and refreshments. AE, D, DC, MC, V.*
Restrictions: *No smoking indoors, no pets; 2-night minimum on weekends.*

The Blue Whale Inn

ike many southern Californians, Fred Ushijima had been visiting the town of Cambria regularly for years, attracted by the laid-back beachfront atmosphere, good restaurants, and the shops and galleries of a growing artists' colony. Cambria's proximity to the Hearst Castle at San Simeon has always meant large numbers of visitors, but the village hasn't become touristy or overdeveloped.

Fred decided to sink roots in Cambria, and he found the perfect location on a triangular point of land jutting out to the sea along Moonstone Beach Drive. A visual delight, the Blue Whale consists of six guest rooms stepped back from the ocean at such an angle that each captures a bit of the view (the best views, surprisingly, are from the rooms farthest back). At the front of the inn is a spacious living room furnished with overstuffed sofas and chairs and a wood-burning stove; it adjoins the dining area, and the two together create a great room with a wall of windows revealing the ever-changing ocean vista.

A tiny Japanese-style garden, created by Fred, separates the guest rooms from the parking lot. Planted with a colorful selection of native plants—including lupine, coreapsis, thyme, and westringa—the garden is punctuated by a series of stepping-stones that lead from the parking area to the decks in front of the guest rooms. Guests often contemplate the beauty of nature while sitting on the garden's wooden bench or watching its tumbling waterfall.

In sharp contrast to the expansive views of sea and sky outside, the inn's interior is a riot of wallpapers and flowered fabrics, mostly in shades of blue; whitewashed pine is the wood of choice. Appointments are comfortable: step-up canopy beds, love seats, desks, a coffee table, and side chair in each room. Skylights punctuate each vaulted ceiling. Bathrooms, also skylit, have adjacent dressing areas complete with a sink set into a long vanity.

Although Fred is often at the inn, gardening and sharing his dining suggestions ("a walking menu," one guest observed), Karleen and Bob Hathcock are the day-to-day innkeepers. Karleen is the breakfast chef, known for her croissant French toast with strawberry sauce.

Address: *6736 Moonstone Beach Dr., Cambria, CA 93428, tel. 805/927–4647.*
Accommodations: *6 double rooms with baths.*
Amenities: *Fireplace, refrigerator, hair dryer, TV, phone in rooms; gift shop.*
Rates: *$135–$170; full breakfast, afternoon refreshments. MC, V.*
Restrictions: *No smoking indoors, no pets; 2-night minimum on weekends and holidays.*

The Cheshire Cat

T wo words sum up these adjacent gray-and-white Victorian-era houses linked by a brick patio: "Laura" and "Ashley." If you like the late designer's delicate floral fabrics, bedding, and wallpapers, then you'll be in heaven here. Owner Christine Dunstan, who once owned and ran a B&B in Scotland, gave her American inn a thoroughly British look, from the picket-fenced flower gardens to the formal entry and fireplace-warmed sitting area. Some masculine English antiques offset the frilly prettiness of the public rooms, most notably the huge refectory-style table and weighty sideboard in the dining room.

Dunstan has the help of a manager, Marti Armstrong, and a small crew of friendly folks to cook the substantial full breakfast and tend to the guests and the property. There's a fair amount to tend to: the main house, all Victorian turrets and bays; the neighboring house, a Georgian-style box with shutters and bay windows; the Tweedledum & Tweedledee house, a simple clapboard cottage, in back; and the various garden areas, including a large brick patio where a first-rate breakfast is served.

Larger and more upscale than most other B&Bs in town, the Cheshire Cat is popular with small groups for retreats or meetings, but most of its customers are couples seeking romance. They generally find it, particularly if they splurge on the Eberle Suite, which has a brick fireplace and a

whirlpool tub for two; the White Rabbit Suite, whose private patio overlooks the gardens; or the swank Tweedledum Suite in the newer back house, complete with living room, dining room, kitchenette, fireplace, TV, king-size bed, and whirlpool tub.

The west-facing rooms in the main house can be a bit noisy, since they're the closest to busy Chapala Street. On the plus side, the inn is a short walk from the shops and restaurants of State Street.

Address: *36 W. Valerio St., Santa Barbara, CA 93101, tel. 805/569–1610.*
Accommodations: *7 double rooms with baths, 7 suites.*
Amenities: *Phone, chocolates, liqueurs in rooms, fireplace in 4 rooms, whirlpool tub in 4 rooms, TV in 2 rooms, meeting room for 8 to 12 with fireplace; mountain bicycles, spa in gazebo.*
Rates: *$89–$169, suites $169–$249; full breakfast, afternoon wine. MC, V.*
Restrictions: *No smoking indoors, no pets; 2-night minimum on weekends.*

El Encanto

Like its rival high-end country inn, the San Ysidro Ranch, El Encanto has had its ups and downs over the years. It's definitely on the ascendance these days, since an extensive renovation dealt with the shabbiness that had crept up on the place in the '80s. Fortunately, a bit of genteel shabbiness remains—too much slickness would most definitely not suit this tumble of cottages in the hills above the Santa Barbara Mission.

The sort of country inns that pepper New England are scarce in California, home of the grand hotel, the tiny B&B, and the faceless motel—which makes this almost-in-the-country inn so welcome. Although red-tile-roofed Spanish villas dominate in the surrounding areas, most of El Encanto's buildings are board-and-batten cottages.

What makes El Encanto as enchanting as its name promises are the view of ocean, trees, and red-tile roofs from the restaurant's huge patio; the 10 acres of grounds (ferns, banana palms, towering eucalyptus, thick lawns, even a lily pond); and the larger cottage suites and villas, done up in a pleasant, generally informal mishmash of French-country fabrics, English-style florals, and updated American-country furniture with a Shaker feeling. Most of the cottages have porches and French doors; some have private patios.

The standard rooms, which can be small, lean more toward the updated American-country look, with Berber carpets, crisp tile bathrooms, and a predominant hunter green and tan color scheme.

The terrace restaurant's lovely views, not to mention its good California–contemporary American cuisine, have made it one of Santa Barbara's most popular brunch spots, so reserve early; it tends to sell out on summer weekends. To work off the food, guests play tennis, swim laps, or walk the hilly streets. Or they snooze in one of the yellow-striped swings dotting the grounds. The beach is a 10-minute drive away, and the State Street shops are even closer.

Address: *1900 Lasuen Rd., Santa Barbara, CA 93103, tel. 805/687–5000 or 800/346–7039, fax 805/687–3903.*
Accommodations: *34 double rooms with baths, 45 suites.*
Amenities: *Phone and cable TV in rooms, fireplace and private patio or deck in many rooms; restaurant, bar, lounge, 9 meeting and banquet rooms, room service 7 AM–9 PM; swimming pool, tennis court, walking paths.*
Rates: *$140–$180, suites $160–$280, two-bedroom suites $360–$660; breakfast not included (except some midweek packages). AE, DC, MC, V.*
Restrictions: *No pets; 2-night minimum on weekends.*

Los Olivos Grand Hotel

Ronald Reagan and Michael Jackson have ranches hereabouts, as do lots of less famous but similarly moneyed folks. Which explains this country inn's haute-bourgeois style and high prices. Those who value rusticity should look elsewhere; those looking for creature comforts (and who don't mind paying for them) are likely to have a memorable stay.

About 45 minutes up a lovely, sharply winding mountain road from Santa Barbara, Los Olivos is tucked into the oak-dotted ochre hills of the Santa Ynez Valley. Vineyards and ranch land occupy most of the valley, and the town isn't much more than a dozen art galleries, a wine shop, a gas station, a saddlery, a couple of restaurants, and this inn. Amusements in these parts are genteel: wine tasting, horseback riding, hiking, dining, gallery hopping, and taking in the night air from the confines of a steaming hot tub.

The Grand Hotel hews to the polished (as opposed to the rustic) French-country style. Classical music wafts through the lobby, with its stone fireplace, gleaming piano, French doors, and various clusters of sofas, wing chairs, and Queen Anne furniture. At one end is Remington's, a good Continental-American restaurant named for the western artist; downstairs, the Wine Cellar, a private dining room, is great for larger parties.

Each of the large suites (set in two low-lying Victorian buildings) is individually styled; vaulted, beamed ceilings, Pierre Deux–style fabrics, iron or brass beds, hand-painted tile fireplaces, and Impressionist paintings are the norm. The Monet Suite, with its bay window, restful blues, and comfy chaise, is particularly lovely, but there isn't a loser in the bunch. Luxurious touches abound, from wet bars to down comforters.

Though the inn lacks the homey, personal feeling of owner-operated B&Bs, the staff exudes friendly professionalism and will tend to most any request, from arranging a private tour of a winery to delivering a freshly brewed cup of tea to your room at 3 AM.

Address: *2860 Grand Ave., Los Olivos, CA 93441, tel. 805/688–7788 or 800/446–2455.*
Accommodations: *21 suites.*
Amenities: *Fireplace, phone, cable TV, wet bar, refrigerator, wine in rooms, whirlpool tub in many rooms; restaurant, lounge, meeting and banquet rooms, room service; swimming pool, spa; bicycles, picnics and backpacks extra.*
Rates: *$160–$325; Continental breakfast. AE, D, DC, MC, V.*
Restrictions: *No pets; 2-night minimum on weekends.*

Old Yacht Club Inn

When former school administrators Nancy Donaldson and Lu Caruso and teacher Sandy Hunt opened Santa Barbara's first bed-and-breakfast in 1980, they set out to provide a homey atmosphere in which guests would feel comfortable putting their feet up—and so pampered that they'd want to return again and again. In addition, there would be the outstanding food prepared by Nancy, a member of the American Wine and Food Institute.

Initially the inn consisted of only the historic 1912 Craftsman house with its broad porches, tiny balcony across the front, white brick fireplace, and colorful gardens. Just a block from the beach, it had been built as a private home, and during the 1920s served as the headquarters for the Santa Barbara Yacht Club. In 1983 the innkeepers acquired the more spacious house next door, which they transformed into the Hitchcock House.

The Hitchcock is a monument to the families of the innkeepers, with its four rooms named and decorated to honor parents and grandparents. The Julia Metelmann is decorated with life-size photographs of the mother of a former inn partner. The photographs depict Julia as a young pioneer in North Dakota, and furnishings include a red lacquer Chinese chest that once belonged to her.

There are five rooms in the main house, four on the second floor, and one downstairs. The upstairs rooms offer a light and airy ambience. In the two front-facing rooms French doors open onto a balcony where guests can sip wine while taking in the afternoon sun. Downstairs, the sunny Captain's Corner opens onto a private patio.

Breakfast and Saturday-night dinners are served in the inn's dining-living room. Nancy uses fresh local ingredients in her five-course gourmet dinners: fresh fish from the bay, artichokes from nearby fields, sorrel grown in the backyard. Breakfast features the lightest of light omelets, pancakes, French toast, home-baked breads, and fresh fruit.

Address: *431 Corona del Mar Dr., Santa Barbara, CA 93103, tel. 805/ 962–1277.*
Accommodations: *8 rooms with baths, 1 suite.*
Amenities: *Phone in rooms, whirlpool tub in 2 rooms; bicycles, beach towels, chairs.*
Rates: *$90–$150; full breakfast, evening refreshments, dinner served to guests on Sat. nights (about $25). AE, D, MC, V.*
Restrictions: *No smoking in guest rooms, no pets; 2-night minimum on weekends.*

The Parsonage

I n 1981, Hilde Michelmore transformed a dreary school for problem
children (formerly the home of the
parson of nearby Trinity Episcopal
Church) into an excellent bed-and-
breakfast, immediately becoming a
leader of Santa Barbara's just-develop-
ing B&B scene. She tried to retire in
1993 but couldn't leave her pride and
joy; now she's trying out semi-retire-
ment, sharing the management of the
inn with her daughter, Jane Fair.

The mother-daughter team have been
immersed in renovating their big, boxy
hillside Queen Anne Victorian (circa
1892), though they haven't tampered
with the uncluttered Victorian look (if
that's not an oxymoron). Most rooms
are wearing new paint, wallpaper, and
upholstery. Whirlpool tubs have been
added to the Honeymoon Suite and
Peacock Room; soon to be added are
some in-room fireplaces and an outdoor whirlpool.

On the ground floor are the large,
bright living and dining rooms, which
combine polished woodwork, Oriental
rugs, subdued antiques, and white-lace
curtains to create a formal yet unfussy
look. Hilde's pride and joy is the Oriental dining room table, with its subtly
beautiful painted top. Her blend of
antiques and styles of several periods—from the Louis XVI dresser and
mirror in the Versailles Room to the
Victorian settee in the Las Flores
Room—emphasizes homeyness, not
museum-style perfection.

The Honeymoon Suite may be one of
the most romantic accommodations in
town. A huge three-room suite that
wraps around a front corner of the
house, it offers stunning views of
ocean, city, and mountains; it also has a
glass-walled solarium. Good sea views
can also be had from the bay windows
of Las Flores, and the other two second-story rooms offer mountain views.

Weather permitting—which is most of
the time—breakfast is served on bone
china on the outdoor deck or in the
stately new gazebo. Jane bakes coffee
cakes and cinnamon rolls and takes
pride in her substantial breakfast
entrées, including soufflés, egg creations, and creative varieties of French
toast. Home-baked cookies are often
set out on the dining-room table, along
with pitchers of iced tea or lemonade.

Address: *1600 Olive St., Santa Barbara, CA 93101, tel. 805/962–9336.*
Accommodations: *5 rooms with
baths, 1 suite.*
Amenities: *Fireplace in 1 room.*
Rates: *$95–$140, suite $185; full
breakfast, afternoon refreshments.
AE, MC, V.*
Restrictions: *No smoking indoors,
children under 12 discouraged, no
pets; 2-night minimum on weekends,
3-night minimum on holidays.*

San Ysidro Ranch

San Ysidro's luxuriousness belies its humble roots as one of the Santa Barbara Mission's working ranches. It became a guest ranch in the late 1800s after cottages were added to the 1825 adobe, which still stands, and became famous in the 1930s, when owners Ronald Colman (the actor) and Alvin Weingand (a state senator) attracted stars, writers, and royalty. Here Vivian Leigh and Laurence Olivier married, John and Jackie Kennedy honeymooned, and Winston Churchill wrote some of his memoirs.

Nestled in the hills above Montecito, one of the country's wealthiest small towns, the Ranch, as it is known to faithfuls, had become shabby by the '60s. New owners restored the cottages and added some luxurious new ones, and Hollywood was once again in residence. In 1987, Claude Rouas, owner of Napa Valley's luxe Auberge du Soleil, took over and set out to bring the atmospheric stone restaurant, the ranch's old packing house, up to France's country-inn standards, a goal he and American chef Gerard Thompson have achieved in spades.

The inn itself remains as swell as ever. Winding paths connect the various board-and-batten cottages, which house everything from smallish double rooms to huge two-bedroom suites with soaring beamed ceilings. The decor is American country gone elegant: clean-lined antiques, down comforters, Oriental rugs, and a lavish use of high-quality pine.

Some highly stressed guests (including many of the very famous) just hide out by their fireplaces and order room service. Others stroll the gardens and orchards, hike through the 540 acres, swim, play tennis, ride horses, play chess in the games room, have a drink in the cozy Plow & Angel bar, or venture into downtown Montecito or nearby Santa Barbara. Families are increasingly in evidence, thanks to the new petting zoo, play area, videos, and kids' menus. Even the family dog is welcome. Everyone gets what they came for: clean air, charm, comfort, pampering, romance, and enough peace and quiet to finish writing that script.

Address: *900 San Ysidro La., Montecito, CA 93108, tel. 805/969–5046 or 800/368–6788, fax 805/565–1995.*
Accommodations: *26 double rooms with baths, 18 suites and cottages.*
Amenities: *Fireplace or wood stove, phone, cable TV, private deck, wet bar, refrigerator in rooms, whirlpool tub in many rooms, restaurant, bar, room service; swimming pool, spa, tennis, horses and picnics extra.*
Rates: *$195–$325, suites $450–$750; breakfast not included. AE, MC, V.*
Restrictions: *2-night minimum on weekends.*

Simpson House Inn

Although red-tile roofs are the norm in Santa Barbara, Victoriana runs rife as well, since so many Brits settled here in the late 1800s. One such emigrant was Robert Simpson, the Scotchman who built this Eastlake-style house in 1874. Glyn and Linda Davies restored the house and made it their home in 1976; more recently, they have transformed it into the finest B&B in the Central Coast.

Set on a quiet, exquisitely landscaped acre in the heart of town, the Simpson House Inn offers something for almost everyone. Traditional B&B fans should stay in the main house, where larger-than-average rooms are paeans to Victorian style, color, and elegance. One room pays tribute to famed Victorian designer Christopher Dresser; another showcases a great William Morris wallpaper. Oriental rugs, English lace curtains, wicker, and claw-foot tubs add to the atmosphere.

Those put off by Victorian primness and the occasional discomforts of 100-year-old bathrooms should consider the newest additions to the property: three cottages and a restored 100-year-old barn. The cottages are among the most romantic quarters in town—each has its own private courtyard (with bubbling fountain), queen feather-bed, love seat set beside a wood-burning fireplace, teak floors, in-room whirlpool, superb shower, hidden TV/VCR, and plenty of privacy. Though a bit less dreamy, the four large suites in the barn are exceptional. Oriental rugs rest on antique pine floors, French doors open to private decks, king-size beds wear high-quality linens, English pine armoires hide TVs and VCRs, showers are modern and roomy, and fireplaces burn real wood, not those ubiquitous metal logs.

Resident innkeeper Gillean Wilson oversees the substantial breakfast, which can be taken on the veranda, in the garden, or in your suite. But it is the early evening that is most memorable, when guests toast the balmy Santa Barbara twilight with local wines and elegant hors d'oeuvres while knocking around croquet balls, stoking the fireplace, or sitting for a spell on a wicker sofa in the gardens.

Address: *121 E. Arrellaga St., Santa Barbara, CA 93101, tel. 805/963-7067 or 800/676-1280, fax 805/564-4811.*
Accommodations: *6 double rooms with baths, 3 cottages, 4 suites.*
Amenities: *Air-conditioning, robes in rooms; fireplace, TV with VCR, and coffeemaker in cottages and suites; bicycles, croquet, beach chairs, towels.*
Rates: *$105–$160, suites and cottages $195–$240; full breakfast, evening refreshments. AE, D, MC, V.*
Restrictions: *No smoking indoors, no pets; 2-night minimum on weekends.*

Union Hotel/ Victorian Mansion

I n the tiny Old West outpost of Los Alamos, some 50 miles north of Santa Barbara, these two inns present a study in fantasy fulfillment. The Union Hotel, a onetime Wells Fargo stagecoach station dating from 1880, was renovated by Dick Langdon in 1970 and turned into one of the first bed-and-breakfasts in California. The whimsical Old West atmosphere, which begins in the lobby peopled with mannequins costumed in frontier finery, is carried into the saloon with its mahogany Ping-Pong table supported by marble statues, and continues in the bedrooms with their French and patriotic wallpapers.

In the neighboring yellow three-story 1864 mansion, mere whimsy gives way to flat-out fantasy. Dick, who passed away in 1994, created a sort of Disneyland for adults here, the spirit of which is kept alive by his children, who now run both facilities. Take the Egyptian Room, designed to make a couple feel like Antony and Cleopatra camping out in the desert. A step-up white bed, canopied with gauze, stands in the middle of the room facing a wall-size mural of a desert. Walls are draped with Near East–motif fabrics, and there's a step-up hot tub and a marble-faced fireplace flanked by floor cushions. The bathroom door is a life-size statue of King Tut, opened by tugging his beard, and the bathroom itself resembles the inside of a pyramid. Hooded desert robes, backgammon, computer-controlled background music, and videotapes of *Lawrence of*

Arabia and *The Wind and the Lion* round out the fantasy.

Other rooms are equally fantastic: Roman, Gypsy, Pirate, '50s Drive-In, and French—each with fitting murals, bed, theme robes, music, movies, games, and menus. Breakfast is delivered to the theme rooms through lockers concealed in the walls.

Over the years, Dick employed a community of artists and artisans who gave life to his fantasy. Among the grounds's distinguishing features are the largest hedge-maze west of the Mississippi and a restored 67-foot yawl that once belonged to the King of Denmark.

Address: *362 Bell St., Box 616, Los Alamos, CA 93440, tel. 805/344–2744 or 800/230–2744, fax 805/344–3125.*
Accommodations: *Hotel has 3 rooms with baths, 11 rooms with sinks share 2 baths; mansion has 6 rooms with baths.*
Amenities: *(in Mansion) TV with VCR, tapes, phone, hot tub, fireplace, robes, refrigerator in rooms; restaurant, saloon, shuffleboard, Ping-Pong, swimming pool, spa in gazebo.*
Rates: *Hotel $60–$160, mansion $180–$220; full breakfast. AE, D, MC, V.*
Restrictions: *No pets; restaurant open Wed.–Sun.*

Ballard Inn

This gray and white updated Cape Cod–style inn looks out of place in the Santa Ynez Valley, home of sprawling horse ranches and the up-and-coming wineries of Santa Barbara County. Standing on a corner in the tiny town of Ballard, the Ballard Inn was built in 1985 by a group of Hollywood celebrities and is now owned by Santa Barbara restaurateur Steve Hyslop and partner Larry Stone.

Each room illustrates a different aspect of local lore. One room feels like a frontiersman's mountain cabin, with a rough stone fireplace and rustic wooden furnishings; another recalls cowboy days, with a collection of chaps, cowboy gear, and early photographs of local cattle ranches. The Vineyard Room honors the wine country with grape colors and willow furni-ture. Comfortable, overstuffed sofas fill the living room, and an Old West ambience prevails in another common room, the Stagecoach. In the evening, the dining room becomes Café Chardonnay, a full-service restaurant.

Address: *2436 Baseline Ave., Ballard, CA 93463, tel. 805/688-7770 or 800/638-2466, fax 805/688-9560.*
Accommodations: *15 double rooms with baths.*
Amenities: *Air-conditioning, fireplace in 7 rooms; bicycle rentals, carriage rides extra.*
Rates: *$160–$195; full breakfast, afternoon wine tasting. AE, MC, V.*
Restrictions: *No smoking indoors, no pets; 2-night minimum on weekends.*

Bath Street Inn

At first glance, the Bath Street Inn, an 1870s Victorian cottage on a quiet street a few blocks off Santa Barbara's main drag, looks deceptively small. There's no clue that it's so much larger than it appears, thanks to a recent expansion.

Most guest rooms are located upstairs, with those on the third floor filling odd-shaped spaces created by the eaves and gables of the steeply pitched roof. Two more luxurious rooms occupy the brand-new Summer House in back. The decor in all is predominantly Victorian, with comfortable, overstuffed sofas, wingback chairs, canopy beds, reading nooks, and cabbage-rose wallpapers. "People say it reminds them of their mother's house," remarks owner Susan Brown, one of Santa Barbara's first innkeepers.

Guests are usually served breakfast in the garden out back. As pleasant as it is to linger here, this inn makes a convenient home base for excursions to the beach or for exploring the shops and sights of nearby State Street.

Address: *1720 Bath St., Santa Barbara, CA 93101, tel. 805/682-9680 or 800/788-BATH, 800/549-BATH in CA.*
Accommodations: *10 rooms with baths.*
Amenities: *Air conditioning and TV in 2 rooms, fireplace in 1 room; bicycles.*
Rates: *$95–$150; full breakfast, afternoon refreshments, evening wine. AE, MC, V.*
Restrictions: *No smoking indoors, no pets; 2-night minimum on weekends.*

Bayberry Inn

he late Carlton Wagner, a
renowned interior designer and
color consultant, created this inn,
reminiscent of the gilded age just after
World War I, within a shingle-covered,
late-19th-century house. You'll find an
abundance of silk, crystal, and porce-
lains throughout. The dining room ceiling is draped in yard after yard of soft
pink silk, with folds brought together
in the center by a crystal chandelier.
The walls in the dining room are covered by beveled mirrors. Beds are
canopied in heavy fabric, with a crystal
chandelier in the center of the canopy.
The rooms tend to be cozy, with the
dramatic bed as the main feature;
lighting in most rooms is subdued, creating a romantic mood.

Innkeeper Keith Pomeroy specializes
in pampering guests. With a background in catering, he prepares breakfasts as pretty as they are tasty,
served on fine china in the opulent dining room.

Address: *111 W. Valerio St., Santa
Barbara, CA 93101, tel. 805/682–3199.*
Accommodations: *8 double rooms
with baths.*
Amenities: *Robes, fireplace in 4
rooms, whirlpool tub in 1 room, phone
in 4 rooms, guest refrigerator, TV
available; bicycles, croquet, badminton.*
Rates: *$85–$135; full breakfast, afternoon refreshments.*
Restrictions: *No smoking, no pets
except for small dogs; 2-night minimum on weekends.*

The Beach House

he outstanding feature of this
aptly named B&B is its location
across the street from Cambria's
gorgeous dark-sand beach. Trails
meander along the bluff above the
sand; you can surf crisp waves at one
end, explore tidal pools at the other, or
lose yourself in a book in one of the
many sunny coves.

The inn, if less impressive than the
beach, is not without comforts. Resembling any number of beach houses lining southern California's shores, it's a
typical '60s contemporary, all wood and
glass, with a steeply pitched roof and
huge second-floor concrete deck. Common areas range from a cramped
ground-floor sitting area to an airy second-floor room. Bedrooms are fairly
nondescript—wall-to-wall carpeting in
greens and browns, knotty-pine ceilings, wicker furniture, new quilts. The
two downstairs rooms have fireplaces
but are rather dark; more impressive
is the high-ceiling king-bedded room
upstairs, boasting ocean views and a
private deck.

Address: *6360 Moonstone Beach Dr.,
Cambria, CA 93441, tel. 805/927–3136.*
Accommodations: *7 rooms with
baths.*
Amenities: *Cable TV in rooms, fire-
place in 2 rooms; mountain bikes.*
Rates: *$120–$150; full breakfast,
evening wine and cheese. MC, V.*
Restrictions: *No smoking indoors, no
pets.*

Bella Maggiore Inn

Designed by famed Los Angeles architect A. C. Martin, this 1925 hotel in Ventura's historic district is a lovely example of the Italianate style, a cool Mediterranean building with an ornamental plaster facade, awnings, and a high-ceilinged, earthtone lobby dotted with comfortably worn sofas and chairs. Toward the rear is a hushed, walled courtyard, which was recently transformed into Nona's Courtyard Cafe.

Though breakfast is served, the Bella Maggiore is more a small hotel than a B&B. Rooms vary in size, but they're similar in appearance, done in a spare Mediterranean style, with simple wood furnishings and shuttered windows. They're notable more for quiet, comfort, and good value than luxury. Just around the corner is Ventura's old-

town shopping street, home to lots of good, cheap antiques stores and book shops. The mission, grand old courthouse, and beach are all nearby.

Address: *67 S. California St., Ventura, CA 93001, tel. 805/652–0277 or 800/ 523–8479.*
Accommodations: *21 rooms with baths, 3 suites.*
Amenities: *Cable TV, phone, ceiling fan in rooms; fireplace in 6 rooms, air-conditioning in 4 rooms.*
Rates: *$75–$150, suites $100–$135; full breakfast, evening hors d'oeuvres. AE, D, DC, MC, V.*
Restrictions: *No pets.*

The Eagle Inn

This modest hotel is notable for three things: its location near the beach and Stearns Wharf; its striking 1930s Spanish architecture; and, most of all, its lack of a two-night minimum on weekends, as hard to find in Santa Barbara as a snowstorm.

Alan and Janet Bullock (she of the red hair and English accent) own and operate this former apartment house in a neighborhood of similar Spanish beauties. Though neither elegant nor antiques-stuffed, the inn offers plenty of comfort and early-California charm for the price. Many of the rooms have full kitchens; some, like the bright number 17, are large enough for a family. Romantics should splurge on the Sunflower Suite in the cottage across the street; it's a small former apartment with a rag rug, pine armoire,

kitchen, and sunflowers splashed on upholstery, curtains, and bedding.

Address: *232 Natoma Ave., Santa Barbara, CA 93101, tel. 805/965–3586 or 800/767–0030, fax 805/966–1218.*
Accommodations: *17 double rooms with baths, 1 suite.*
Amenities: *Cable TV, phone, coffeemaker, refrigerator, kitchen in many rooms; access to health club.*
Rates: *$70–$130, suite $95–$145; Continental breakfast. Weekly rates offered. AE, MC, V.*
Restrictions: *Smoking only in some rooms, no pets.*

Garden Street Inn

Nostalgia is the theme at this Stick-style Italianate inn near Mission San Luis Obispo and only a few steps from the town's Old California–style downtown. Innkeepers Dan and Kathy Smith retained the 1887 structure's high ceilings, skylit grand staircase, 8-foot-tall wooden doors, stained glass, and squared bay windows. The thematic decor draws from the Smiths' family histories as well as that of the community. The Field of Dreams Room is dedicated to Kathy's sportswriter father and contains baseball memorabilia; Walden, sporting family wood carvings and New Zealand art, honors Dan's dad, who loved the outdoors; and the Ah Louis Room, containing an antique Oriental curio cabinet, celebrates an early Chinese labor leader who organized Central Coast railroad workers.

The couple are a good source of information about local history, beaches, restaurants, and the Thursday-night farmers' market that takes place nearby.

Address: *1212 Garden St., San Luis Obispo, CA 93401, tel. 805/545–9802.*
Accommodations: *9 double rooms with baths, 4 suites.*
Amenities: *Air-conditioning, radio with tape deck in rooms, fireplace in 5 rooms, whirlpool tub in 6 rooms.*
Rates: *$90–$120, suites $140–$160; full breakfast, afternoon refreshments. AE, MC, V.*
Restrictions: *No smoking indoors, no pets; 2-night minimum on holiday and special-event weekends.*

Glenborough Inn

Aficionados of the turn-of-the-century Arts-and-Crafts movement, which put American architecture on the map, will want to check out the Glenborough, a fine example of Craftsman design. Leaded windows, dark burnished wood on ceilings and around doorways, Batchelder tile fireplace in the living room, solid oak beams, an easy flow from room to room—all the signature design touches are there. Unfortunately, the furniture runs to typical Victorian instead of the more suitable Arts-and-Crafts pieces, but one can't have everything.

Each of the rooms and suites in the main house and two cottages across the street has a different look: country, art nouveau, nautical, wicker, formal Victorian, and so on. Most are well appointed, though some bathrooms are

uncomfortably small. Co-owner Ken Armstrong's green thumb is evident in the several gardens, one of which holds a totally private hot tub.

Address: *1327 Bath St., Santa Barbara, CA 93101, tel. 805/966–0589 or 800/962–0589, fax 805/564–2369.*
Accommodations: *4 rooms with baths, 4 rooms share 2 baths, 3 suites.*
Amenities: *Fireplace in 3 rooms; hot tub.*
Rates: *$80–$165; full breakfast, afternoon and evening refreshments. AE, MC, V.*
Restrictions: *No smoking indoors, no pets; 2-night minimum on weekends.*

Inn at Summer Hill

The best-known landmark in Summerland, a small seaside town just south of Santa Barbara, had long been the Big Yellow House restaurant, but the 1989 opening of the Inn on Summer Hill changed the status quo. Built as a showcase for the talents of interior designer Mabel Schults, the newly constructed Craftsman-style inn consists of two long, narrow buildings with rooms on the first and second floors, each with a motel-style private entrance.

All rooms have private balconies and ocean views and are lavishly decorated—practically overflowing with furniture, much of it rattan with floral fabrics. White pine is used in the ceilings, wainscoting, paneling, and most of the furniture. Guest rooms on the second level have pine-paneled vaulted ceilings, feel larger, and seem to get less highway noise.

Address: *2520 Lillie Ave., Box 376, Summerland, CA 93067, tel. 805/969–9998 or 800/845–5566, fax 805/969–9998.*
Accommodations: *15 rooms with baths, 1 suite.*
Amenities: *Air-conditioning, TV with VCR, 2 phones, fireplace, refrigerator, robes, hair dryer, and ironing board in rooms, irons available; spa.*
Rates: *$160–$195, suite $225–$275; full breakfast, afternoon and evening refreshments. AE, MC, V.*
Restrictions: *No smoking indoors, no pets; 2-night minimum on weekends and holidays.*

J. Patrick House

This inn is set on a pine-shaded acre above East Village Cambria, in an area known as Lodge Hill, and is convenient to shops, galleries, and restaurants, though it's some distance from the beach. The inn consists of two buildings connected by a garden and a trellised arbor. The front building is a contemporary log cabin, where new innkeepers Barbara and Mel Schwimmer greet guests, tend to the living-room fireplace, and cook up breakfast.

There is one bright, spacious guest room upstairs. The remaining rooms and a separate guest sitting room are in the cedar-sided two-story building out back. Each of the rooms is named for a county in Ireland: Cork, Clare, Galway, Dublin. Furnishings are simple and eclectic. Beds are of wicker, willow, or painted wood, and guest rooms are adorned with floral wallpapers and spreads. Flowers abound, and woodland bouquets are tucked into every corner throughout the inn—in rooms, on tables in hallways, on windowsills. Each room has a window seat with a garden view.

Address: *2990 Burton Dr., Cambria, CA 93428, tel. 805/927–3812.*
Accommodations: *8 rooms with baths.*
Amenities: *Fireplace or wood-burning stove in rooms, guest refrigerator.*
Rates: *$100–$120; full breakfast, afternoon refreshments. MC, V.*
Restrictions: *No smoking, no pets.*

La Mer

La Mer offers a bit of European ambience in a distinctly southern California seaside setting. Presided over by German-born Gisela Baida, the inn is visible from afar on its perch high up on a hillside and is decorated with a collection of European flags. The inn has five rooms, each decorated in a theme of a different European country. The French Room is powder blue, with an antique carved walnut bed and a ceiling-tall ficus tree. The Norwegian Room has a nautical theme, with a ship's bed, wood paneling, and brass fixtures in the bathroom. The bright and airy rooms are surrounded by balconies and porches.

Gisela serves a sumptuous Bavarian-style breakfast in the parlor, with its view of the ocean; the buffet features cheeses and Black Forest ham in addition to fruit, pastries, and beverages. She promotes the inn as a romantic midweek getaway by offering attractive packages that include dinners, visits to nearby Wheeler Hot Springs, and therapeutic massages.

Address: *411 Poli St., Ventura, CA 93001, tel. 805/643–3600.*
Accommodations: *5 rooms with baths.*
Amenities: *Old-fashioned radio in rooms, fireplace in 1 room; beach towels, antique carriage rides and picnic baskets extra.*
Rates: *$105–$155; full breakfast, afternoon refreshments. MC, V.*
Restrictions: *No smoking indoors, no pets.*

Montecito Inn

Like the San Ysidro Ranch, this small hotel is located in swank Montecito and has a show-biz history, having been built by Charlie Chaplin and Fatty Arbuckle in 1928. But it's more urban than country, situated on the edge of one of Montecito's two main shopping streets (great for strolling) and backing up to the freeway (which can be heard from the rear-facing rooms). An admirable small hotel, it combines the friendliness of an inn with the amenities of a hotel.

Years of renovation have led to a new sleekness, particularly in the meandering lobby, replete with marble floors and columns, muted sponge-painted walls, and rich damask upholstery. Guest rooms have dark-wood armoires, shuttered windows, and subtle French provincial fabrics on beds and upholstery. The small pool/spa area is charming, if a bit sullied by freeway noise, and there are lots of other sporting extras. Best of all is the Montecito Cafe, a handsome, affordable spot serving California cuisine.

Address: *1295 Coast Village Rd., Montecito, CA 93108, tel. 805/969–7854 or 800/843–2017, fax 805/969–0623.*
Accommodations: *48 double rooms with baths, 5 suites.*
Amenities: *Air-conditioning in public rooms; cable TV, phone, ceiling fan in rooms; refrigerator, VCR in some rooms; some nonsmoking rooms, room service, swimming pool, spa, sauna, fitness center, bicycles.*
Rates: *$150–$195, suites $205–$265; Continental breakfast. AE, DC, MC, V.*
Restrictions: *No pets; 2-night minimum on weekends.*

Olallieberry Inn

Where time stands still" is the motto of this 1873 Greek Revival house, but that's not entirely accurate—modernity is much in evidence in the spiffy new kitchen and the new French doors and deck connecting the dining room and backyard. Run by owners CarolAnn and Peter Irsfield (who's still commuting to his L.A. law practice) and innkeeper Colleen Busch, this small inn glows with the sort of personal warmth that first put B&Bs on the map.

At the edge of Cambria's cutesy downtown, the Olallieberry is decorated in a style that suits its era. The front parlor's crystal chandelier and Victorian sofa are rather formal for funky Cambria; the white-wicker, fireplace-warmed Gathering Room is more casual and popular. The Cambria Room has a raised fireplace, high ceilings, and Queen Anne furniture; bathers will love the huge tub in the low-ceilinged Olallieberry Room. The grassy backyard leads to a thicket of trees and Santa Rosa Creek.

Address: *2476 Main St., Cambria, CA 93428, tel. 805/927-3222, fax 805/927-0202.*
Accommodations: *3 double rooms with attached baths, 3 with detached baths.*
Amenities: *Fireplace in 3 rooms.*
Rates: *$85–$120; full breakfast, evening wine and hors d'oeuvres. MC, V.*
Restrictions: *No smoking indoors, no pets.*

The Olive House

In 1987, Lois Gregg and her then-husband sold their Hearthside Inn in Bar Harbor, Maine, and bought this 1904 shingled Craftsman-pattern house in the bougainvillea-draped foothills near the mission. Lois is a hands-on innkeeper, and her warm, relaxed style (she's typically attired in shorts and running shoes) perfectly suits laid-back Santa Barbara.

Lois spruced up Olive House by adding thick, forest-green wall-to-wall carpeting and Victorianish floral wallpapers that are more delicate than fussy. The turn-of-the-century details—darkwood beams, paneling, and headboards—throughout are offset by such lightening touches as miniblinds and simple white curtains. The best room is Bella Vista, a large corner room with ocean breezes and a bit of a view. A buffet breakfast—fruit, pastries, eggs, cereals—is served in the dining room, furnished with American antiques. Extras include a studio grand piano in the living room and a sunny little patio in the side yard.

Address: *1604 Olive St., Santa Barbara, CA 93101, tel. 805/962-4902 or 800/786-6422.*
Accommodations: *6 rooms with baths.*
Amenities: *Private deck and hot tub in 2 rooms, fireplace in 1 room.*
Rates: *$105–$175; full breakfast, evening wine and hors d'oeuvres. AE, MC, V.*
Restrictions: *No smoking indoors, no pets; 2-night minimum on weekends.*

Pickford House

The small town of Cambria dates back to the 19th century, but this residential subdivision is a product of the early 1980s. Perhaps in order to compensate for its newness, Pickford House is a riot of American antiques and reproductions: Headboards are carved and heavy, tubs are claw-footed, carpets are floral; fussy lace doilies are scattered about. Off the ordinary lobby an extraordinary parlor is replete with a brass-railed 175-year-old bar and loads of antiques.

It might be out-of-place and rather musty, but the Pickford House offers a lot of comfort for the price, along with views and easy access to Hearst Castle (its rooms are named for the celebrities who visited the publishing magnate there). And owner Anna Larsen makes a mean plate of *aebleskive* (Dan-

ish pancakes) for breakfast. Perhaps the best Victorian-style room, large and bright, is named for Mary Pickford. If you're not a fan of the period, try the spacious, king-bedded Fairbanks room, with subdued art-deco furniture, a fireplace, and a lovely view of the hills.

Address: *2555 MacLeod Way, Cambria, CA 93428, tel. 805/927–8619.*
Accommodations: *8 rooms with baths.*
Amenities: *Cable TV in rooms, fireplace in 3 rooms.*
Rates: *$85–$120; full breakfast, evening wine and hors d'oeuvres. MC, V.*
Restrictions: *Smoking in lobby only, no pets.*

The Squibb House

The trend in new California inns is toward opulence and romance, but Bruce Black has a different agenda. It's not that his newly opened Squibb House lacks creature comforts or romantic appeal—it has enough of both. But more than that, it radiates history, community, and pride of place, with a careful eye toward good design.

Built in 1877 by Cambria's school principal, this butter-yellow Gothic Revival Italianate structure in the heart of the village went on to become the home of several of Cambria's leading citizens. Black purchased the house in 1993 and thoroughly restored it, respecting its purity of design and changing little in the structure. His craftsmen built pine furniture in the 100-year-old carpentry shop next door, while Black himself sought out old glass at flea markets,

restored the gardens, and painted layers of soft colors in the bedrooms, resulting in extraordinary patinas. This new inn is well worth a visit.

Breakfast, served in your room or a downstairs parlor, includes fresh fruit and still-warm pastries, bread, and muffins from a nearby bakery.

Address: *4063 Burton Dr., Cambria, CA 93428, tel. 805/927–9600.*
Accommodations: *5 double rooms with baths.*
Amenities: *Fireplace in all rooms.*
Rates: *$95–$125; Continental breakfast, afternoon refreshments. DC, MC, V.*
Restrictions: *No smoking, no pets.*

Summerland Inn

Summerland lives up to its name: It's a fetching little sun-washed town with a staggering number of antiques shops and plenty of beach cottages sprinkled alongside the coastline, intersected by train tracks and Highway 101. There are only two B&Bs in town, and this is the more modest of the two, built as an inn in the '80s. Just across the highway from the sparkling sea (which is accessed via an underpass), the inn offers generic charm but a goodly amount of comfort and location for the price.

Rooms are done in an American country style, with pencil-post or brass beds, quilts, and small bathrooms. A few have fireplaces, all have small TVs, and some have partial ocean views, though those tend to be the noisiest. Breakfast is served in the rooms, because common areas are limited to a small lobby and a pleasant garden.

Address: *2161 Ortega Hill Rd., Summerland, CA 93067, tel. 805/969–5225.*
Accommodations: *11 double rooms with baths.*
Amenities: *Phone, TV in rooms, fireplace in 2 rooms; croquet.*
Rates: *$65–$140; full breakfast. AE, D, DC, MC, V.*
Restrictions: *No smoking indoors, no pets; 2-night minimum on weekends.*

Tiffany Inn

Prim, pretty Victorians may seem anomalous in Spanish-mad Santa Barbara, but this neighborhood just west of State Street's shops and cafés is positively thick with them. This tan-and-green Stick-style model from 1898 is particularly well restored, with its hipped roof, shingled second and third floors, large front porch, jutting bays, and covered rear patio furnished with high-quality green wicker. The only fly in the ointment is the street traffic outside.

Owners Carol and Larry MacDonald respect the interior's Victoriana but aren't slaves to it—puffy floral curtains valances, white walls, and solid pastel bedspreads add a welcome touch of English cheerfulness. Up a steep staircase on the third floor is the marvelous Penthouse Suite, a rambling, nook-filled hideaway complete with fireplace, ceiling fan, love seats, view-rich deck, and a second bedroom with twin bed and whirlpool tub.

Address: *1323 De la Vina St., Santa Barbara, CA 93101, tel. 805/963–2283 or 800/999–5672.*
Accommodations: *3 rooms with baths, 2 rooms share bath, 2 suites.*
Amenities: *Fireplace in 5 rooms, whirlpool tub and refrigerator in suites.*
Rates: *$75–$190; full breakfast, evening wine and hors d'oeuvres. AE, DC, MC, V.*
Restrictions: *No smoking indoors, no pets; 2-night minimum on weekends.*

The Upham

AVictorian Italianate building topped with a cupola, wrapped with porches, and cheered by rose gardens, the Upham was built in 1871 by a Boston banker turned hotelier. Over the years additions have been made, including several cottages behind the main building. One of the cottages holds the extravagant Master Suite, complete with fireplace, wet bar, and large private yard. The rest of the quarters are humbler but comfortable in a masculine sort of way: wall-to-wall carpeting, white shutters, ginger-jar lamps, reproduction four-poster Colonial beds, wing chairs.

The public areas are equally eclectic. One large, comfortable sitting area looks like an English drawing room, and the grassy courtyard is dotted with Adirondack chairs. Perhaps most charming of all is the veranda seating at Louie's, the admirable California-cuisine restaurant.

Address: *1404 De la Vina St., Santa Barbara, CA 93101, tel. 805/962–0058 or 800/727–0876, fax 805/963–2825.*
Accommodations: *46 double rooms with baths, 3 suites.*
Amenities: *Cable TV and phone in rooms, fireplace in 7 rooms and 1 suite, restaurant, conference and banquet rooms.*
Rates: *$105–$195, Master Suite $325; Continental breakfast, evening wine and cheese. AE, D, DC, MC, V.*
Restrictions: *No smoking indoors, no pets; 2-night minimum on weekends.*

Villa Rosa

An antidote to Santa Barbara's many Victorian B&Bs, this small inn pays proud tribute to the city's Spanish architectural heritage, with its tile roof, archways, wrought-iron balconies, rough-hewn beams, and saltillo-tile courtyard. A low-key, sophisticated place, Villa Rosa is a short walk from the beach and from Stearns Wharf.

In the lobby areas and guest rooms, colors are muted and earthy, upholstered chairs and sofas are straight-lined and contemporary, and wood furniture is southwestern in style. The accommodations all pretty much look alike. Some lower-floor rooms have shutter-clad French doors opening to the courtyard and small pool, but they can be rather dark; upper-floor rooms are more cheerful. On the down side, the breakfast is pretty unimpressive and service can be amateurish; on the plus side, the inn is cool, quiet, and very comfortable. It's a good place for those who prefer chic monochromaticism to color and antiques.

Address: *15 Chapala St., Santa Barbara, CA 93101, tel. 805/966–0851 or 800/727–0876, fax 805/962–7159.*
Accommodations: *18 rooms with baths.*
Amenities: *Phone, fireplace in 4 rooms; pool and spa.*
Rates: *$80–$190; Continental breakfast, afternoon wine and cheese, evening port and sherry. AE, MC, V.*
Restrictions: *No pets; 2-night minimum on weekends.*

Monterey Bay

Monterey Bay
Including Santa Cruz and Carmel

A semicircle about 90 miles across, Monterey Bay arcs into the California coast at a point about two hours' drive south of the San Francisco Bay Area. Santa Cruz sits at the northern end of the curve, and the Monterey Peninsula, containing Monterey, Pacific Grove, and Carmel, occupies the southern portion. In between, Highway 1 cruises along the coastline, passing windswept beaches piled high with sand dunes. Along the route are fields of artichoke plants, the towns of Watsonville and Castroville, and Fort Ord, the army base where millions of GIs got their basic training.

A beneficent climate, stunning scenery, and the sweep of history have combined to bring visitors to this area for hundreds of years. Although evidence suggests that Native Americans lived here 10,000 years ago, the first written records date from 1542, when Portuguese explorer Juan Rodríguez Cabrillo sighted the beaches and pine forests where Carmel now lies. The Spanish later settled here, building missions in Carmel and Santa Cruz, and eventually naming Monterey the capital of Alta California. Monterey remained the center of government for California until 1850.

During the late 1800s, the cool summers attracted a seasonal colony of Methodists who came to Pacific Grove on retreat; they later built the Victorian homes for which the town is now famous. At about the same time, wealthy easterners discovered Monterey's splendid scenery and mansions sprang up along Pacific Grove and Pebble Beach.

The Monterey Bay area has attracted artists and writers for more than a century. The best known on the long list of names include novelists Robert Louis Stevenson, Mary Austin, and John Steinbeck; poet Robinson Jeffers; and photographers Edward Weston and Ansel Adams. Carmel's heritage as an

*art colony lives on in dozens of art galleries scattered
throughout the town.*

*As Monterey was becoming a mecca for artists and the
wealthy, Santa Cruz was developing as a working community
with logging, fishing, tanning, and farming being the major
industries. The arrival of the railroad brought visitors from
San Francisco and the hot inland valleys to the seaside
pleasures of Santa Cruz and Capitola, and the establishment
of the University of California at Santa Cruz added yet
another dimension to the town's character.*

*Monterey Bay is one of the loveliest spots on the West Coast.
With its combination of rugged natural beauty and sophisticated local culture, this remarkably diverse area offers fine
restaurants, bed-and-breakfast inns, tourist attractions (both
natural and man-made) that reflect and respect its history
and heritage, a lively arts community, and varied shopping.*

Places to Go, Sights to See

Big Sur. A 26-mile drive south of Carmel via Highway 1 yields breathtaking
views at every turn: The rugged Santa Lucia Mountains rise sharply on one side
of the highway, and the Pacific pounds against the shore on the other. Big Sur's
intractable landscape was home to author Henry Miller and many famous artists.

Cannery Row (765 Wave St., Monterey, tel. 408/649–6690) is a restored area of
shops, restaurants, and galleries where the 16 sardine canneries immortalized in
John Steinbeck's novel *Cannery Row* once stood.

Carmel Mission (3080 Rio Rd., Carmel, tel. 408/624–3600). With beautifully landscaped gardens, this is one of the loveliest of the 21 California missions. Buried
here is Father Junípero Serra, founder of nine of the missions.

Monterey Bay Aquarium (886 Cannery Row, Monterey, tel. 408/648–4888). The
centerpiece of Cannery Row, this sealife museum houses more than 6,500 marine
creatures. Exhibits include a 28-foot-tall kelp forest, a shark display, and examples of the undersea life of Monterey Bay.

Monterey State Historic Park (525 Polk St., Monterey, tel. 408/649–7118). This
is a collection of adobe structures and other historic buildings from the Spanish
and Mexican eras, when Monterey was the capital of California.

Point Lobos State Reserve (Hwy. 1, Carmel, tel. 408/624–4909) is an outdoor
museum of unmatched beauty. Nearly 10 miles of trails weave along the shore-

line, and there are 750 acres of underwater reserve, a portion of which is open to scuba and skin divers with permits. The many tidal pools contain starfish, anemones, and other examples of marine life; sea lions, otters, and harbor seals are in residence most of the time.

Seventeen Mile Drive. Running along the outer rim of the Monterey Peninsula, this scenic drive offers some of the most photographed ocean vistas in the world. The route passes through the famous Pebble Beach and Cypress Point golf courses, Lone Cypress, Restless Sea, and numerous magnificent estates. Entrance gates are at Lighthouse Avenue in Pacific Grove, and off Highway 1 and North San Antonio Avenue in Carmel. The $6 fee is well worth it.

Tor House (26304 Ocean View Ave., tel. 408/624–1813) is the unique house and tower built by poet Robinson Jeffers during the early 1900s from stones gathered on Carmel beach. Docent-led tours cover the early history of Carmel as an artists' colony.

Restaurants

Central 159 (tel. 408/655–4280) in Pacific Grove is known for its eclectic menu featuring the lighter side of new American cuisine. Also in Pacific Grove, **El Cocodrilo** (tel. 408/655–3311) features spicy Central American and Caribbean cuisines. **Fresh Cream** (tel. 408/375–9798), in Monterey, is acclaimed for its classic French cuisine and outstanding service. In Santa Cruz, **Gilbert's on the Wharf** (tel. 408/423–5200) offers casual seafood dining with an ocean view. **Shadowbrook Restaurant** (tel. 408/475–1511) in Capitola serves Continental cuisine. Locally popular for its atmosphere, it is reached by cable car. In Aptos, the Bayview Hotel's **Veranda Restaurant** (tel. 408/685–1881) offers inventive California cuisine in a Victorian setting.

Tourist Information

Big Sur Chamber of Commerce (Box 87, Big Sur, CA 93920, tel. 408/667–2100); **Monterey County Visitors & Convention Bureau** (380 Alvarado St., Box 1770, Monterey, CA 93942–1770, tel. 408/649–1770, fax 408/649–3502); **Santa Cruz County Conference and Visitors Council** (701 Front St., Santa Cruz, CA 95060, tel. 408/425–1234 or 800/833–3494); **Santa Cruz Winegrowers** (Box 3000, Santa Cruz, CA 95063, tel. 408/479–WINE).

Referral Service

B&B Innkeepers of Santa Cruz County (Box 464, Santa Cruz, CA 95062, tel. 408/425–8212).

Apple Lane Inn

Diana and Doug Groom acquired Apple Lane Inn in a romantic moment. They were celebrating their wedding anniversary at the inn where they were married a couple of years earlier, when they learned that the property might be for sale if the right buyers could be found. "The right buyers were sitting there in the parlor," Diana laughs. Before long, the elementary school teacher and flight instructor—plus kids and animals—had moved into the inn and put their own stamp on it.

This four-story, gray-and-blue farmhouse, built in the 1870s, is perched on a 3-acre ocean-view hillside, once part of a Spanish land grant. It's surrounded by a Victorian cutting garden, rows of vegetables, and old apple orchards. Alongside the lane, a large red barn contains a horse corral and a chicken house where hens lay tomorrow's breakfast.

Of the guest rooms, Blossom in the back of the house is the most interestingly furnished. A huge, 150-year-old reproduction of a 14th-century bed once owned by Diana's Aunt Mildred is flanked by a pair of Eastlake chairs and stands on a 400-year-old Persian carpet next to an amazing buffet with 22 beveled mirrors. Uncle Chester's Room, also on the second floor, contains a 40-inch-high, 400-year-old four-poster bed that Doug's uncle found in Spain during World War I. One large suite consisting of two bedrooms and a bathroom fills an unfinished attic on the third floor,

unusual because it has exposed rafters and shingles. The Attic Suite offers the inn's best view of meadows, gazebo, and distant Monterey.

Common rooms are comfortably Victorian. A long double parlor contains a dining table set up for breakfast at one end and a sitting room-library at the other. A player piano and stacks of games and books are available for guest use.

Food is an essential part of the experience at this inn. Diana loves to cook, and breakfast is likely to feature ham-and-cheese soufflé, eggs Christy, or morning Monte Cristo accompanied by fruit, coffee cake, cereal, and beverages. Home-baked desserts are offered after dinner in the upstairs sitting room.

Address: *6265 Soquel Dr., Aptos, CA 95003, tel. 408/475–6868.*
Accommodations: *3 double rooms with baths, 1 suite.*
Amenities: *TV room, guest phone, fireplace in parlor; picnic baskets available.*
Rates: *$70–$175; full breakfast, afternoon and evening refreshments. D, MC, V.*
Restrictions: *No smoking indoors, limited pet accommodations.*

Babbling Brook Inn

Presided over by the vivacious Helen King, this inn offers a combination of romantic setting, California history, and a convenient location for business travelers. In the heart of Santa Cruz, the inn's wooded grounds and gardens make it appear to be worlds away from the city.

The inn consists of four cedar-shingle-sided buildings set on different levels of the hillside property. Portions of the main house's stone foundation date from 1796, when the mission fathers built a gristmill for grinding corn. In 1981, when it became a bed-and-breakfast inn, three cottages were added. Last year, the historic waterwheel was returned after a seven-decade absence to its original pond setting in front of the main building.

The rooms are decorated in French-country style: soft colors, floral-print curtains, and iron beds covered with floral spreads. The most charming are in the main house: The romantic Honeymoon Suite hideaway offers couples seclusion as well as a view from a private deck that overlooks the waterfall. The expansive Garden Room has a wood-burning stove, a great garden view, and complete privacy. The rooms in the outbuildings get more street and parking-lot noise, but they also have decks facing the garden. The Babbling Brook's gardens are often the setting for weddings, with the big wrought-iron white gazebo as the centerpiece, the brook meandering through the

property, and flowers adorning every inch of hillside.

Helen King, a onetime organizer of international tours, is acutely aware of business travelers' needs; she accommodates them by offering an early breakfast, late check-in, and copies of the *Wall Street Journal*. And in the afternoon, Helen hosts a congenial wine-hour gathering in front of the fire in the comfortable living room.

The buffet-style breakfast of frittatas or other egg dishes, fruits, and fresh muffins and croissants with jam is set out in the living room, although guests can go either into the adjacent dining room or outside to enjoy their meals in the shade of the redwood trees.

Address: *1025 Laurel St., Santa Cruz, CA 95060, tel. 408/427-2437 or 800/866-1131, fax 408/427-2457.*
Accommodations: *12 double rooms with baths.*
Amenities: *Cable TV and phone in rooms, fireplace in 10 rooms, whirlpool tub in 4 rooms; picnic baskets available.*
Rates: *$85–$165; full breakfast, afternoon refreshments. AE, D, MC, V.*
Restrictions: *No smoking indoors, no pets; 2-night minimum on weekends.*

Green Gables Inn

The Green Gables Inn, a striking landmark along the oceanfront of Pacific Grove, dates from 1888, when Los Angeles businessman William Lacy built the two-story, half-timbered and gabled Queen Anne for his lady friend, Emma Murdoch.

Lacy was also an amateur architect, and he probably designed this elegant house in which nearly every room has a three-sided bay window that takes in the ocean view just across the street. Framed entirely of redwood, it has solid maple floors, countless angles, slopes and nooks, exposed ceiling beams, intricate moldings, woodwork and arches, and even stained-glass windows framing the fireplace and set into pocket doors dividing rooms in what's now the Lacy Suite. The windows, fixtures, and woodwork all date from the original construction.

Roger and Sally Post bought the house as a family home for their four daughters. The Posts began renting out rooms to summer visitors, and in 1983 the Green Gables became a full-time inn (and the cornerstone of the Four Sisters collection of seven large inns in California, operated by the Roger Post family).

Guest rooms in the carriage house, perched on a hill out back, are larger than those in the main house and have more privacy as well as views of the ocean. They also offer more modern amenities, but the rooms in the main house, with their intricately detailed molding and woodwork, have more charm. The Lacy Suite on the main floor, doubtless a converted parlor and library, has a fireplace, built-in bookshelves, and a claw-foot tub in the bathroom. Upstairs in the Gable Room, a window seat under leaded-glass windows overlooks the ocean. The Balcony Room is like a sleeping porch, and the Chapel Room actually resembles a church, with a vaulted ceiling and a pewlike window seat stretching across the front of the room.

The food, always fresh, is served in a family-style setting. The ample buffet breakfast includes frittatas, a fruit plate, an assortment of breads and scones, and apple pancakes. Afternoon refreshments include wine and hors d'oeuvres. The young staff is gracious and can offer assistance with dinner reservations and sightseeing information.

Address: *104 5th St., Pacific Grove, CA 93950, tel. 408/375–2095.*
Accommodations: *6 double rooms with baths, 4 doubles share 2 baths, 1 suite.*
Amenities: *Fireplace in carriage-house rooms; picnic baskets available, bicycles, limited parking.*
Rates: *$100–$160; full breakfast, afternoon refreshments. AE, MC, V.*
Restrictions: *No smoking, no pets.*

Inn at Depot Hill

Innkeeper Suzie Lankes and her partner, Dan Floyd, have created one of the most beautiful bed-and-breakfasts in California—perhaps anywhere. And they provide guests with exquisite pampering to complement the splendid surroundings.

Once a historic railroad station in the beachside village of Capitola, the Inn at Depot Hill is now a vision of turn-of-the-century European-style luxury. Most rooms have a Continental theme: Dutch Delft, a corner suite, includes a big blue-and-white sitting room, a bedroom with a huge featherbed draped in Battenberg lace and real linen, a private patio filled with tulips and irises, and a gray-marble bathroom with double shower. Romantic Paris, a study in black and white, has walls upholstered in French toile, windows curtained in lace, and a bath done in gray marble. Portofino captures a sunny Italian mood, with a vine-and-leaf-decorated bed and a private Mediterranean garden planted with orange and lemon trees. Departing from the European motif, the Railroad Baron's room honors local history. This masculine accommodation, resembling a posh railroad car, has deep red brocade upholstery, a red-and-gold sitting room, rich woods with gold leaf, a circular lit dome over the bed—and an eagle presiding over all.

This is first and foremost a romantic inn. While Suzie and her staff encourage guests to mingle, most prefer to retreat to the privacy of their rooms.

Thus guests are likely to have private use of the inn's gardens, the parlor-library with piano tucked into one corner, and even the dining room, where an unusual glass-topped table can fit 10.

The food here is ample and well prepared. A late-afternoon hors d'oeuvre buffet features local wines, a canapé tray, meatballs, and crudité and dip. A dessert buffet and sherry welcome guests returning from dinner. For breakfast there are breads, fruit, cereal, and an egg entrée. Service is elegant, with silver, linens, and china displaying the inn's logo.

Address: *250 Monterey Ave., Box 1394, Capitola by the Sea, CA 95010, tel. 408/462-3376 or 800/572-2632, fax 408/462-3694.*
Accommodations: *4 double rooms with baths, 4 suites.*
Amenities: *TV with VCR, stereo, phone with modem, hair dryer, robes, steamer, coffeemaker, fireplace in rooms, private landscaped patio and hot tub in 5 rooms.*
Rates: *$165–$250; full breakfast, afternoon and evening refreshments. AE, MC, V.*
Restrictions: *No smoking indoors, no pets; 2-night minimum on weekends.*

The Jabberwock

"T hings are not always as they seem," observes Alice in *Through the Looking Glass*. That's certainly the case at this delightful inn, perched on a quiet residential street in the hills above Monterey Bay and just a short walk from Cannery Row and the Aquarium. Take breakfast, for example, where you're likely to sit down to a repast of Snarkleberry Flumptious or Brundt Blumbleberry. Or have a look at the clocks, all of which run backward. Guest rooms have names from the pen of Lewis Carroll. If you need to make a call, you'll find the phone in the Burbling Room.

This fantasy is the creation of Jim and Barbara Allen, who left jobs in Los Angeles—he was a fire fighter, she worked in the hotel industry—in 1982 to open an inn in "a better climate." The 1911 building they bought had seen better days, but the Allens tackled the needed restoration with the humor that now pervades the inn.

In short order, they had the place fixed up, with rooms as comfortable as they are engaging. Momerath, for example, has a superking-size bed with an elaborately carved mahogany headboard as its centerpiece; the private bathroom has a claw-foot tub. Borogrove is a huge corner room with an expansive ocean view and a telescope for scanning the horizon, a Victorian settee, and a fireplace. The best view can be had from the third-floor tower, where two rooms share a bath and a small sitting area. The Mimsey room is tiny, but it has

wall-to-wall windows and the oldest piece of furniture in the house, a wood-frame bed bought in 1886 for $6.45.

One of the most pleasant spots is the huge wraparound sun porch, from which guests can watch otters and sea lions frolicking in the bay. Should you want a closer perspective on marine life, the Allens have prepurchased tickets to the famous nearby Aquarium on hand, so patrons can bypass the oft-lengthy lines.

Guests usually drift into the comfortable living room after dinner to discuss their dining adventures and sample the milk and cookies guarded by Vorpal Bear, who warns, "Before bedtime . . . not dinner. Vorpal Bear attacks if you cheat."

Jim and Barbara keep up to date on the local restaurants. Fresh Cream, for example, is described as "where Jim takes Barbara when he's in trouble."

Address: *598 Laine St., Monterey, CA 93940, tel. 408/372-4777.*
Accommodations: *3 double rooms with baths, 4 doubles share 2 baths.*
Amenities: *Off-street parking.*
Rates: *$100–$180; full breakfast, afternoon refreshments. MC, V.*
Restrictions: *No smoking indoors, no pets; 2-night minimum on weekends, 3-night minimum on holidays.*

Mangels House

Once the country home of California sugar barons Claus Mangels and his brother-in-law Claus Spreckels, Mangels House is set on 4 acres of lawn and orchard. The big, white square Italianate structure with deep verandas is close to the entrance of the Forest of Nisene Marks State Park and surrounded by nearly 10,000 acres of second-growth redwoods.

The Mangels family built the house in 1886 as a retreat from San Francisco; each summer the family—with children, governess, and servants—would move to the then logged-out forest for a three-month stay. At the time of its construction, the house boasted some of the most modern conveniences, including fully plumbed marble-topped vanities, still in use in the bedrooms today. Vintage gaslight fixtures in the ceilings have more recently been converted to electricity.

English-born innkeeper Jackie Fisher is the force behind the inn's genteel ambience. She came to the business naturally, after raising children, living abroad with radiologist husband Ron, and serving as hostess on many occasions. "I love meeting new people," she explains as she pours late-afternoon tea for guests in the inn's 40-foot-long sitting room. Usually conversation turns to shared experiences and personal adventures, such as the time the family lived in Zaire.

Indeed, the inn reflects the family's life. One African-themed bedroom displays artifacts collected in Kenya and Zaire, including a collection of carved animals, banana-leaf art, dolls, and medicine men. By contrast, Timothy's Room features a pair of beautiful, locally thrown vases and a unique carved wooden headboard that Jackie herself designed.

Guests gather each morning in the dining room for a hearty English breakfast, which Jackie serves family-style. It starts with Jackie's homemade crumpets, "a vehicle for getting melted butter to your mouth." Accompaniments include fruit compote, spicy cheese-egg puff, oatmeal scones, and dessert—plenty to keep one going on a long morning hike through the forest.

Address: *570 Aptos Creek Rd., Box 302, Aptos, CA 95001, tel. 408/688–7982.*
Accommodations: *6 double rooms with baths.*
Amenities: *Guest phone, fireplace in sitting room and 1 guest room; English garden, games including table tennis and darts.*
Rates: *$105–$135; full breakfast, afternoon refreshments. AE, MC, V.*
Restrictions: *Smoking in sitting room only, no pets; 2-night minimum on weekends.*

Martine Inn

legance and grace are the keys to
the Martine Inn, a nearly 100-
year-old mansion perched on a
hillside above the tiny cove of the Monterey Bay that frames Pacific Grove.
Originally a Queen Anne with turrets
and towers, the home was owned until
World War II by Laura and James
Parke (of Parke Davis Pharmaceutical
Co.), who remodeled it in Mediterranean style, with a stucco exterior
and windows framed by arches. Don
Martine's family acquired the house in
1972; by 1984 he and wife Marion had
opened it as an inn.

Don and Marion have assembled one
of the most extensive antiques collections to be found in any California bed-
and-breakfast inn, mostly American
pieces dating from 1840 through 1890:
an Eastlake suite used by publisher
C.K. McClatchy; a mahogany suite
exhibited at the 1893 Chicago World's
Fair; Academy Award costume
designer Edith Head's bedroom suite;
and an 1860 Chippendale Revival four-
poster bed.

Guest rooms are located on the
ground and second floors of the main
house, with stunning views of the
water through arched front windows
upstairs in the Parke, Victorian, and
Maries rooms. Other rooms are in
what was once the carriage house off
the courtyard.

The inn has many common areas. The
parlor, which occupies the glassed-in

front of the house's main floor, lures
guests to savor the stunning ocean
view. A small library contains a personal collection of books and magazines, and two small solarium sitting
rooms adjoin guest rooms on the
ground and second floor. A games
room contains an 1870 oak slate pool
table, a 1917 nickelodeon, and a slot
machine from the 1930s.

Breakfast may be the best time of the
day at the Martine. In the dining room,
Marion serves up a lavish spread,
including eggs poached in cream sauce,
cereal, muffins, and fruit. Guests eat at
large lace-clad tables set with Marion's
best Sheffield silver and look out at a
sweeping sea vista that competes with
the food and decor for their attention.

Address: *255 Ocean View Blvd.,
Pacific Grove, CA 93950, tel.
408/373-3388, fax 408/373-3896.*
Accommodations: *19 double rooms
with baths.*
Amenities: *Phone, refrigerator, and
robes in rooms, fireplace in 7 rooms,
conference facilities; picnic meals
available, garden, whirlpool tub.*
Rates: *$125-$230; full breakfast, afternoon refreshments. MC, V.*
Restrictions: *Smoking in fireplace
rooms only, no pets; 2-night minimum
on weekends, 3-night minimum on
holidays.*

Old Monterey Inn

Ann and Gene Swett have elevated the business of innkeeping to a high art, offering their guests quietly elegant accommodations in a historic home—and the type of pampering that anticipates every need. Just a few blocks from downtown Monterey, a woodsy, flower-lined driveway leads to the English Tudor–style home built in 1929 by Carmel Martin, then the mayor of Monterey.

When Gene Swett was transferred to Monterey from the Bay Area in 1968, the family needed a house that was big enough for eight. Although the Martin house was run-down, the Swetts purchased it, renovated it, and created what would become one of the loveliest inns in California.

Outside, Gene made an oasis of year-round color. The house was Ann's domain. She began haunting flea markets as well as garage and yard sales. The quest continues, and the themes and color schemes of guest rooms are always subject to change. Thus the room once known as Madrigal is now Serengeti, evoking a turn-of-the-century African safari, with mosquito netting over the bed, rattan chairs, pith helmets, antique leather hatboxes, and a brass-elephant bird-cage stand. In the Library Room, floor-to-ceiling bookshelves contain volumes of nostalgic children's literature. The Garden Room feels almost like a tree house set in the upper branches of the massive oak just outside the window.

Guests have the option of having breakfast in bed. But unless you're honeymooning, don't take it. Breakfast is served in front of the fireplace in the formal dining room, at a table set for 14 with exquisite Oriental china. Guests dine on fruit, breads, quiche, or stratta served course by course. Gene is the consummate host, mingling and getting to know each and every guest to determine food preferences before sending everyone off to dinner. He can recommend a half dozen romantic picnic spots and can advise guests on which galleries and shops they should visit.

The Swetts offer guests a chance to get away from it all. "You come to our inn to talk to each other . . . to get your life back together," says Gene.

Address: *500 Martin St., Monterey, CA 93940, tel. 800/350–7344, fax 408/375–6730.*
Accommodations: *8 double rooms with baths, 1 suite, 1 cottage suite.*
Amenities: *Fireplace in 8 rooms, whirlpool bath in 1 room, robes; picnic baskets available.*
Rates: *$170–$240; full breakfast, afternoon and evening refreshments. No credit cards.*
Restrictions: *Smoking in garden only, no pets; 2-night minimum on weekends, 3-night minimum on holidays. Closed Christmas Day.*

Post Ranch Inn

A significant new addition to northern California's high-end getaway circuit, Post Ranch Inn is located on 98 secluded acres overlooking the Big Sur coastline. It blends elements of country inn, resort spa, and nature retreat into one seamlessly innovative package. "We don't fit any particular mold," declares general manager Larry Callahan. "We just fit Big Sur."

The redwood-and-steel individual units rest on either side of a quiet ridgetop trail; six more rooms are located in the three-story Butterfly House. All include the same plentiful amenities, which range from king-size beds and hand-carved walking sticks to whirlpool tubs whose sliding windows yield a strictly private nature view.

As the first such venue approved by local politicos in 20 years, Post Ranch has embraced environmentally kind precepts and then some. Oceanside cottages are built into the slope, their earth-covered roofs blending into the landscape—deer occasionally nibble at the wildflowers that grow there. "Mountainside" dwellings are mostly "tree-houses," built on stilts so as not to disturb existing ground vegetation. Floor plans are unique to each structure, decor handsome and not fussy. The effect is both luxurious and in harmony with the tranquil surroundings.

Complementing the panoramic coastal views are commissioned artworks, scattered throughout the property. Their uniquely Californian style is echoed in room furniture, in the tree-carved "living benches" along paths, and in Dan Wood's "rust"-ic custom grillwork. Next to the spectacularly situated Sierra Mar restaurant, where complimentary breakfast and optional prix fixe dinners are served, are a sun deck and trellis-obscured Jacuzzi pool. Down the hill, past architect Mickey Muennig's striking reception/craft-store building, you'll find a 20-by-60-foot lap pool.

Up and running just since 1992, Post Ranch is still in the process of adding some elements, like a fully equipped health spa. But this "work-in-progress" is already one of the most distinctively designed, romantically secluded spots to be found anywhere.

Address: *Hwy. 1, Box 219, Big Sur, CA 93920, tel. 408/667–2200 or 800/527–2200, fax 408/667–2824.*
Accommodations: *29 double rooms with baths, 1 suite.*
Amenities: *Fireplace, whirlpool tub, private deck, stereo system, massage table, coffeemaker, hair dryer, robes, walking sticks in rooms; basking and lap pools, guided walks/stargazing, yoga/exercise classes, picnic lunches, massage, aroma therapy, facials, tarot readings, gift shop, limousine service (fee) from Monterey.*
Rates: *$265–$525; expanded Continental breakfast, complimentary wine tastings. AE, MC, V.*
Restrictions: *No smoking in rooms, no pets; 2-night minimum on weekends, 3-night minimum on holidays.*

Stonepine

o enter this fabulous 330-acre Carmel Valley estate, originally the weekend home of the Crocker banking family, you'll pass through two electronically controlled gates, drive by the Equestrian Center with its adjacent paddock, survey acres of oak-covered hillsides, and eventually pull into the parking area where a Phantom V Rolls-Royce waits to whisk guests to the far corners of the property.

The Mediterranean-style château, built in the 1920s, was designed for lavish entertaining. The elegantly appointed public rooms have graceful stone arches, Roman columns, and gracious gardens shaded by rare Italian stonepines. Antiques abound: a hand-carved limestone fireplace from Italy in the grand living room; 18th-century French tapestries in the living room, the foyer, and the spiral staircase; a carved French writing desk in the Cartier bedroom; 19th-century burnished-oak paneling in the library and dining room.

Guest rooms in the château are elegantly but simply furnished with over-stuffed chairs and canopy beds. Bathrooms are dramatic, offering sweeping garden views, sunken marble Jacuzzis, and expansive marble countertops with double sinks. Tattinger, the original master bedroom done in black and white, offers a sitting room–office, separate his and hers bathrooms, and a hidden tower room. Four bedrooms in the Paddock House

are done in casual country plaids with horsey themes.

Following an evening champagne reception, guests are escorted to dinner in the château dining room, where tables are set with Baccarat crystal, Limoges china, and sterling silverware. A typical six-course menu offers choices such as roasted Chateaubriand and sautéed salmon dill–beurre blanc accompanied by soup, salad, dessert, Stilton, and port.

Service here, as one might expect, is attentive and discreet.

Address: *150 E. Carmel Valley Rd., Carmel Valley, CA 93924, tel. 408/659–2245, fax 408/659–5160.*
Accommodations: *8 rooms with baths, 4 suites, 1 two-bedroom cottage.*
Amenities: *TV with VCR, fireplace, Jacuzzi, phone, robes in rooms; video and book library, restaurant, room service, honor bar; picnic baskets, gardens, tennis, pool, croquet, archery, health club, hiking and riding trails, equestrian center.*
Rates: *$225–$750; full breakfast, dinner ($55) available. AE, MC, V.*
Restrictions: *No pets; 2-night minimum on weekends and holidays.*

Bayview Hotel

This striking mansard-roofed hotel looks a bit out of place on a busy corner in historic Aptos Village. A three-story building dominating the single-story shops surrounding it, the Bayview (which has no view) dates back to the 1870s, when, as the Anchor House, it provided luxury accommodations in this tiny lumber town. Some remnants of the era remain: guest rooms with 10-foot-tall ceilings adorned with ornate plaster rosettes, massive hand-painted wood furnishings imported from Spain, and brass lighting fixtures.

The first floor contains a popular local restaurant, the Veranda (where breakfast is served), and a small Victorian parlor for inn guests. Bedrooms on the second floor are generally spacious with simple Victorian furnishings,

carved wooden beds, straight-back chairs, and Battenberg lace. The four newly renovated third-story rooms, two of which feature gas fireplaces, have a slightly more modern feel—their sloping ceilings preclude use of the high antique bedboards that catch the eye downstairs and date from the hotel's earliest heyday.

Address: *8041 Soquel Dr., Aptos, CA 95003, tel. 408/688–8654.*
Accommodations: *10 double rooms with baths; 2 rooms can combine for family suite.*
Amenities: *Phone in rooms, fireplace in parlor and 2 rooms, TVs available, restaurant; gardens.*
Rates: *$90–$155; full breakfast. AE, MC, V.*
Restrictions: *No smoking, no pets; 2-night minimum on weekends.*

Blue Spruce Inn

This pair of Victorian farmhouses, tucked behind a white picket fence on a busy city street, offers comfortable, no-nonsense bed-and-breakfast accommodations—plus a few surprises. There are outdoor fountains in secret corners; interconnecting decks adorned by colorful rose gardens; birdbaths; an enormous green-tiled shower lit by a full-length, stained-glass mural; skylights above the beds; a full-body shower described as a "human car wash"; handmade Amish quilts in Irish chain and broken star patterns; work of local artists on the walls; window seats; and a cozy common area filled with books and magazines.

Innkeeper Pat O'Brien, a former teacher, presides with Irish charm,

offering a ready smile and laugh for all who cross her threshold.

Address: *2815 S. Main St., Soquel, CA 95073, tel. 408/464–1137, fax 408/475–0608.*
Accommodations: *6 double rooms with baths.*
Amenities: *Phone and computer-modem capacity in rooms, fireplace in 5 rooms, whirlpool tub in 2 rooms, TV with VCR in 2 rooms; gardens with outdoor hot tub, picnic baskets available.*
Rates: *$85–$135; full breakfast, afternoon refreshments. AE, MC, V.*
Restrictions: *No smoking indoors, no pets; 2-night minimum on weekends.*

The Centrella

The Centrella was built in 1889, the same year that Methodist Christian retreat Pacific Grove was incorporated as a city—though laws discouraging behavior the church frowned upon lasted well into the 1960s. Many extant structures echo that religious-community past, none more than this charming "cottage," whose spacious three stories retain much of their original flavor as a proper Victorian boarding house.

The main building's 17 rooms are simply but comfortably appointed, with wrought-iron headboards and antique armoires; attic suites have dormer windows and skylights. Breakfast and early-evening refreshments are served in a large, pleasant parlor downstairs. A garden courtyard separates three bungalows; these afford a more intimate experience than the main building's rooms and have gas fireplaces and fenced-in private sun decks. A fourth bungalow at the back of the property offers similar accommodations on two floors.

Address: *612 Central Ave., Pacific Grove, CA 93950, tel. 408/392-3372 or 800/233-3372, fax 408/371-2036.*
Accommodations: *16 double rooms with baths, 2 doubles share bath, 8 suites.*
Amenities: *Phone in rooms; cable TV, refrigerator, wet bar in suites; fireplace in 5 suites.*
Rates: *Rooms $90–$125, suites $150–$185; full breakfast, afternoon refreshments. AE, MC, V.*
Restrictions: *Smoking in courtyard only, no pets; children under 12 in garden suites only; 2-night minimum on weekends.*

Cliff Crest Bed and Breakfast Inn

Innkeeping may seem an unlikely retirement career choice for an aerospace engineer and a recipe tester for Carnation foods, but it's the one Bruce and Sharon Taylor made when they moved from Los Angeles to this seaside town in 1986, purchasing Cliff Crest.

A smallish, modest Queen Anne, Cliff Crest was the home of William and Jenny Jeter. William was a mayor of Santa Cruz, lieutenant governor of California from 1895 to 1899, and founder of a local bank. Historic photographs on the walls illustrate the active life the Jeters led.

Like the Jeters, the Taylors enjoy visiting with guests in the parlor or in the sunny solarium. The guest rooms on the first and second floors contain antiques from the Taylors' personal collection: an Eastlake bedroom suite, an original Morris chair, an antique walnut dresser.

Sharon's penchant for experimenting with recipes continues, and results in such unusual breakfast entrées as chili egg puff, one of her most popular creations.

Address: *407 Cliff St., Santa Cruz, CA 95060, tel. 408/427-2609.*
Accommodations: *5 double rooms with baths.*
Amenities: *Robes; fireplace in 1 room.*
Rates: *$85–$135; full breakfast, evening refreshments. AE, D, MC, V.*
Restrictions: *No smoking indoors, no pets; 2-night minimum on weekends.*

Country Rose Inn

I nnkeeper Rose Hernandez has fashioned a remote retreat out of this big, white Dutch colonial farmhouse, just a few miles south of bustling Silicon Valley. It's set back on a country lane and surrounded by fields, ancient oaks, and flowering magnolias.

Many of the furnishings and decor come from Rose's family: her mother's wedding dress hanging in an antique armoire; a marriage trunk; a *metate y mano* stone Rose's mother used for grinding corn during the early days of her marriage; a baby grand piano in the music room. The Rambling Rose suite offers a lavish, romantic cathedral-ceiling hideaway comprising a bedroom and separate sitting room with Franklin stove, and a huge bathroom featuring a double Jacuzzi, over-size steam shower, and an enormous double-sink vanity.

Common areas include a large dining room–bar, where Rose serves breakfast, and a cozy antiques-filled sitting room with fireplace and baby grand piano. Rose is always ready with recommendations for restaurants and theater events in nearby Gilroy.

Address: *455 Fitzgerald Ave., No. E, San Martin, CA 95046, tel. 408/842–0441.*
Accommodations: *4 double rooms with baths, 1 suite.*
Amenities: *Air-conditioning, fireplace, Jacuzzi in 1 room; gardens, picnic baskets available.*
Rates: *$79–$169; full breakfast, afternoon refreshments. MC, V.*
Restrictions: *No smoking, no pets.*

Gatehouse Inn

T his Italianate Victorian house has a somewhat literary history. John Steinbeck, whose grandparents lived across the street, used to visit with owner Alice Langford to discuss poetry and King Arthur. The house dates from 1884 and is one of the oldest in Pacific Grove.

The original decor has either been retained or re-created: lincrusta on the walls, Bradbury & Bradbury silk-screen wallpapers, and antique white wicker furnishings, lending both the main house and the sympathetic addition an airy feel. About half of the rooms are faithfully decorated in the Victorian style; the others are done up in fantasy themes: One is like a sultan's tent, with Persian carpet, brass headboard with inlaid mother-of-pearl, and a chair made from a camel saddle.

Some rooms have claw-foot tubs set in their corners or alcoves.

Manager Lois De Ford presides over a buffet breakfast that includes quiches, homemade muffins, and coffee cake.

Address: *225 Central Ave., Pacific Grove, CA 93950, tel. 408/649–1881 or 800/753–1881.*
Accommodations: *9 double rooms with baths.*
Amenities: *Radio and tape player, phone in rooms, fireplace in 5 rooms, guest kitchen.*
Rates: *$110–$150; full breakfast, afternoon refreshments. AE, MC, V.*
Restrictions: *No smoking indoors.*

Gosby House

The Gosby House is a gabled and turreted landmark dating from 1887, when J. E. Gosby built one of the first boardinghouses in town. The addition of the turret tower, a bay window with stained glass, white spindled gingerbread adorning the front porch, and the shingled exterior transformed the homely building—ugly duckling–style—into a graceful Queen Anne Victorian.

Guest rooms vary in size, and all are decorated with late Victorian antiques and period reproductions. The inn has an informal, country air about it, and at breakfast guests feel comfortable choosing among the buffet offerings of cinnamon rolls, quiche, muffins, scones, omelets, and Mexican eggs, and taking them out to the garden; in the afternoon, they can enjoy a glass of wine and hors d'oeuvres in the parlor. The young innkeepers are knowledgeable and can offer tourism or restaurant suggestions.

Address: *643 Lighthouse Ave., Pacific Grove, CA 93950, tel. 408/375-1287.*
Accommodations: *20 double rooms with baths, 2 doubles share bath.*
Amenities: *Phone in rooms, whirlpool tub in 2 rooms, fireplace in 12 rooms; picnic baskets and wine available, bicycles.*
Rates: *$85–$150; full breakfast, afternoon refreshments. AE, MC, V.*
Restrictions: *No smoking, no pets.*

Happy Landing Inn

This 1920s inn is a collection of pastel-colored Hansel and Gretel cottage-like rooms linked together and set in a sea of flowers. Flagstone paths wind through the gardens, which include a beckoning lily pond and a lattice gazebo. Stone benches and lawn statuary abound.

Designed by Hugh Comstock, the architect responsible for many of Carmel's "storybook"-style structures, the two master suites and five bedrooms share the gardens, the great room, and the kitchen. The rooms have cathedral ceilings, lace curtains, brass beds, and an eclectic assortment of antiques. Each room has its own garden entrance. A breakfast of quiche, coffee cake, and fresh fruit or yogurt will be served to the rooms when "you raise the shade to let us know you're ready," according to owner Dick Stewart.

Coffee and tea are served by a great stone fireplace. The inn is within easy walking distance of the beach, shops, and art galleries of Carmel.

Address: *Monte Verde St. between 5th and 6th Aves., Box 2619, Carmel, CA 93921, tel. 408/624-7917.*
Accommodations: *5 double rooms with baths, 2 suites.*
Amenities: *Cable TV in rooms, fireplace in suites and 1 room.*
Rates: *$90–$155; expanded Continental breakfast, afternoon refreshments. MC, V.*
Restrictions: *No smoking indoors, no pets; 2-night minimum on weekends.*

Sandpiper Inn

Longtime innkeepers Graeme and Irene Mackenzie, originally from Scotland, are true to the spirit of hospitality conveyed by the Gaelic motto hanging in the Sandpiper Inn's spacious, bay-view living room: "Ceud Mile Failte: A hundred thousand welcomes."

The prairie-style inn, located near scenic Carmel Point and built in the 1920s, features bands of horizontal casement windows, a stucco finish, and a long, flat roofline. It offers a selection of spacious rooms, many with sweeping ocean views, on the first and second floors of the main house and in two garden cottages. There are open-beam ceilings, skylights, fireplaces, reproduction and antique furnishings, canopy beds, and local art on the walls.

Lovely gardens, with sitting areas tucked in all corners, are filled with pink, white, and red rhododendrons, camellias, azaleas, and geraniums.

Address: *2408 Bayview Ave., Carmel, CA 93923, tel. 408/624–6433.*
Accommodations: *16 double rooms with baths.*
Amenities: *TV in 1 room, fireplace in 3 rooms, fireplace in living room, guest phone, gardens; German spoken.*
Rates: *$95–$180; expanded Continental breakfast, afternoon refreshments. AE, MC, V.*
Restrictions: *No smoking indoors; 2-night minimum on weekends, 3-night minimum on some holidays.*

Sea View Inn

A few blocks from the madding crowd that sometimes overwhelms Carmel, the Sea View typifies what longtime visitors to Carmel come for: peaceful seclusion amid stunning natural beauty. Diane Hydorn and husband Marshall, a former airline pilot and now a writer and artist (whose paintings grace many of the inn's rooms), have been the hosts here since 1975.

Inside the Craftsman cottage there's lots of dark woodwork in open-beam ceilings, paneled walls, milled moldings, hardwood floors topped with Oriental rugs, overstuffed chairs, sofas in subdued colors, and brick fireplaces that keep the living room and games room warm on cool days (in other words, most of the time). Books, maga-

zines, and games abound, and classical music plays softly in the background.

Breakfast, which consists of quiche, home-baked breads, fruits, and cheeses, is served by candlelight.

Address: *Camino Real between 11th and 12th Aves., Box 4138, Carmel, CA 93921, tel. 408/624–8778.*
Accommodations: *6 double rooms with baths, 2 doubles share bath.*
Rates: *$80–$115; Continental breakfast, afternoon refreshments. MC, V.*
Restrictions: *No smoking indoors, no pets; 2-night minimum on weekends, 3-night minimum on holidays.*

Seven Gables Inn

This inn is actually a collection of four yellow, gabled clapboard buildings that share a corner lot and a breathtaking view of the ocean. The main house was built in 1886, one of the first of the many showy Victorian homes in Pacific Grove; the three outbuildings were put up during the 1910s and 1940s.

The Flatley family (who opened the Green Gables Inn during the 1950s) has filled the buildings with a collection of European antiques from various periods, marble statues, and bric-a-brac. Gold-leaf mirrors, picture frames, a Tiffany window, crystal chandeliers, inlaid wood furnishings, beveled-glass armoires, and Oriental rugs and marble statues create a formal European atmosphere. Susan Flatley, who manages the inn day to day, grew up in this house and is quite knowledgeable about the area; she happily provides advice and insight on visiting nearby Cannery Row, the Aquarium, and various Monterey historic sites.

Address: *555 Ocean View Blvd., Pacific Grove, CA 93950, tel. 408/ 372–4341.*
Accommodations: *14 double rooms with baths.*
Amenities: *Picnic baskets, refrigerators.*
Rates: *$105–$205; full breakfast, afternoon tea. MC, V.*
Restrictions: *Smoking in garden only; 2-night minimum on weekends, 3-night minimum on holidays.*

Stonehouse Inn

This handcrafted stone cottage dates back to 1906, when San Francisco socialite Nana Foster hosted Bay Area artists and writers at her weekend retreat. Rooms named for those notables—Jack London, Sinclair Lewis, Lola Montez—are smallish, some tucked in gables, others with ocean views lined up across the front; furnishings include brass and canopy beds, hand-carved armoires, and skylights.

The common areas, with distinctive Craftsman architectural touches, are particularly inviting. The centerpiece of the board-and-batten living room is a great stone fireplace flanked by shelves of books, a Victorian sofa, and a pair of wing chairs. An indoor garden–sun room is furnished with a rattan sofa and an antique wicker perambulator. Innkeeper Loretta Rolleri serves homemade breads, Stonehouse granola, quiche, and egg dishes in the sunny breakfast room, which opens to the cottage's backyard.

Address: *8th Ave. below Monte Verde St., Box 2517, Carmel, CA 93921, tel. 408/624–4569.*
Accommodations: *6 double rooms share 3 baths.*
Amenities: *Fireplace in living room, guest phone; gardens.*
Rates: *$95–$135; full breakfast, afternoon refreshments. MC, V.*
Restrictions: *No smoking indoors, no pets.*

San Francisco

San Francisco
From North Beach to the Sunset District

Sailboats gliding past Alcatraz Island, the hand-tooled finial of a restored Victorian, the clang of a cable-car bell, the aroma of Italian roast coffee, the spices of Szechuan cooking, the old '60s holdover and the new '90s individualist—San Francisco dazzles, provokes, and never disappoints. A jewel on the tip of a peninsula, the city is surrounded by water—the Pacific to the west of the Golden Gate Bridge, San Francisco Bay to the east. Victorian "painted ladies" cling to hills so steep they rival any roller coaster. Although driving can be nerve-racking and walking challenging, panoramic views reward at every turn.

Many visitors begin their tour of San Francisco at the vibrant waterfront. On a sunny weekend day, tourists and residents alike throng the unique shops, T-shirt stands, historic and hokey museums, and bay-view restaurants. Pier 39, a two-story wooden boardwalk of boutiques, eateries, and an old-fashioned carousel, juts into the ocean. Just up the street are the Cannery and Ghirardelli Square, a former chocolate factory, with more fun shops and restaurants. Along the way, you'll be enticed by the catch of the day cooked and sold at sidewalk stalls along Fisherman's Wharf. This is the northern terminus of the cable car, the nation's only moving National Historic Landmark.

The cable car climbs and dips over the city's hills to North Beach, the Italian neighborhood. Open-air cafés, pastry shops, delis, coffee-roasting companies, bakeries, and pizza parlors ensure that visitors never go hungry as they explore the Italian import shops and the Romanesque-Gothic cathedral of Saints Peter and Paul. Many of these businesses have been run for generations by the same Italian families that started them. On the adjacent Telegraph Hill, residents have some of the best views of San Francisco as well as the most difficult ascent to their aeries.

The next stop is Chinatown, alive and exotic with crowds of Chinese and more recently arrived Southeast Asians scrutinizing the abundant vegetable stands and snapping up bargains on embroidered linens, jade, and ceramics in the import shops along Grant Avenue. Roast ducks hang in restaurant windows, Chinese characters cover marquees, and teahouses offer cups of steaming ginseng, reputed to induce good health. Nearby is Union Square, the heart of downtown and the city's premier shopping district. Within a few blocks are Macy's, Neiman-Marcus, F.A.O. Schwarz, Gump's, Shreve & Co., a spate of world-famous retailers, and many smaller, exclusive boutiques. Chances are that many of the shoppers who frequent these pricey establishments live in Pacific Heights, where many-splendored mansions and town houses dominate some of San Francisco's most expensive real estate.

Continuing on the west side of the city, you'll find the stunning Golden Gate Park, home to world-class museums and delightful gardens. Although the park stretches from Stanyan Street to the sea, several highlights are clustered in one section. The M. H. de Young Memorial Museum, known for its American works, and the renowned Asian Art Museum share the same building. Next door is the serene four-acre Japanese Tea Garden, with its winding paths, a 200-year-old Buddha, a bonsai forest, and the always busy Tea House, where fortune cookies were invented. Across the street, the Strybing Arboretum is a microcosm of the plant kingdom, divided into such theme plantings as the New World Cloud Forest and the Scent Garden. The California Academy of Sciences and its magnificent aquarium are across the concourse.

Due north is another urban oasis, the 1,500-acre Presidio, an area of rolling hills, majestic woods, and attractive redbrick army barracks. Just outside its eastern boundary is the rosy and rococo Palace of Fine Arts, which houses the Exploratorium, an innovative science museum. Crowning the Presidio is the Golden Gate Bridge.

Since its bawdy, boomtown birth in the wake of the 1849 gold rush, San Francisco has pulsed with ethnic diversity, free enterprise, a thirst for the good life, and a love for the natural beauty of the West. Take a stroll away from the tourist spots and you'll discover this spirit still very much alive. Although occasional earthquakes may rattle the city temporarily, San Francisco remains unsinkable.

Places to Go, Sights to See

Alcatraz Island. Al Capone, Machine Gun Kelly, and Robert Stroud, the "Birdman of Alcatraz," were inmates at this former maximum-security federal penitentiary. You can walk through the prison and grounds on a self-guided tour. Seating on the ferries of the Red and White Fleet (tel. 415/546–2882), which leave from Pier 41, is in great demand—deservedly so, as this is a delightful excursion—and should be reserved in advance.

Asian Art Museum (Golden Gate Park, tel. 415/668–7855). With an estimated 12,000 works spanning 6,000 years, this is the largest museum outside Asia that is devoted to Asian art. Highlights include the Magnin Jade Room and the Leventritt collection of blue-and-white porcelain. The adjoining *M. H. de Young Memorial Museum* (tel. 415/863–3330) is especially strong in American art, including works by Sargent, Whistler, Cassatt, and Remington.

California Academy of Sciences (Golden Gate Park, tel. 415/750–7145). One of the top museums of natural history in the country, the Academy encompasses the first-rate *Morrison Planetarium*, featuring star and laser shows; *Steinhart Aquarium*, with its 100,000-gallon Fish Roundabout, which is home to 14,000 creatures; and such exhibits as an "earthquake floor," which enables visitors to ride a simulated California quake.

Coit Tower (atop Telegraph Hill, tel. 415/362–0808). Take an elevator to the top of this art-deco monument, decorated with murals dedicated to the workers of California, to enjoy panoramic views of the city and the bay.

Golden Gate Bridge. For the best views of this international symbol of San Francisco, see it from Lincoln Boulevard, on the western edge of the Presidio, or drive across the bridge to the parking lot on the Marin side.

Golden Gate Park. The best way to see this 1,000-acre park is by car. Highlights include the *Conservatory* (tel. 415/641–7978), an elaborate Victorian crystal palace that was designed after one in London's Kew Gardens, and the *Japanese Tea Garden* (tel. 415/752–1171), a 4-acre village of small ponds, streams, and flowering shrubs created for the 1894 Mid-Winter Exposition. Visitors especially enjoy paddle-boating on Stow Lake, the expansive picnic grounds, and the park's first-class museums (*see above*).

Lombard Street (between Hyde and Leavenworth Sts.). Cars line up to zigzag down this "crookedest street in the world," where pedestrians negotiate stairs instead of sidewalks. Note: The street is scheduled to close for part of 1995.

Mission Dolores (16th and Dolores Sts., tel. 415/621–8203). The sixth of 21 missions founded in California by the Franciscans and the oldest building in the city, this structure, dating from 1776, retains the appearance of a small-scale outpost, dwarfed by the towers of the adjacent basilica.

San Francisco Museum of Modern Art (151 3rd St., tel. 415/357–4000). SFMOMA moved into its stunning new Mario-Botta—designed building in 1995. Two floors are devoted to temporary exhibitions; early modernist works, photography, and post-World War II California art are among the strengths of the permanent collection.

Yerba Buena Gardens. The block surrounded by 3rd, Mission, Howard, and 4th streets—across from SFMOMA and above the underground addition to *Moscone Center*—holds an attractive expanse of green surrounded by a circular walkway lined with benches and outdoor sculptures. On the eastern side of the block is the *Center for the Arts* (701 Mission St., tel. 415/978–2278), a complex of galleries and performance spaces.

Restaurants

San Francisco's culinary delights are legendary and abundant. Among the restaurants near the B&Bs listed are three downtown spots: reputed California cuisine inventor Jeremiah Tower's **Stars** (tel. 415/861–7827); L.A. wizard Wolfgang Puck's **Postrio** (tel. 415/776–7825); and the bustling **City of Paris** (tel. 415/441–4442) bistro. For a Southeast Asian treat, try the inexpensive **Burma's House** (tel. 415/775–1156). The specialty at North Beach's **Buca Giovanni** (tel. 415/776–7766) is pasta made on the premises. **Fog City Diner** (tel. 415/982–2000), below Coit Tower, is chic yet informal. **Alain Rondelli** (tel. 415/387–0408) is worth the trek to the Richmond District. Its namesake is a three-star French chef who has been influenced by California's Asian and Hispanic heritage. **Zuni Cafe** (tel. 415/552–2522) serves a perfect Caesar salad—and loads of atmosphere. The nearby **Hayes Street Grill** (tel. 415/863–5545) is noted for its charcoal-grilled fresh fish plates. Chef Reed Hearon's colorful **Cafe Marimba** (tel. 415/776–1506) serves up the Marina District's snappiest Mexican cuisine. Craving a big, juicy steak? Head to **Harris'** (tel. 415/673–1888). Not a carnivore? **Greens at Fort Mason** (tel. 415/771–6662) has creative vegetarian dishes—and one of the best views of the bay.

Tourist Information

San Francisco Convention and Visitors Bureau (lower level of Hallidie Plaza at Powell and Market Sts., tel. 415/391–2000).

Reservation Services

Bed & Breakfast International (Box 282910, San Francisco, CA 94128–2910, tel. 415/696–1690, fax 415/696–1699); **Bed & Breakfast San Francisco** (Box 349, San Francisco, CA 94101, tel. 415/931–3083, fax 415/921–2273).

Archbishops Mansion

T he Archbishops Mansion is an elegant European manor reborn in San Francisco. The Second Empire–style residence, built in 1904 for Archbishop Patrick Riordan, faces Alamo Square and its "postcard row" of restored Victorians. Designers Jonathan Shannon and Jeffrey Ross have restored the home, now managed by Joie de Vivre Hotels, to that era of opulence. Ornate Belle Epoque furnishings and reproductions fill the rooms, such as the crystal chandelier that hung in Scarlett O'Hara's beloved Tara in *Gone with the Wind*. Everything about the mansion—the scale, the ornamentation, the Napoleon III antiques—is extravagant.

A three-story redwood staircase rises majestically from the coffered foyer. Above, sunlight filters through a 16-foot-wide, oval leaded-glass dome, which miraculously survived the 1906 earthquake. While you sip your complimentary evening wine in the front parlor, dominated by a massive redwood fireplace with fluted Corinthian columns, you'll be serenaded from the hall by a 1904 ebony Bechstein piano once owned by Noel Coward.

Inspired by the Opera House several blocks away, guest rooms are unabashedly romantic. The gold-hued Don Giovanni Suite conveys a Renaissance formality and, not surprisingly, has a huge bed. The zebrawood canopy four-poster bed found in a castle in southern France was masterly carved during the Napoleonic period.

The Carmen Suite's outstanding feature is its bathroom: A claw-foot tub sits in front of a fireplace to enhance your soaking pleasure. A second fireplace warms the Carmen's bedroom, where the 1885 settee has its original horsehair covering. Billowing draperies, canopied beds, and ceramic-tile fireplaces are routine here.

A breakfast of bakery muffins, bundt cakes, and tea or coffee is brought to your room in a picnic basket, or you can join the other guests in the formal dining room for an expanded Continental breakfast. Complimentary wine and hors d'oeuvres are offered in the early evening in the parlor.

Address: *1000 Fulton St., San Francisco, CA 94117, tel. 415/563-7872 or 800/543-5820, fax 415/885-3193.*
Accommodations: *10 double rooms with baths, 5 suites.*
Amenities: *Phone and cable TV in rooms, fireplace and robes in many rooms, whirlpool tubs in 2 suites; elevator, laundry service; room service for wine, beer, and snacks; conference facilities, limited parking.*
Rates: *$115–$189, suites $205–$385; Continental breakfast, evening refreshments. AE, MC, V.*
Restrictions: *Smoking only in one downstairs common area, no pets; 2-night minimum on weekends.*

Chateau Tivoli

Astay in this ornate fin de siècle château in the historic Alamo Square district may forever alter your decorating sensibilities. Built in 1892, this historic painted lady wears no fewer than 22 colors, from raisin brown to turquoise, with ornamentation picked out in 23-karat gold leaf.

The château's past is even more colorful than its exterior. Designed by 19th-century British architect William Armitage, the house once belonged to lumber-baron Daniel Jackson and later to Mrs. Ernestine Kreling, owner of San Francisco's Tivoli Opera House. Over the past few decades, when the Alamo Square district saw some rough times, the building was everything from a halfway house to a famed ashram. Current owners Rodney Karr and Willard Gersbach purchased the château from new-age guru Jack Painter in 1985.

Rodney and Willard have carried the flamboyant appearance of the exterior inside, tightly packing every room, hallway, and wall with antique furnishings and art (some from the estates of Cornelius Vanderbilt and Charles de Gaulle), housewares, knickknacks, and a somewhat haunting taxidermy collection. Competing for attention are the cornices and carved oak paneling of the entrance hall, double parlor, and staircase.

The riotous, museumlike quality of the château's busy public areas is carried over into the guest rooms. A sultan and his elephant could both stay comfortably in the glorious Mark Twain suite; its Renaissance Revival–style parlor alone is 500 square feet. Romantics will relish the Luisa Tettrazine suite's marble bath with double shower head, huge French Renaissance canopy bed, and frescoed ceilings. Five additional bedrooms are equally spacious. From the bowed windows and Aesthetic Movement furniture in the Joaquin Miller room to the intimate tower dining nook and French wash walls of the Jack London room, there's something at the Chateau Tivoli for anyone open to the owners' flair for dramatic decorating. The only drawback is the neighborhood, which can be a tad dicey at night and is sometimes noisy.

A Continental breakfast of scones, cereals, juices, and fresh fruit is served at a grand dining room table that seats more than a dozen.

Address: *1057 Steiner St., San Francisco, CA 94115, tel. 415/776–5462 or 800/228–1647, fax 415/776–0505.*
Accommodations: *1 double room with bath, 4 doubles share 2 baths, 1 suite, 1 double suite.*
Amenities: *Phone in rooms, fireplace in 1 room and 1 suite.*
Rates: *$80–$125; suites $160–$200; Continental breakfast weekdays, full breakfast weekends, complimentary wine. AE, MC, V.*
Restrictions: *No smoking indoors.*

Hotel Triton

Although certainly not a traditional bed-and-breakfast, the Triton just may be the zaniest hostelry in town. Guests enter via a whimsical lobby of shimmering silk-taffeta furniture, star-studded carpeting, and inverted gilt pillars, stylized spoofs of Roman columns.

The result of a $10 million makeover of the old Beverly Plaza Hotel, a former haven of Japanese businessmen, today's Triton caters to fashion, entertainment, music, and film-industry folks, who seem to like the iridescent pink-and-gold-painted rooms, harlequin diamonds on the walls, and s-curved dervish chairs with tassels. Indeed, it's right in the downtown gallery district, several blocks from Union Square, just steps from the Chinatown Gate, and an uphill hike to the coffeehouses and celebrated nightlife of North Beach. The South of Market area, home to the Showplace Design Center and other smart fashion-design outlets, is a five-minute drive away.

A team of local artists coordinated the Triton look, installing original art in every room and an assortment of curly-necked lamps and oddball light fixtures. Geometric patterns dominate—diamond-shaped, gilt-painted end tables and beige checkerboard-painted walls. These themes and unexpected color combinations, such as big navy silk pillows with magenta buttons, give the rooms an avant-garde appeal.

Such playfulness makes you forgive the rooms' diminutive dimensions. For enough space to stretch out, try the junior suites. The roomy master suite, number 221, includes a whirlpool bath tucked in a mirror-lined side room with its own TV. Comfort has not suffered for the sake of trendiness. Asymmetrical wooden armoires offer plenty of closet space, and beds covered with duvets are extremely comfortable.

Aioli, a Mediterranean restaurant, and the coffeehouse–newsstand Café de la Presse, which serves as a gathering place for foreign visitors to the city, are attached to the hotel.

Address: *342 Grant Ave., San Francisco, CA 94108, tel. 415/394–0500 or 800/433–6611, fax 415/394–0555.*
Accommodations: *133 double rooms with baths, 7 junior suites.*
Amenities: *Phone, TV, and minibar in rooms, CD stereo and VCR in suites, whirlpool bath in 1 suite, fireplace in lobby; conference facilities, room service 6 AM–9 PM, valet-laundry service, business-secretarial services, fitness center, complimentary limousine service to South of Market design community, valet parking.*
Rates: *$99–$169, suites $189–$239; complimentary morning coffee, tea, and evening wine. AE, MC, V.*
Restrictions: *No pets.*

Inn at the Opera

Half-hidden behind the Opera House and the Veterans Building, near the Civic Center, this impeccable inn with its lavish floral arrangements and elegant furnishings manages to be a paradigm of superb taste without being stuffy. In 1986, owner-manager Tom Noonan turned a neglected seven-story hotel into a resplendent hideaway for performing artists and their fans: Mikhail Baryshnikov, Luciano Pavarotti, Herbie Hancock, and Dizzy Gillespie are among the notables who have stayed here. Noonan is a congenial host, overseeing every detail and maintaining the inn's reputation for fine service and hospitality.

The plush little lobby, all pale green with Oriental porcelain and damask chairs, resembles the foyer of a European inn. Excellent California-Mediterranean cuisine is served in the adjoining Act IV restaurant, against the swank backdrop of wood paneling, tapestry-covered walls, leather chairs, and a green marble fireplace; a formally dressed pianist plays old standards on a glossy black grand. The inn offers a package including show, dinner, dessert and champagne, and overnight accommodations.

The hotel's 48 rooms are discreetly romantic, glowing with pastel colors and Old World finesse, from the half-canopy beds and fluffy pillows to the handsome antique armoires and gorgeously framed color reproductions of delicately etched flowers and birds. Subtle grace notes abound, such as a basket of red apples and armoire drawers lined with sheet music. Under filmy curtains and drawn-back drapes, window shades gently let in the morning light through a lacy diamond-shaped cutout near the bottom. Larger suites have two bedrooms, each linked to its own bath, and a central sitting room with a well-stocked minibar and microwave. Guests can have breakfast brought to their rooms with a morning newspaper or head for Act IV's buffet breakfast. Those in the know prefer the rooms in the back, as the front ones do get street noise.

Address: *333 Fulton St., San Francisco, CA 94102, tel. 415/863–8400 or 800/423–9610 (in CA), fax 415/861–0821.*
Accommodations: *30 double rooms with baths, 18 suites.*
Amenities: *2-line phone with data port, minibar, robes, cable TV in rooms, microwave in suites, irons and ironing boards, hair dryers available, fireplace in restaurant/bar, morning newspapers, complimentary pressing on arrival, overnight shoeshine, 24-hour room service, business-secretarial service, laundry service, packing service, staff physician, complimentary limousine service to financial district, valet parking.*
Rates: *$110–$155, suites $175–$205; Continental breakfast. AE, MC, V.*
Restrictions: *Pets by application only; 4 no-smoking floors.*

The Mansions Hotel

I f inns were awarded prizes for showmanship, the Mansions Hotel would win top honors. First, there's the decapitated head of the resident ghost who reads minds. And where else can you see the innkeeper, clad in sequined dinner jacket, play the saw? They're just part of the live "magic extravaganzas" held every weekend at the Mansions.

The inspiration behind this zaniness is the aforementioned innkeeper, Bob Pritikin. The author of *Christ Was an Adman*, Pritikin isn't afraid of innovation in his hotel, two adjacent Queen Anne Victorians a short walk from the chic boutiques and eateries of Pacific Heights. The cabaret, free to overnight guests, also draws diners from the highly praised hotel restaurant.

The Mansions Hotel is as visually flamboyant as its entertainment, although the west wing has a simpler, country-inn look. In the public areas no surface has been left unembellished. Objects, wall murals, curios (a selection of ugly ties, for example), and sculptures, many by Beniamino Bufano, are everywhere. The porcine theme in the breakfast dining room is tough to miss, surrounded as you are by an old wooden carousel pig and wall painting depicting a swine-filled picnic in progress.

All of the west-wing rooms have murals that depict the famous San Francisco personage for whom the room is named. The authentic and Victorian reproduction decor might include a rolltop desk, four-poster canopy bed, and Tiffany-style lamp. The west-wing rooms have Laura Ashley flower-print wallpaper and matching bedding, with a preponderance of pine furniture. Particularly lavish is the Louis IV room, where such guests as Barbra Streisand, Robert Stack, and Michael York have enjoyed the immense gold-leaf half-tester bed and wardrobe and private redwood deck.

A full breakfast of fresh fruit, cereal, eggs cooked to order, crumpets, bangers, potatoes, and juice can be delivered to your room. There you'll find a replica of a Victorian silk rose to take home—and a little chocolate version of the Mansions that, chances are, will never leave the premises.

Address: *2220 Sacramento St., San Francisco, CA 94115, tel. 415/929–9444, fax 415/567–9391.*
Accommodations: *13 double rooms with baths, 8 suites.*
Amenities: *Phone in rooms, fireplace in some suites, whirlpool tub in 1 room; restaurant, evening entertainment, complimentary newspaper and coffee, limited room service, laundry service, billiard table.*
Rates: *$129–$159, suites $189–$350; full breakfast. AE, D, DC, MC, V.*

The Queen Anne

This majestic, four-story Victorian ranks among the loveliest of San Francisco's classic painted ladies. Its rose and green gables and distinctive corner turret rise proudly above a neighborhood of vivid Victorians in lower Pacific Heights; walking tours of this colorful district can be arranged at the hotel. Japantown with its restaurants and the Fillmore shopping area are just around the corner.

The building's roots as a luxurious boarding school for girls, constructed by silver-mogul and Senator James G. Fair in 1890, still show in its rich cedar and oak paneling and the lofty staircase winding four flights up past stained-glass windows to an antique skylight. A sprawling lobby full of Victoriana—from brocade chairs to crimson walls—encompasses most of the ground floor. Guests can curl up with coffee or sherry before a crackling fire or partake of the breakfast buffet here each morning (many prefer to take a tray back to their room). This spacious public area, which fans into adjoining conference chambers, makes the hotel ideal for weddings and business meetings.

All the rooms and suites are different, blending contemporary comforts with historic accents. The plush carpeting, modern bedspreads, and hair dryers in the baths are offset by old-fashioned details like brass-necked lamps, English antiques, and lacy curtains. Fireplaces warm many quarters; one enormous room has two brick hearths at either end. The accommodations, large for a small hotel, range from a two-bedroom, split-level town house with a private deck to a snug top-story room with slanted ceilings and a framed picture of George Washington.

Address: *1590 Sutter St., San Francisco, CA 94109, tel. 415/441–2828 or 800/227–3970, fax 415/775–5212.*
Accommodations: *45 rooms with baths, 3 suites, 1 town house suite.*
Amenities: *Phone and TV in rooms, fireplace and wet bar in many rooms, minifridge in suites; fireplace in parlor, irons and ironing boards available, conference and reception facilities, concierge-secretarial service, laundry service, morning newspaper, complimentary morning limousine downtown, off-street parking.*
Rates: *$99–$150, suites $175–$275; Continental breakfast, afternoon tea and sherry. AE, D, DC, MC, V.*
Restrictions: *No pets.*

The Sherman House

The words "crème de la crème" best describe this French-Italianate white mansion in Pacific Heights a block off Union Street. More showcase than home-sweet-home, the Sherman House exudes old money, from the silken-striped Empire chairs of the second-floor gallery-salon and the sweeping staircase to the Old World splendor of the music hall.

Built in 1876 by music lover–instrument maker Leander Sherman, the house once attracted patrons and world-class musicians such as Enrico Caruso and pianist Jan Paderewski, who performed in the magnificent music hall; string quartet and piano concerts still make the chandeliers quiver today. Iranian economist Manouchehr Mobedshahi and his art historian wife, Vesta, saved this urban palace from demolition when they bought and restored it in 1980. Designer William Gaylord added antiques and objets d'art from estates and auctions, largely in French Second Empire style. A solarium with diamond-shaped windowpanes and a connecting chamber lit by a flickering fire make up the petite (and expensive) in-house restaurant, which serves California cuisine.

Great care went into the guest rooms, one more sumptuous than the next. Marble fireplaces with gas jets, bowls of heady potpourri, and featherbeds enclosed in heavy drapery are common denominators. The dark, wood-beamed, and wainscoted look of the Biedermeier and Paderewski suites contrasts sharply with the airy feel of the Leander Sherman Suite; its enormous rooftop terrace could hold a party of 25. Behind the main house, half an acre of garden—a princely estate in land-pinched San Francisco—encircles a carriage house containing the hotel's largest, priciest quarters, the Garden Suite. Decorated in a rattan motif, with a house-in-the-country aura and its own gazebo and private garden, this set of rooms is popular for wedding parties.

Address: *2160 Green St., San Francisco, CA 94123, tel. 415/563–3600 or 800/424–5777, fax 415/563–1882.*
Accommodations: *8 double rooms with baths, 6 suites.*
Amenities: *Phone, cable TV with stereo, robes, hair dryer in rooms; whirlpool bath or Roman-style tub in some rooms, fireplace in 13 rooms and in main salon and restaurant; garden, restaurant, music room, conference and wedding facilities, personal valet service, massage service, private chauffeur available, laundry service, 24-hour room service, business-secretarial services, valet parking.*
Rates: *$250–$375, suites $575–$825. AE, D, MC, V.*
Restrictions: *No smoking in restaurant and some public areas, no pets.*

Victorian Inn on the Park

Overlooking Golden Gate Park's Panhandle, this Queen Anne Victorian is a riot of gables, finials, and cornices. The most unusual feature is the open belvedere in a cupola, one of only two existing in the city; it's a private retreat for guests in the Belvedere Suite.

Renowned San Francisco architect William Curlett designed the mansion in 1897 for a prominent lawyer. In 1980, Paul and Shirley Weber purchased the building. Their daughter, attorney Lisa Benau, and her husband William, looking for a way to raise their children while working at a job they love, transformed the house into one of San Francisco's first bed-and-breakfasts.

If you've ever wanted to experience the more luxurious aspects of life in the Gay '90s, this is the place to do it. Step across the threshold to a grand entrance of rubbed mahogany paneling and oak parquet floors; they look even more burnished when a fire is lit in the immense brick fireplace framed by a sculpted wood mantel. The parlor is rather formal, with a graceful Rococo Revival fainting couch in floral brocade and a velvet settee. Wine is served here in the evening by the white-tile and painted-wood hearth, which almost touches the ceiling. Light filters through period fringed and embroidered lamp shades.

Guest rooms, decorated with Rococo Revival and Eastlake antiques and peppered with modern reproductions, are most noteworthy for their wall treatments. The wallpapers, combining different floral motifs in rich blues, purples, greens, and gold, are reproductions of William Morris designs, meticulously hand-silkscreened by Bradbury & Bradbury, a local firm.

Piles of pillows, marble bathroom counters, Victorian-era prints and photos, and a decanter of sherry in every room are some of the inn's special touches. The rooms on the street level are quiet and removed but a bit dark. This, however, is a small complaint that never overshadows the friendly ambience and elegant presentation at the Victorian Inn on the Park.

Address: *301 Lyon St., San Francisco, CA 94117, tel. 415/931–1830 or 800/435–1967, fax 415/931–1830.*
Accommodations: *12 double rooms with baths, 1 suite, 1 double suite with 2 baths.*
Amenities: *Phone and clock radio in rooms, fireplace in some rooms, TV available, meeting facilities; parking available.*
Rates: *$99–$159, suites $159–$315; expanded Continental breakfast. AE, D, DC, MC, V.*
Restrictions: *No smoking in breakfast room, no pets; 2-night minimum on weekends, 3-night minimum on holiday weekends.*

White Swan Inn

Fireplaces in every room, romantic furnishings, delicious food, top-notch amenities, and a location just two blocks from Union Square make the White Swan Inn one of the premier bed-and-breakfasts in San Francisco. This circa-1908 building has the look of a London town house, and the decoration is studiously English. Walk into the library, and you'll think you've been admitted to an exclusive gentleman's club, with tufted wing chairs; rich, dark wood; sparkling brass fixtures and hardware; hunting scenes on the pillows; and a red tartan couch.

The guest rooms, predominantly green and burgundy with touches of yellow and rose, have a more informal look than the public rooms. All are similarly furnished with reproduction Edwardian pieces in cherry and other dark woods. Four-poster beds, wingback or barrel chairs, TVs enclosed in an armoire or a cabinet, wooden shutters, and Laura Ashley–style floral wallpaper are standard. A bedside switch allows you to control the gas fireplaces.

The hotel is one of the Four Sisters Inns, owned and operated by the Post family, and each evening and morning, a family member greets guests in the common rooms. At the White Swan, it's usually Kim, one of the four Post sisters for whom their family business was named. Their trademark teddy bears cuddle in the reception area, peeking through banisters and perched on the mantel over the perpetually lit fire. A plush bear also adorns each guest room.

The Four Sisters properties are known for their food, so you're urged to find an excuse to be back at the White Swan in the afternoon. You'll be rewarded by such complimentary snacks as lemon cake, vegetables with curry dip, stuffed grape leaves, and specialty cheeses, accompanied by wine, sherry, and other drinks. Typical breakfast fare includes Mexican quiche, soda-bread toast, Swiss oatmeal, fresh fruit, granola, and dough-nuts. Everything is homemade. Guests have made so many requests for the recipes that the family has released its own cookbook.

Address: *845 Bush St., San Francisco, CA 94108, tel. 415/775–1755, fax 415/775–5717.*
Accommodations: *23 double rooms with baths, 3 suites.*
Amenities: *TV, wet bar, refrigerator, hair dryer, robes, phone in rooms; laundry service, conference and catering facilities, wine-only room service, complimentary newspaper and shoeshine service; valet parking available.*
Rates: *$145–$160, suites $195–$250; full breakfast, afternoon refreshments. AE, DC, MC, V.*
Restrictions: *No smoking, no pets.*

The Alamo Square Inn

his inn spans three buildings encircling a flower-filled patio overlooking a small garden. The most attractive of the three is the 1895 Neo-Classical Revival Baum House, with delicate relief work in the form of wreaths and ribbons.

In the guest rooms, innkeepers Wayne Morris Corn and Klaus Ernst May have opted for reproduction and contemporary furnishings. One upstairs suite features an ultramodern black-laminate bedroom set and a sunken whirlpool bath. Another bright attic suite with dormers has white wicker furniture and opens onto a rooftop sun deck. Several rooms overlook Alamo Square.

The second building is an 1896 Tudor Revival, but the rooms are darker, with small windows. The third house features a modern garden apartment with full kitchen.

Address: *719 Scott St., San Francisco, CA 94117, tel. 415/922–2055 or 800/345–9888, fax 415/931–1304.*
Accommodations: *9 double rooms with baths, 3 suites, 1 housekeeping suite.*
Amenities: *Phone in rooms, Jacuzzi in 1 suite, TV in 4 rooms, fireplace in 4 rooms, conference room; off-street parking.*
Rates: *$85–$135, suites $175; full breakfast, afternoon refreshments. AE, DC, MC, V.*
Restrictions: *No smoking indoors, no pets; 2-night minimum on weekends, 3-night minimum on some holidays.*

Albion House Inn

ucked away several blocks from the Civic Center and two blocks off Market Street, the cozy Albion is within walking distance of many restaurants and the city's opera, ballet, and symphony. Formerly a flop-house for 1960s rock stars, this pre-quake Victorian, now owned by Aziz and Regina Bouagou, was restored and fitted out with bird-print wallpaper and Turkish kilim rugs. An enormous and inviting lobby-living room has teak beams, a grand piano, a marble fire-place, and a table where a generous breakfast steams every morning.

The rooms, though small, are cheerful, decorated with an English-country flair. The rather inappropriately named Janis Joplin suite—a favorite of honeymooners—has sweet floral fabrics and a half-canopy bed and thronelike wicker chair. Other rooms complement the peach, green, and ivory color scheme with a warm mix of antiques and rattan, brightened by floral arrangements. Although the revital-ized Hayes Valley area is a few blocks away, traffic on Gough Street is intense and this stretch slightly rundown.

Address: *135 Gough St., San Francisco, CA 94102, tel. 415/621–0896 or 800/625–2466, fax 415/621–3811.*
Accommodations: *7 double rooms with baths, 1 suite.*
Amenities: *Phone in rooms, fireplace in living room, TV available, restaurant.*
Rates: *$75–$135, suite $180; full breakfast, complimentary brandy, afternoon tea. MC, V.*
Restrictions: *No smoking in common areas and some rooms.*

The Bed and Breakfast Inn

The three 100-year-old Italianate Victorian row houses that comprise the Bed and Breakfast Inn are nestled in a quiet mews just off Union Street and may be the closest you'll come to staying in a native's home. Although owners Bob and Marily Kavanaugh don't reside here, most of the furniture and cherished antiques have descended through their two families.

Guest rooms are cozy, with traditional pieces (some of them love seats), the family china on display, and impressionistic landscape paintings by Marily. Fresh flowers perfume each room. The inn's most popular suite, Celebration, a favorite of honeymooners and other romantics, boasts Laura Ashley wallpaper and curtains and an intimate, sunken double tub. Most rooms that have private bathrooms also have phones and TVs. Pension rooms that share a bath are simple but affordable.

Address: *4 Charlton Ct., San Francisco, CA 94123, tel. 415/921–9784.*
Accommodations: *5 double rooms with baths, 4 doubles share 3 baths, 2 housekeeping suites.*
Amenities: *Phone in 7 rooms, TV in 6 rooms, complimentary coffee, sherry in rooms with baths and in parlor.*
Rates: *$70–$140, suites $190–$275; Continental breakfast. No credit cards.*
Restrictions: *Smoking on deck only, no pets.*

Bock's Bed and Breakfast

Situated in Parnassus Heights—just blocks from Golden Gate Park, the University of California at San Francisco Medical Center complex, and the shops and restaurants of Cole Valley—this 1906 Edwardian bed-and-breakfast, family home of native San Franciscan Laura Bock, offers an oasis of serenity in an attractive residential setting. Slightly off the beaten path, Bock's provides a very reasonably priced respite from the hurly-burly of the city, yet excellent public transportation connections are nearby to take you anywhere in San Francisco.

This small (three units), gay-friendly establishment is simply but comfortably furnished, and the deck off the living room gives views of Buena Vista Park and downtown in the distance.

Typical period features of the house include diamond windows, high pillow ceilings, virgin redwood paneling on the main floor, and mahogany inlaid oak floors in the entrance room. The Mary Ellen Pleasant Room has its own private deck complete with a dramatic Parnassus Heights view.

Address: *1448 Willard St., San Francisco, CA 94117, tel. 415/664–6842.*
Accommodations: *1 double room with bath, 1 double and 1 single share bath.*
Amenities: *Phone and TV in rooms, coffee/tea service.*
Rates: *$40–$75; expanded Continental breakfast. No credit cards.*
Restrictions: *No smoking; 2-night minimum.*

Golden Gate Hotel

The family-run Golden Gate Hotel is ideal for budget-conscious visitors. With rooms as low as $59 for a shared bath (with sink in each guest room), this circa-1913 Edwardian is just two blocks from Union Square. Hosts John and Renate Kenaston and their Moroccan assistant Halim provide complimentary afternoon tea and cookies, served in the cozy parlor, which is simply decorated with ivory-sponged walls, gray-blue carpeting, a contemporary, "deconstructivist" fireplace, and Rococo Revival love seat and coffee table—all presided over by the house cat, Nemo. Coffee lovers can look forward to what is billed as "the city's strongest coffee."

Guests reach their rooms by riding the town house's original birdcage elevator whose shaft is festooned with amusing paintings and murals. The rooms are small, clean, and reasonably quiet given the hotel's downtown location. Each is cheerfully furnished, with white or blue wicker chairs, wicker headboards, and 19th-century mahogany wardrobes.

Address: *775 Bush St., San Francisco, CA 94108, tel. 415/392-3702 or 800/835-1118.*
Accommodations: *14 double rooms with baths, 9 doubles share 3 baths.*
Amenities: *TV in rooms, phone in 10 rooms.*
Rates: *$59-$89; Continental breakfast, afternoon refreshments. AE, DC, MC, V.*

Hotel Griffon

With its clean, contemporary design and proximity to San Francisco's financial district, the Hotel Griffon attracts mostly corporate clients, but its setting on the historic Embarcadero, its glittering views of the bay, and its restaurant also make it a romantic getaway on weekends.

Occupying a five-story 1906 building, transformed—at a cost of $10 million—from a run-down sailor's inn several years ago, the hotel now has a spare European look. Rooms and suites are quietly elegant, most done in ivory and beige with exposed-brick walls, rich cherry and mahogany furniture, tapestried window seats, and, in the bathrooms, marble vanities and sinks. Bayside rooms, only slightly more expensive, offer beautiful vistas of the Bay Bridge; protected from traffic noises by two sets of double-paned windows, these get snapped up quickly.

Address: *155 Steuart St., San Francisco, CA 94105, tel. 415/495-2100, fax 415/495-3522.*
Accommodations: *12 single rooms with bath, 47 double rooms with bath, 3 suites.*
Amenities: *Phone with modem, cable TV, and minibar in rooms, terrace in penthouse suites, VCR available, complimentary newspaper, boardroom, laundry service, room service 11:30 AM-2:30 PM and 5:30-10 PM, use of nearby fitness center, garage available for extra fee.*
Rates: *$130-$160, suites $225; Continental buffet breakfast. AE, MC, V.*
Restrictions: *No pets.*

Inn at Union Square

A half block west of Union Square, the Inn at Union Square is a friendly, more personal alternative to the area's skyscraping hotels. Interior designer Nan Rosenblatt, who owns the inn with husband Norman, has endowed the guest rooms and parlors with the rich, inviting ambience of a gracious country home.

At the end of each of five floors is a cozy sitting area warmed by a wood-burning fireplace. High tea, complete with a generous selection of cucumber sandwiches, cakes, and cookies, is served here.

Guest rooms feature furniture in Chippendale and Federal styles, heavy draperies, and floral-print canopies and half-canopies. Don't expect a view in this crowded part of town, where buildings are squeezed next to one another.

Address: *440 Post St., San Francisco, CA 94102, tel. 415/397–3510 or 800/288–4346, fax 415/989–0529.*
Accommodations: *23 double rooms with baths, 7 suites.*
Amenities: *Phone and TV in rooms, fireplace in 2 rooms, wet bar in 2 rooms, whirlpool bath, sauna, and refrigerator in 1 suite; complimentary newspaper and shoeshine service, laundry service, room service, honor bar, catered dinner in room available, valet parking.*
Rates: *$120–$180, suites $150–$300; Continental breakfast, refreshments. AE, DC, MC, V.*
Restrictions: *No smoking, no pets.*

Inn San Francisco

T he Inn San Francisco in the Mission District is quintessential northern California: a beautifully restored 1872 Italianate Victorian with a hot tub out back. Featherbeds, 19th-century British and American furnishings throughout, a delightful garden and cottage, and a rooftop patio complete the picture.

The spacious double parlor is elegantly decorated in true Victorian fashion with forest-green walls, rubbed redwood trim, velvet side chairs, a tapestried fainting couch, and Oriental rugs. One popular guest room opens onto a private, sheltered deck with its own traditional redwood hot tub. Another room has a double whirlpool bath beneath a stained-glass skylight. Owners Marty Neely and Connie Wu add their own special touches: fresh flowers and truffles by San Francisco chocolatier Joseph Schmidt in every room.

Address: *943 South Van Ness Ave., San Francisco, CA 94110, tel. 415/641–0188 or 800/359–0913, fax 415/641–1701.*
Accommodations: *17 double rooms with baths, 5 doubles share 2 baths.*
Amenities: *Phone, TV, refrigerator and clock radio in rooms, hot tub on deck of 1 room, whirlpool tub in 5 rooms, fireplace in 4 rooms; hot tub in garden, limited off-street parking.*
Rates: *$75–$195; full buffet breakfast; complimentary tea, coffee, and sherry. AE, D, DC, MC, V, personal checks.*
Restrictions: *No smoking in parlor, no pets in public areas.*

Jackson Court

T his charming, old 1900 brownstone in the heart of Pacific Heights houses an exemplary San Francisco bed-and-breakfast: tasteful, personal, and serene. From the walk-in courtyard, doors open into a cordial sitting room where red velvet sofas catch the glow of a blazing fire. Floors are parquet and ceilings wood-beamed.

Each room has its own personality and color scheme. Some are done in old-fashioned ivory, others in lush burgundy; some have marble basins in the rooms, and all have antique writing desks. Off the main parlor, the spacious Executive Room is sophisticated in a masculine way with its brass bed and coatrack. The bed-and-breakfast's wood-paneled conference room is right next door. The Garden Court Room looks out on a private garden.

Upstairs, the library wins raves for its sunny grandeur and gracious hearth. Breakfast is served in the small, bright upstairs kitchen, where guests can stash perishables in the fridge or prepare their own simple meals.

Address: *2198 Jackson St., San Francisco, CA 94115, tel. 415/929–7670.*
Accommodations: *10 double rooms with baths.*
Amenities: *Phone and TV in rooms, fireplace in 2 rooms, fireplace in lobby; off-street parking.*
Rates: *$108–$150; expanded Continental breakfast, afternoon tea and cookies. AE, MC, V.*
Restrictions: *No smoking, no pets.*

James Court Hotel

O ne block off Polk Street and two from bustling Van Ness Avenue, the 1907, post-quake James Court Hotel, site of a former Gump's specialty store, is a haven for artists and especially musicians (like the group Counting Crows) visiting San Francisco. Owned by local modern-rock musician Rudy Colombini, the newly renovated, 36-room hotel's appeal includes its "boho" flavor, cheap rates, and a location central to the California Street cable-car line, Union Square, North Beach, Chinatown, Fisherman's Wharf, Nob Hill, and other tourist meccas.

Be forewarned that the James Court does have 17 basement rehearsal spaces available for use between 6 and 10 PM—and the music does indeed travel up. The rooms themselves are

perhaps best described by Colombini— he dubs them "Days Inn classic." They are sparsely and simply furnished with double beds (either one or two) and a blond wood desk and chest of drawers. The four suites each have their own kitchenette.

Address: *1353 Bush St., San Francisco, CA 94109, tel. 415/771–2409, fax 415/921–1648.*
Accommodations: *14 double rooms with baths, 18 doubles with shared baths, 4 suites.*
Amenities: *Phone and cable TV in rooms, laundry facilities, $5 all-day parking.*
Rates: *$40–$50; Continental breakfast. MC, V.*
Restrictions: *Smoking in one wing only.*

The Monte Cristo

Originally a bordello, the Monte Cristo occupies a deep burgundy, 1875 Italianate building with white awnings and window boxes. At the edge of Presidio Heights, this now modest, low-key guest house is within a few blocks of chic shopping on Sacramento Street and about 10 minutes from downtown San Francisco.

Though it lacks the drama and personality of many other small inns, the Monte Cristo offers good value in a peaceful environment. The Chinese wedding room features a unique carved Cantonese bed, as well as a deep tiled tub, tasseled lamp, and other Oriental accoutrements. A grandiose four-poster bed dominates the secluded upstairs Georgian room. The other rooms are simpler and more Victorian, with sunny bay windows,

crocheted bedspreads, and antiques. Breakfast is served downstairs in a pretty, flowery parlor at tables for two, and complimentary wine is offered in the tiny sitting room.

Address: *600 Presidio Ave., San Francisco, CA 94115, tel. 415/931–1875, fax 415/931–6065.*
Accommodations: *11 double rooms with baths, 3 doubles share bath, 1 deluxe suite.*
Amenities: *Phone in some rooms, TV in some rooms, minifridge in deluxe suite, TV rentals, pay phone.*
Rates: *$63–$98, suites $108; Continental breakfast. AE, MC, V.*
Restrictions: *No pets.*

Petite Auberge

Just two blocks from Union Square, this circa-1915 Baroque Revival inn is a romantic retreat with a small garden patio in the heart of downtown. Owned and operated by the Four Sisters Inns (*see* the White Swan Inn, *above*), the Petite Auberge features dainty floral wallpaper, French-country oak armoires and matching headboards carved in flower and vine reliefs, fireplaces framed with hand-painted floral tiles, and whimsically costumed teddy bears. Other eye-catching accents include glazed terra-cotta tiles in the lobby and Pierre Deux fabrics in some of the rooms.

The lace-curtained guest rooms, predominantly peach, French-country blue, and rose, have thoughtful features, such as reading lights above each side of the bed, a selection of old

books, fresh apples, hair dryers, and a wine list. Color TVs are tucked away in armoires. Some rooms have bay windows with sitting areas; others have charming tables with hand-painted flowers.

Address: *863 Bush St., San Francisco, CA 94108, tel. 415/928–6000, fax 415/775–5717.*
Accommodations: *26 double rooms with baths.*
Amenities: *Phone in rooms, fireplace in many rooms, whirlpool tub in 1 room; laundry service, wine-only room service, catered dinner in room available, valet parking.*
Rates: *$110–$160, suites $220; full breakfast, afternoon refreshments. AE, DC, MC, V.*
Restrictions: *No smoking, no pets.*

Savoy Hotel

San Francisco is blessed with nearly as many small, European-style hotels as Paris, and this newcomer is one of the very best for the money. Named for the Savoy region of France and housed in one of the many late-Victorian, postearthquake buildings surrounding Union Square, the hotel is exceptionally comfortable given its modest scale and price. Featherbeds, down pillows, and cotton Matelasse bedspreads help ensure a good night's sleep; etchings, polished Provençal-style furniture, and Toile de Jouy fabrics with bucolic country scenes set the French-country tone. The suites, with their modest vestibules, black-granite bathrooms, and sitting rooms with Louis-Philippe sleeper sofas, are worth the few extra dollars.

Off the tiny lobby, Brasserie Savoy has had a rebirth under chef Dean Coddem and now, along with its always excellent seafood, specializes in hearty, European-inspired brasserie fare.

Address: *580 Geary St., San Francisco, CA 94102, tel. 415/441–2700 or 800/227–4223.*
Accommodations: *70 rooms with baths, 13 suites.*
Amenities: *Phone, cable TV, hair dryer, minibar, robes in rooms; restaurant, concierge, conference center; valet parking.*
Rates: *$89–$109, suites $139–$159; Continental breakfast; complimentary afternoon tea, sherry, and other refreshments. AE, D, DC, MC, V.*
Restrictions: *No smoking on certain floors, no pets.*

Spencer House

A short walk from Golden Gate Park and the hippie haven of Haight-Ashbury, this classic 1887 Queen Anne Victorian just off Buena Vista Park was once the residence of a San Francisco milliner and gold-mine speculator.

Innkeepers Barbara and Jack Chambers purchased the Spencer House as their home in 1984 and spent two years restoring it before opening their inn in 1986. The French château influence can be seen in the elegant silk wall coverings, Louis XVI antiques, and half-canopy beds suitable for royalty. Rooms are also outfitted with old-fashioned light fixtures and linens trimmed with antique lace. Many of the original features of the house are still present, including faceted stained-glass windows, and combination gas-and-electric brass chandeliers. Guests are greeted as if they were long-lost friends, and many of them are. The Spencer House doesn't have a listed telephone number; Barbara and Jack rely on word of mouth and repeat business. Light sleepers may want to request an interior room rather than one facing either Haight or Baker Street.

Address: *1080 Haight St., San Francisco, CA 94117, tel. 415/626–9205, fax 415/626–9208.*
Accommodations: *6 double rooms with baths.*
Amenities: *Fireplace in parlor, limited parking.*
Rates: *$95–$155; full sit-down breakfast (by candlelight). No credit cards.*
Restrictions: *No smoking; 2-night minimum on weekends, 3-night minimum on holiday weekends.*

Union Street Inn

Window-shopping in San Francisco's most fashionable shopping district, one would never guess that it possesses a garden carriage house, the favorite retreat of Diane Keaton and other celebrities when they visit the city. Of course, guests needn't stay in the cottage to have a view of Union Street Inn's beautiful backyard English-style garden.

The parlor of Helen Stewart's 1901 Edwardian features a brick and redwood gas fireplace and padded salmon-colored velvet walls with wainscoting; French doors open onto a gardenside redwood deck. Certainly the cottage accommodations are the most sybaritic: In the center of the 300-square-foot room is an indulgent double whirlpool Jacuzzi glowing beneath a skylight and hemmed by greenery. The Wildrose Room, with its king-size brass bed and persimmon-mauve decor, affords a garden view that can be seen from *its* Jacuzzi. The English Garden Room's French double doors open onto a private deck overlooking the garden.

Address: *2229 Union St., San Francisco, CA 94123, tel. 415/346–0424.*
Accommodations: *6 double rooms with baths.*
Amenities: *Phone and robe in rooms, TV on request, whirlpool in 2 rooms; limited off-street parking.*
Rates: *$125–$175, carriage house $225; Continental breakfast, evening refreshments. AE, MC, V.*
Restrictions: *Smoking in garden only, no pets.*

Washington Square Inn

One of San Francisco's prettiest small, modern hotels, this inn overlooks verdant Washington Square and the cathedral of Saints Peter and Paul in North Beach.

This property of Nan and Norman Rosenblatt (who also own the Inn at Union Square; *see above*) has the ambience of a gracious country home, with dramatic floral draperies, half-testers, bedspreads, sofas, and bay-window seats. There isn't a bad view to be had: Some rooms look out over Washington Square, while others face an inner patio filled with potted plants and flowers.

In the afternoon, complimentary high tea with cucumber sandwiches is served by the fireplace in the downstairs parlor, followed by evening wine and hors d'oeuvres. Breakfast is served in your room or at the dining table in the parlor, from where you can watch the locals performing their morning *t'ai chi* exercises in the square.

Address: *1660 Stockton St., San Francisco, CA 94133, tel. 415/981–4220 or 800/388–0220, fax 415/397–7242.*
Accommodations: *10 double rooms with baths, 5 doubles share 2 baths.*
Amenities: *Phone in rooms; complimentary newspaper and shoeshine service, laundry service, room service for beer, wine, and soft drinks; valet parking available.*
Rates: *$85–$180; expanded Continental breakfast, afternoon refreshments. AE, DC, MC, V.*
Restrictions: *No smoking, no pets.*

Bay Area

Bay Area
Marin, East Bay, and the Peninsula

Like a twilight fog, the Bay Area beyond San Francisco's city limits defies set boundaries. The peninsula, the East Bay, and Marin are names used knowingly by locals and terms dictated somewhat by geography, but they tell only part of the story. These three areas, all within a 30-mile radius of downtown San Francisco, encompass forested coastal mountains, high-tech industrial centers, majestic shorelines, enclaves of academia, quiet seaside villages, sunny inland suburbs, and one-of-a-kind nature preserves.

The peninsula stretches south from San Francisco, through Silicon Valley and down to San Jose, and is the only part of the Bay Area that's reachable from the city without crossing a bridge. Along the Pacific coastline here, the air is often moist with fog in the morning and late afternoon but bright with sunshine during midday. Commercial florists and backyard gardeners make much of this mild climate. In South San Francisco you can take a greenhouse tour at Rod McClellan's, the world's largest hybridizer of orchids, and around Half Moon Bay you'll find one of the most prolific flower-growing regions in the world. Here, too, you can shop in boutiques or head to the beach for a picnic or horseback ride on the sand. Swimmers, however, will find the Pacific waters goose-bumpingly cold at any time of the year. To the southeast is Filoli, whose magnificent estate and gardens were used as the setting for the TV series Dynasty.

San Jose is inland, just below the southern curve of San Francisco Bay. High-tech industry has pumped new life into this city, and a museum called the Tech Museum of Information offers a fun, hands-on peek into computers, including a simulated "clean room," where silicon chips are made. From San Jose north along the bay toward San Francisco there's a string of high-tech–oriented towns, including Mountain View, where you can take tours of wind

*tunnels and prototypical aircraft at the Ames Research Center,
and Palo Alto, home to Hewlett-Packard, Apple, and the
elegant Spanish Revival–style campus of Stanford University.*

*The East Bay is just that: the area east of San Francisco Bay
beginning at Oakland and Berkeley. The University of
California at Berkeley holds a long-standing rivalry with
Stanford in both football and academics. Berkeley's reputation
as a hotbed of radical thinking has always spilled off campus,
and during the past decade the city has become known for
spawning a generation of innovative young chefs of the
"California cuisine" school, their inspiration being Alice
Waters and her Chez Panisse restaurant.*

*Oakland boasts such attractions as the Oakland Museum, a
microcosm of the Golden State's cultural heritage, art, and
natural history. The parks and gardens around Lake Merritt,
pleasant hillside and bayside neighborhoods, shopping at Jack
London Square along the revitalized waterfront, and generally
warmer-than-San Francisco weather offer as much to the
visitor as to the commuting resident.*

*North of the Golden Gate Bridge is Marin, with its redwood
forests, well-preserved coastline, and golden-brown hills,
interspersed with clusters of suburban towns. Artsy, upscale
Sausalito, just across the bridge, is a favorite getaway for both
locals and tourists. Whimsical shops and art galleries line the
main street, and restaurants cantilevered over the water offer
panoramic views of San Francisco Bay and the skyline.
Curving mountain roads lead west to the tallest living things
on earth—redwood trees—in Muir Woods. Nearby is Muir
Beach, a secluded cove along the Pacific, and Stinson Beach,
one of the most popular—and crowded—strips of shore in
northern California. Point Reyes National Seashore is an
expansive coastal preserve encompassing rolling hills, long,
nearly deserted sandy beaches, a lighthouse built in 1870, a re-
created Miwok Indian village, an interpretive walk along the
San Andreas Fault, and a free-roaming herd of tule elk. Many
consider Point Reyes to be northern California at its best.*

Places to Go, Sights to See

Filoli (Canada Rd., Woodside, tel. 415/364–2880). This 654-acre estate is one of California's best-loved gardens and is open by tour only. Advance reservations are required.

Muir Woods National Monument (off Hwy. 1, 17 miles northwest of San Francisco, tel. 415/388–2595). This awe-inspiring grove of coastal redwoods, the tallest living things on earth, has some specimens that are 250 feet high, with diameters of more than 12 feet.

Oakland Museum (10th and Oak Sts., Oakland, tel. 510/834–2413). The museum is devoted to California's natural history, man-made heritage, and art.

Point Reyes National Seashore (off Hwy. 1, Point Reyes, tel. 415/663–1092). Encompassing 74,000 acres of rolling hills, forests, pastureland, estuaries, and beaches, the preserve has a visitor center, re-created Miwok Indian village, the Morgan Horse Ranch (where horses are bred and trained for the National Park Service), and Earthquake Trail, which traces the San Andreas Fault.

Rod McClellan's Acres of Orchids (1450 El Camino Real, South San Francisco, tel. 415/871–5655). Orchid cultivation is explored in daily tours through this 35-acre complex of greenhouses.

Winchester Mystery House (525 S. Winchester Blvd., San Jose, tel. 408/247–2101). The eccentric heiress to the Winchester Arms fortune designed this mansion to baffle evil spirits with 160 rooms, 2,000 doors, 10,000 windows, blind closets, secret passageways, and 40 staircases.

Beaches

You can stop at virtually any spot along Highway 1 within an hour's drive north or south of San Francisco for some spectacular coastline scenery. The beaches tend to be fairly narrow strips of sand, backed either by craggy bluffs or rolling hills. The water is often much too cold for swimming; sunbathing is catch-as-catch-can and usually possible only very early in the afternoon.

Point Reyes, Muir Beach, and **Stinson Beach,** to the north, are well-kempt and popular; to the south, the beaches along **Half Moon Bay** skirt quaint seaside villages.

Restaurants

In Marin County, the small town of Inverness is a good place to stop for lunch on the way out to the seashore, or dinner on the way back. At **Manka's** (tel. 415/669–1034), California cuisine is served up in a dining room warmed by a huge fireplace. The **Gray Whale Inn** (415/669–1244) is a great spot for a tasty but casual meal. Restaurants and cafés line Sausalito's main street, and seafood, plain or fancy, is the specialty in most. **The Spinnaker** (tel. 415/332–1500) offers fresh seafood and homemade pasta dishes in a spectacular setting near the yacht club. Off Sausalito's well-worn tourist path is the low-key, generous **Sushi Ran** (tel.

415/332–3620). Celebrity chef Bradley Ogden's **Lark Creek Inn** (tel. 415/924–7766) is worth a trip to Larkspur, up Hwy. 101 a bit from Mill Valley. The selection of brews and the mellow atmosphere are the main draws at Stinson Beach's **Sand Dollar** (tel. 415/868–0434). Devotees of California cuisine pay homage at Berkeley's landmark **Cafe at Chez Panisse** (tel. 510/548–5049) for fresh and innovative light lunches and dinners from a daily changing menu of grilled dishes, pastas, pizza, and salads. Also in Berkeley, crowds flock to famous **Spenger's Fish Grotto** (tel. 510/845–7771), but we suggest the delicate east-meets-west fare at **Ginger Island** (tel. 510/644–0444) down the street. Near the magnificent Filoli estate in Woodside, the **Village Pub** (tel. 415/851–1294) features California fare, including a variety of main-course salads, pastas, and seafood. **Il Fornaio Cucina Italiana** (tel. 415/853–3888) in Palo Alto is located in the classy Garden Court Hotel. Gourmet Italian pizza is the least of the fine fare here, though its California variations are the chief lure at **Vicolo Pizzeria** (tel. 415/324–4877). Even if San Jose were not the fast-food franchise capital of California (no mean feat), the **Lion and Compass** (tel. 408/745–1260) would be popular for its good and extensive menu, ranging from pork chops and prime rib to such lighter fare as ahi tuna and generous salads. More sophisticated palates will appreciate **Emile's** (tel. 408/289–1960), one of San Jose's finest restaurants. You can smell the salt-sea air from your table at **Barbara's Fish Trap** (tel. 415/728–7049) in Princeton-by-the-Sea. The food's straightforward but tasty. The subtle sauces at **Pasta Moon** (tel. 415/726–5125) make it a good choice in Half Moon Bay.

Tourist Information

Half Moon Bay Coastside Chamber of Commerce (225 S. Cabrillo Hwy., Box 188, Half Moon Bay, CA 94019, tel. 415/726–5202); **San Jose Convention and Visitors Bureau** (333 W. San Carlos St., Suite 1000, San Jose, CA 95110, tel. 408/295–9600); **Sausalito Chamber of Commerce** (333 Caledonia St., Sausalito, CA 94965, tel. 415/332–0505); **West Marin Chamber of Commerce** (Box 1045, Point Reyes Station, CA 94956, tel. 415/663–9232).

Reservation Services

Bed & Breakfast International (Box 282910, San Francisco, CA 94128–2910, tel. 415/696–1690, fax 415/696–1699); **Bed & Breakfast San Francisco** (Box 420009, San Francisco, CA 94142, tel. 415/931–3083 or 800/452–8249); **Inns of Point Reyes** (Box 145, Inverness, CA 94937, tel. 415/663–1420).

Casa del Mar

This pale stucco Mediterranean-style villa perches at the top of a landscaped knoll a scant block from the Pacific Ocean. The original structure on this site was built in 1906 as the Buckeye Lodge, named after a tree common to the area. A two-story cabin, it was favored by hikers who would frequently ferry from San Francisco across the Golden Gate (before the bridge was built) and then traipse across the wild slopes of Mt. Tamalpais. The trailhead near the inn is as popular now as it was then, but today most visitors arrive by car.

The place was purchased in 1987 by Rick Klein, a local lawyer and sometime builder. Klein bought it as a private home but found that making it an inn was the only way he could support his passion for restoring the gardens, which cascade down to sea level, a riot of flowering bulbs, citrus trees, and other vegetation common to the Mediterranean. Klein has also added a vegetable garden and, in the shaded corner that backs up to the mountain slope, a dell of trillium, ferns, and other shade-loving plants. Indeed, Klein has become so enamored of his greenery that he offers occasional tours, charging a nominal fee that he hopes will help bankroll maintenance and expansion of the grounds.

Inside, the crisp decor is also a refreshing antidote to those hot and sticky summer days when the fog fails to roll in at sunset. The entry level has an open-space floor plan, with a breakfast room at one end flanked on two sides by large windows and warmed by sunlight or heat from a dark-blue tile, wood-burning stove. Here guests are served the morning meal. The Mexican paver floor extends to the parlor area, which has its own built-in fireplace. Everywhere are selections from Klein's extensive collection of local artwork, bright paintings (many seascapes), and amusing animal sculptures. The rather small upstairs accommodations are made to seem larger by the use of pale painted walls, lots of windows, and simple furnishings. The rooms derive their names from the charming motifs (shell, passionflower, etc.) painted on the tilework within each shower stall. Two rooms face the ocean; two, the forest behind.

Address: *37 Belvedere Ave., Box 238, Stinson Beach, CA 94970, tel. 415/ 868-2124.*
Accommodations: *4 double rooms with baths.*
Amenities: *Fireplace in public rooms.*
Rates: *$100–$225 ($6 less for singles); full breakfast. AE, MC, V.*
Restrictions: *No smoking, no pets; 2-night minimum on weekends, 3-night minimum on holiday weekends.*

Casa Madrona Hotel

The Casa Madrona was a decaying 1885 Victorian mansion that was on the verge of tumbling from its steep hillside perch above the Sausalito Marina until John Mays renovated and reopened it as a hotel during the late 1970s. The New Casa, a multilevel addition, is stepped down to the street below like an Italian hill town.

The New Casa's guest rooms all share a magnificent view of the marina across the street, Belvedere and Angel islands, and the forested hills of Tiburon beyond. Many rooms have private balconies. Each room of the New Casa has a distinct personality. The Renoir Room, hung with prints of the artist's work, has a window seat, large deck, fireplace, and, in the bathroom, a claw-foot tub surrounded by an impressionistic mural of a flower garden. In the Artist's Loft, an easel and watercolor paints, set beneath a skylight, await your talents.

Guest rooms in the original Victorian building are decorated in period style, with high ceilings, Victorian-era American furniture, and four-poster or brass beds. Rooms facing east or south have views. There are also three private cottages done up as rustic mountain cabins.

Casa Madrona is more small hotel than homey bed-and-breakfast, and except for a large outdoor deck of the New Casa, the Victorian's parlor and balcony are the inn's only common areas. In the evening, wine, cheese, and fruit are served in the parlor, and guests can relax in the antique settees or in the balcony's wicker chairs while taking the night air.

A buffet-style breakfast is served in the award-winning Casa Madrona Restaurant, which is attached to the original building. In warm weather the glass walls and ceiling of this terrace dining room slide open to enhance the already panoramic view, which on a clear day can include the San Francisco skyline. The contemporary American cuisine makes much of the area's ethnic influences, and specialties include pan-fried sugar snap peas with shiitake mushrooms and chili-ginger glaze, ahi tuna grilled rare and served with coconut rice, and whole roasted Dungeness crab with Thai spices. The hotel's bakery, where the restaurant's excellent desserts are prepared daily, is on an upper level.

Address: *801 Bridgeway, Sausalito, CA 94965, tel. 415/332–0502 or 800/288–0502, fax 415/332–2537.*
Accommodations: *29 double rooms with baths, 3 suites.*
Amenities: *Phone in rooms, TV in 23 rooms, fireplace in 18 rooms, minibar in 17 rooms; room service during restaurant hours, conference facilities; outdoor hot tub, valet parking.*
Rates: *$105–$185, suites $225; Continental breakfast. AE, MC, V.*
Restrictions: *No smoking in restaurant; 2-day minimum on weekends.*

The Mill Rose Inn

Set amid a lush flower garden, the Mill Rose Inn is one of the most indulgent, romantic hostelries in northern California. The word *pampered* takes on new meaning here— guests are provided virtually everything they need for a carefree stay. Most of the guest rooms have Eastlake and Arts and Crafts antique furnishings, brass beds, down comforters, billowing draperies, and fireplaces framed with hand-painted tiles. All come equipped with a stereo, TV with VCR, refrigerator stocked with beverages, fruit and nut basket, candies, coffeemaker with herb teas and cocoa, sherry and brandy, hair dryer, and more. Sinfully rich desserts are always available in the parlor, and you'll wake to a generous champagne breakfast.

The Mill Rose Inn is 30 miles south of San Francisco, in the oceanside hamlet of Half Moon Bay. Innkeepers Eve and Terry Baldwin both hold degrees in horticulture and take full advantage of the gentle climate. The front garden is an explosion of color, with more than 200 varieties of roses, lilies, sweet peas, daisies, Iceland poppies, irises, delphiniums, lobelias, and foxgloves, all framed by the inn's crisp white exterior. Tourists and local residents stop by just to photograph the spectacular floral displays. Located in the town's historic district, the inn is five blocks from Half Moon Bay and a short drive to Pacific coast beaches.

In contrast to the building's spare exterior, virtually no corner of the guest rooms has gone undecorated. Each is done in rich, deep tones with floral-patterned wall coverings, burgundy carpeting, custom-made brass chandeliers and wall sconces, and watercolor paintings. All have private entrances opening to a balcony that faces the back courtyard, with its hanging potted flowers, brick patio, and whirlpool spa secluded in an old-fashioned gazebo.

In the breakfast room, bouquets on each table and a fire in the hearth, with its hand-painted tiles reading "Welcome All to Hearth and Hall," set the stage for evening desserts and sumptuous breakfasts. Courses might include an orange-banana frappé, fresh fruit, raspberry crème fraiche soufflé, crisp bacon, enormous croissants, local champagne, and Mexican hot chocolate made with cinnamon and almonds.

Address: *615 Mill St., Half Moon Bay, CA 94019, tel. 415/726–8750, fax 415/726–3031.*
Accommodations: *4 rooms with baths, 2 suites.*
Amenities: *Phone, TV with VCR, stereo, clothes steamers in rooms, fireplace in 5 rooms, conference facility.*
Rates: *$165–$265; full breakfast, afternoon wine and snacks. AE, D, MC, V.*
Restrictions: *No smoking, no pets; 2-day minimum on weekends.*

The Pelican Inn

Upon first seeing the Pelican Inn, you may think you've taken a wrong turn and somehow stumbled into the English countryside. Just off Highway 1 in Marin County, the Pelican Inn is fronted by a formal English garden and set in an expanse of lush lawn. This whitewashed Tudor with black timbers is a replica of a 16th-century British inn—the realized dream of Englishman Charles Felix, who built it in 1977.

Now run by Englishman Barry Stock, the hostelry is a favorite stopping place for San Franciscans out to celebrate a special occasion and for tourists visiting the nearby Muir Woods. Muir Beach is just a short walk from the inn.

Guests are especially drawn to the Pelican's pub. Amiable bartenders, a dart board, an assortment of beers, stouts, and ales, and an inviting selection of ports, sherries, and British dishes create a convivial setting. The aptly named Snug is a parlor set aside for registered guests only. English-country antiques, old books, prints and curiosities that Stock has brought back from his homeland, as well as a comfortable sitting area by the woodburning fireplace, make this an ideal sanctuary.

The inn's restaurant is right out of Merry Olde England, with heavy wooden tables, and a dark, time-worn atmosphere, enhanced by foxhunt prints and an immense walk-in hearth with large cast-iron fittings. During dinner and breakfast, the room is lit only by the fireplace, the tall red tapers on each table, and cut-tin lanterns on the walls. Tasty, moderately priced meals include beef Wellington, prime rib, and chicken dishes. Breakfast, served here or in your room, is hearty fare, with eggs cooked to order, breakfast meats, and toasted breads. Lunch specialties include bangers and mash and fish-and-chips as well as pastas and salads. In the backyard beer garden, sunlight filters through a greenery-entwined trellis, and a brick fireplace keeps things cozy.

Planked doors with latches open to the guest rooms, some of which are decorated with antiques from different periods. Each room has leaded, multipane windows, Oriental scatter rugs, English prints, heavy velvet draperies, hanging tapestries, and half-tester beds. Even the bathrooms are special, with Victorian-style hardware and hand-painted tiles in the shower.

Address: *Star Rte. (Hwy. 1), Muir Beach, CA 94965, tel. 415/383–6000.*
Accommodations: *7 rooms with baths.*
Amenities: *Restaurant.*
Rates: *$140–$155; full breakfast. MC, V.*
Restrictions: *No pets; closed Christmas Eve and Christmas Day.*

Union Gardens

Situated in the heart of historic Benicia, this unusual inn has a charm that has less to do with particulars than with its overall personality. It fits no one genre, and that is part of its low-key appeal. Like the old town itself, Union Gardens is well suited to its waterfront location on the Carquinez Strait between San Pablo Bay and the inland delta. The pell-mell pace of development elsewhere in the Bay Area has largely bypassed Benicia, which enjoyed its heyday in the 1850s, when it served briefly as the state capital.

Formerly known as Captain Dillingham's Inn, the property was taken over by the nearby Union Hotel in mid-1994. Although still attractive, it has lost a bit of its warmth in the process. The main house was built in the 1850s as a residence for Captain William Wallace Dillingham, who sailed from Massachusetts around Cape Horn and out to Hawaii before settling here. He married a local widow, and they made a home in this clapboard Cape Cod–inspired residence behind a storybook white-picket fence. Given the inn's salty heritage, it would be easy to imagine that its eclectic assortment of furnishings was collected by the old captain as he sailed the seven seas. How else to explain the presence of, say, a headboard from Brittany or a bridal chest from Yugoslavia or navigational charts from the 1800s? The truth is a bit more prosaic. The previous innkeeper, who also owned an antiques store, more or less

cannibalized his shop for the treasures that give Union Gardens much of its character.

As a result, no room is like any other. The one common trait of the accommodations is that they are all spacious. In the original structure, the Captain's Quarters boasts a working fireplace fashioned from black onyx and can be coupled with an adjacent room to form a suite in space once occupied by a parlor. The four rooms in the newer wing (built in 1984) all have cathedral ceilings. The second-floor accommodations share a deck sheltered by trees; the lower two have brick patios fronting a garden carefully planted for successive blooms, from the bright marigolds of summer to the more subdued chrysanthemums of autumn. A 12-foot-long antique French pine table makes the morning meal memorable.

Address: *145 E. D St., Benicia, CA 94510, tel. 707/746-7164.*
Accommodations: *8 double rooms with baths, 1 suite.*
Amenities: *Phone, TV, spa tub, minifridge in some rooms, fireplace in 1 room; garden, off-street parking, walking distance to shops, restaurants, and marina.*
Rates: *$70–$125; full breakfast. AE, DC, MC, V.*
Restrictions: *No pets.*

Bancroft Hotel

The Bancroft Hotel is so close to Boalt Hall at the University of California at Berkeley that students could toss their law books onto the front porch. Built in 1928 for the College Women's Club, the hotel was leased in the 1980s as a sorority house. In the 1990s, the local Ross family lavished $2 million to restore all three stories and to add a rooftop garden.

The hotel's interiors are completely in synch with the Arts and Crafts exterior designed by architect Walter T. Steilberg, an associate of Berkeley's own Julia Morgan. A 4,000-square-foot great room with high, coffered ceilings consumes most of the ground floor. This meeting space doubles as an extra-large social room for guests.

Accommodations are relatively small, in shades of rose, apricot, and moss green, but leaded windows, reproduction headboards made from a Steilberg design, framed Chinese paintings, and other touches lend the rooms an inviting period feel. Unusually handsome armoires can be converted into desks.

Address: *2680 Bancroft Way, Berkeley, CA 94704, tel. 510/549–1000 or 800/549–1002, fax 510/549–1070.*
Accommodations: *22 double rooms with baths.*
Amenities: *Cable TV with HBO in rooms, balconies off some rooms; conference facilities, next-door parking ($6 per day), café adjacent.*
Rates: *$89–$109; Continental breakfast. AE, MC, V.*
Restrictions: *No smoking, no pets; 2-night minimum on weekends.*

Blackthorne Inn

The Blackthorne Inn is an adult-size fantasy tree house. A four-story spiral staircase winds its way to the guest rooms, and secluded balconies nest in the treetops. The adventurous can slide down a fireman's pole from one of the inn's decks to the driveway.

Handcrafted in 1978 by owner Bill Wigert, the imaginative structure is highlighted by a 3,500-square-foot deck with stairways to higher decks. A single, 180-foot Douglas fir was milled to create the planks in the living room's vaulted ceiling. Boulders in the room's fireplace were gathered from eight counties. The solarium was made with timbers from San Francisco wharves; the outer walls are salvaged doors from a railway station. The inn is crowned with a glass-sheathed octagonal tower called the Eagles Nest. Guests there pay a price for the drama: They must traverse an outdoor walkway to reach the private bath. They are, however, near the inn's hot tub. Guest rooms are uncluttered, with redwood trim, and floral-print comforters.

Address: *266 Vallejo Ave., Box 712, Inverness Park, CA 94937, tel. 415/663–8621.*
Accommodations: *3 rooms with baths, 2 rooms share bath.*
Amenities: *Outdoor hot tub.*
Rates: *$105–$185; full breakfast, afternoon dessert and tea. MC, V.*
Restrictions: *Smoking on decks only, no pets; 2-day minimum on weekends, closed Christmas Day.*

Cowper Inn

T he Cowper Inn encompasses two homes, their front porches connected by a wide, painted Plexiglas deck. One is an 1893 Queen Anne Victorian, and the other is an 1897 Craftsman house. Many guests choose the Cowper for its location, a five-minute walk from downtown Palo Alto and ¼ mile from the train to San Francisco.

Innkeeper Peggy Woodworth has created a home away from home for frequent visitors to nearby Stanford University and Silicon Valley; they appreciate the quiet neighborhood and unfussy atmosphere inside.

The largest common room is in the Craftsman house: an open living room that's arranged so guests can either join each other in conversation or set-tle into a secluded corner. A long dining table is set near a row of windows overlooking the elaborately restored Queen Anne Victorian across the street. The guest rooms in both houses are furnished simply, decorated in warm, light tones, and have wicker chairs, unobtrusive floral wallpaper, and Amish quilts on the beds.

Address: *705 Cowper St., Palo Alto, CA 94301, tel. 415/327–4475, fax 415/329–1703.*
Accommodations: *12 rooms with baths, 2 rooms share bath.*
Amenities: *Phone and cable TV in rooms, kitchenette in 3 rooms, conference facility.*
Rates: *$60–$110; Continental breakfast. AE, MC, V.*
Restrictions: *No smoking indoors; no pets.*

East Brother Light Station

G etting away from it all takes on new meaning at this one-of-a-kind inn, located on a tiny island in San Pablo Bay. Accessible only by the inn's private launch, East Brother Island has unsurpassed views of most of the Bay Area, including the city of San Francisco to the south.

Guests have a choice of four rooms, each with a unique view, in a two-story buff-colored clapboard building, the island's largest structure. The decor of each room differs, with lace curtains, antiques, and fresh flowers a constant. The San Francisco Room is recommended for its view of the city.

A young married couple, Lore Hogan and John Barnett, share inn-keeping duties. Barnett, who has an ocean-navigator's license, ferries visitors from the San Pablo Yacht Harbor across the swirling bay waters to the island's dock; Hogan is in charge of the four-course dinners, which include complimentary wine.

Those in search of urban—or any other—distractions should head elsewhere. There is little to do on the island but read, relax, watch the seabirds, and climb up the lighthouse.

Address: *117 Park Pl., Point Richmond, CA 94801, tel. 510/233–2385.*
Accommodations: *4 rooms, 2 with baths.*
Rates: *$235 single, $295 couples; full breakfast, dinner. No credit cards; personal checks accepted.*
Restrictions: *No smoking indoors, no pets; closed Mon.–Wed.*

Gramma's Inn

A ten-minute walk from Berkeley's university campus, this inn is a complex of five buildings. The two oldest, the 1903 Shingle-style Fay House, and the Main House, an 1899 half-timber, sit at a corner, and a garden area connects them with the other buildings.

The inn is a blend of well-worn comfort and more upscale luxury. The common rooms, in the Main House, have a lived-in feel. The parlor's pink-and-white checkered wing chairs and floral-print overstuffed sofas face the fireplace. The breakfast room resembles a greenhouse and opens to the patio, with umbrella-covered tables and the garden beyond. A full breakfast of omelets and fresh-baked breads is served here.

The newer buildings are somewhat quieter. Rooms in the Garden House are sunlit, with modern bleached-wood furnishings, tile fireplaces, brass beds, and private entrances. The Carriage House rooms all have fireplaces but lack the character of the older buildings. The Cottage House offers larger rooms, all with fireplaces, desks, and sitting areas.

Address: *2740 Telegraph Ave., Berkeley, CA 94705, tel. 510/549–2145, fax 510/549–1085.*
Accommodations: *40 rooms with baths.*
Amenities: *Phones and TV in rooms, fireplace in 20 rooms; off-street parking.*
Rates: *$85–$150; full breakfast. AE, MC, V.*
Restrictions: *No smoking, no pets.*

The Hensley House

T his 1884 Queen Anne Victorian, with its steeply pitched roof and witch's hat tower, is a short walk to the light rail for the five-minute ride to downtown San Jose.

A stately grandfather clock graces the entryway, and in the parlor, velvet brocade high-back chairs, a rosewood settee, and red-velvet side chairs surround an ivory-hued grand piano. The room leads out to a sunny backyard deck. The full breakfast includes such entrées as eggs Florentine and waffles and is sometimes served in the library, dominated by an 11-foot-high walnut vestment cabinet from a Jesuit monastery and a 500-year-old stained-glass window.

Deep, cool color schemes and Victorian antique and reproduction wardrobes

highlight the guest rooms. The largest room is in the tower and features a corner gas fireplace, whirlpool tub, half-canopy bed, and a bay-window sitting area.

Address: *456 N. 3rd St., San Jose, CA 95112, tel. 408/298–3537, fax 408/298–4676.*
Accommodations: *5 rooms with baths.*
Amenities: *Air-conditioning; phone, TV with VCR, clock radio, hair dryer, robes in rooms; fireplace, spa, refrigerator in 1 room; conference facility, off-street parking.*
Rates: *$75–$140; full breakfast. AE, D, DC, MC, V.*
Restrictions: *No smoking indoors.*

Mill Valley Inn

The furnishings are so intriguing at the Mill Valley Inn that some guests may sit up all night trying to figure out if that lamp really is made of a manzanita branch and whether the bathroom mirror was originally a wooden window frame. The answer in both cases is yes. The owners and decorators of this inn, which opened in fall 1994 in downtown Mill Valley, tried to be as ecologically sensitive and environmentally correct as possible. The result is a very sophisticated look with elegant earth tones that coordinate well with the redwood trees and mountain views that give the town its Old World–village ambience. Butter-cream walls, terracotta bathroom floors, and accents of gold and green provide a mellow background for salvaged or commissioned pieces such as the old-looking new armoires. Most of the works, including the tawny, textured linen window coverings, are by local artisans. Wrought-iron balconies grace the stucco exterior; an atrium rises from the street-level garage to the third floor. Open passageways between rooms and easy access to the tree-flanked sun terrace allow plenty of fresh air and some glimpses of Mt. Tamalpais.

Address: *165 Throckmorton Ave., Mill Valley, CA 94941, tel. 415/389–6608.*
Accommodations: *16 rooms with baths, 2 cottages.*
Amenities: *Fireplace or wood stove in some rooms, concierge, in-room dining service from nearby restaurant, off-street parking.*
Rates: *$110–$135, cottages $150; Continental breakfast. AE, MC, V.*
Restrictions: *No smoking, no pets.*

Mountain Home Inn

Early in the century, hikers and railroad passengers had their choice of lodgings on Mt. Tamalpais. The only recommended inn on the mountain now is this architectural wonder, built in 1912 by a Swiss couple who must have pined for their Alpine homeland. A group of investors bought the property after a fire in the mid-1980s and transformed it into a slightly rustic inn.

Four slim redwood trunks shoot up through the airy, high-ceilinged lobby, which shares the top floor with a lounge and a deck cantilevered 1,000 feet above San Francisco Bay, visible in the distance. The floors below are oddly angled to encompass a number of small accommodations and two larger, deluxe rooms. Despite handmade hickory furniture and lovely views, the rooms don't look as fresh as they did in the early days. Still, they are comfortable, decorated in combinations of pastels. Most romantic is number 6, a spacious, secluded room with a fireplace.

Address: *810 Panoramic Hwy., Mill Valley, CA 94941, tel. 415/381–9000, fax 415/381–3615.*
Accommodations: *10 double rooms with baths.*
Amenities: *Phone in rooms, fireplace and Jacuzzi in 4 rooms, private terraces in 2 rooms, TV available on request, restaurant, lounge; off-street parking.*
Rates: *$131–$215; full breakfast. MC, V.*
Restrictions: *No pets.*

Old Thyme Inn

This understated Queen Anne house's rosy hues and white-picket fence set a tone of comfort and good cheer. Innkeepers Marcia and George Dempsey, who took over the inn in 1992, carry on many of the traditions of the former owners, most notably the extraordinary herb garden. More than 80 varieties of herbs sweeten the air and add excitement to many of the specialties guests enjoy at breakfast. Guests are invited to take a sprig or two home with them.

The Garden Suite features a four-poster bed and whirlpool tub beneath skylights. The Thyme Room has a whirlpool, fireplace, and a half-canopy bed. Even with its up-to-the-minute luxuries, the inn retains a genuine air of old-fashioned friendliness and hospitality.

A full breakfast of home-baked breads, fruit, yogurt, granola, a hot item such as English crumpets, and a dessert of, say, hot cherry flan is served family-style.

Address: *779 Main St., Half Moon Bay, CA 94019, tel. 415/726–1616.*
Accommodations: *6 rooms with baths, 1 suite.*
Amenities: *Fireplace, whirlpool tub in 2 rooms; TV with VCR, fireplace, whirlpool tub, refrigerator in suite; health club next door.*
Rates: *$75–$135, suites $220; full breakfast, refreshments. D, MC, V.*
Restrictions: *Smoking in garden only.*

Pillar Point Inn

One of few California inns with an ocean view, Pillar Point sits on a tiny harbor just north of Half Moon Bay, separated from the sea by a breakwater visible through the bobbing masts of fishing boats. Built in 1986 to resemble the homes on Cape Cod, it is now run by a management group.

The gray-blue, two-story inn has immaculate rooms decorated in shades of blue with white accents. Linens are Laura Ashley style, but the seminautical decor stops just short of being precious. Café curtains flanking the window seats leave plenty of room for sunlight to flood the rooms. Aside from the white metal-and-brass bedframes, all the furniture is oak reproduction. Blue and white tiles surround the fireplaces. Close to restaurants, shops, and

the marina, the inn gets a good deal of foot traffic on weekends.

A cozy parlor, separated from the breakfast room by a glass-enclosed fireplace, is stocked with cookies, port, and sherry. Upstairs, a small deck is available for sunning and barbecuing.

Address: *380 Capistrano Rd., Princeton-by-the-Sea, CA 94018, tel. 415/728–7377.*
Accommodations: *11 double rooms with baths.*
Amenities: *Phone, TV with VCR, minifridge, fireplace in rooms; off-street parking.*
Rates: *$145–$175; full breakfast. AE, MC, V.*
Restrictions: *No smoking, no pets.*

Roundstone Farm

Owner Inger Fisher describes Roundstone Farm as "my hillside haven." Nestled among the hills near Point Reyes National Seashore, this farmhouse was constructed in 1987. From the rambling shed-style building, you'll see pastoral scenes of Inger's horses grazing by the pond, meadows stretching to wooded hillsides, and a glimmer of Tomales Bay.

A 16-foot-high skylighted and beamed cathedral ceiling and tall windows keep the living room bright. The wood stove, country-casual furniture, and stone floors confirm that you've gotten away from it all. The decor throughout the inn is low-key, in keeping with—perhaps creating—the relaxed atmosphere. Guest rooms are uncluttered, with floral-print curtains and bedspreads, a Windsor side chair or two,

and white wood headboards fashioned after garden gates, all harmonizing with antique armoires from England and Denmark. Breakfast is served family-style in the dining room, whose sliding glass doors lead to a patio and garden.

Address: *9940 Sir Francis Drake Blvd., Box 217, Olema, CA 94950, tel. 415/663–1020.*
Accommodations: *5 rooms with baths.*
Amenities: *Fireplace in 4 rooms.*
Rates: *$115–$135; full breakfast. AE, MC, V.*
Restrictions: *Smoking on deck only, no pets; 2-night minimum on weekends, closed first 2 weeks of Dec.*

Ten Inverness Way

Veteran innkeeper and columnist Mary Davies has created a coastal country-style bed-and-breakfast in Inverness, on Tomales Bay. The weathered 1904 Shingle-style house is convenient to the Point Reyes National Seashore and close to the fine Czechoslovakian and French restaurants in town.

The inn's living room is warmed by a large stone fireplace, and the walls are lined with bookshelves. Windows look out onto the trees and gardens.

The atmosphere is country-cottage casual, and the decor takes its cues from the stone fireplace, redwood interior, and Oriental rugs. Hand-sewn quilts enhance the guest rooms. There's nothing fancy or fussy here,

but then again, people come to get away from fancy and fussy.

Breakfasts feature banana-buttermilk buckwheat pancakes and chicken-apple sausage.

Address: *10 Inverness Way, Box 63, Inverness, CA 94937, tel. 415/669–1648.*
Accommodations: *4 rooms with baths, 1 suite.*
Amenities: *Hot tub.*
Rates: *$145–$150; full breakfast, complimentary beverages. MC, V.*
Restrictions: *Smoking in garden only; 2-day minimum on weekends, 3-day minimum on holidays.*

Wine Country

Wine Country
Napa, Sonoma, Southern Mendocino Counties

Less than an hour north of the cosmopolitan streets of San Francisco lies the gateway to California's wine country, the premium grape-growing region in the United States. Well-traveled highways gradually give way to country roads that meander through lush valleys, along hillsides dotted with orchards, and past thousands of acres of vineyards whose color and character change dramatically with the season.

The counties of Napa and Sonoma, which garner the lion's share of wine-tasting awards, are separated by the majestic Mayacamas Mountains. To the north of them, Mendocino County is best known for its rugged coastline and for the quaint New England–style town of Mendocino. More recently, however, the area has been gaining a reputation for the grapes that are grown inland, particularly in the scenic Anderson Valley, which may one day become as famous as its Napa and Sonoma cousins.

The 21-mile-long Napa Valley, which stretches from the top of San Francisco Bay to the unassuming town of Calistoga, boasts more than 200 wineries. But it is dwarfed by its neighbor to the west. Sonoma's 1,600 square miles consist of rolling hills, scenic valleys, and five distinct wine-growing regions, including one that straddles the dynamic Russian River as it wends its way west to meet the waters of the Pacific Ocean.

It has been said that Napa is reminiscent of parts of the French countryside while Sonoma resembles Italy, especially Tuscany. The analogies with Europe are particularly apt, given the local emphasis on fine wines and extraordinary cuisine. Moreover, many of the region's earliest wineries were established during the 1800s by immigrants from France and

*Italy as well as from Germany and Hungary. Gradually
orchards of apples, pears, walnuts, and plums were replanted
with grapes, though Sonoma is still famous for its apples and
other produce. Sonoma's numerous ranches and farms
produce everything from beef and poultry to strawberries and
melons, and it's all available at the hundreds of produce
stands scattered along the county's 1,450 miles of roadsides.*

*The wine country's abundant open space is endangered,
however, by encroaching development. The county seat itself
has mushroomed, making it difficult to travel easily between
the Sonoma Valley and the Russian River area.*

*Despite recent urban growth, particularly in the vicinity of
Santa Rosa, the wine country is still largely rural—fertile
ground for dozens of small inns that attract a constant stream
of visitors year-round. In Napa, summer weekends find cars
snaking along Highway 29, the main north-south
thoroughfare. An increasingly popular option is the Silverado
Trail, a two-lane road that parallels the highway on the
eastern side of the valley.*

*Sonoma bears myriad reminders of the county's mission
heritage; in Napa, the hot springs and mud baths bear
testimony to the valley's volcanic history. Napa has a
reputation for elitism, whereas Sonoma remains close to its
agricultural heritage. Combined, the two areas constitute one
of California's prime attractions.*

*The Anderson Valley is the strongest lure of the lesser-known
Mendocino wine country, encompassing the area around
Ukiah along the four- to six-lane Highway 101. Located some
100 miles north of San Francisco, the 25-mile-long valley lies
on either side of Highway 128, which zigzags through rocky
outcroppings as it leads west into more open countryside. Still
known for its apples, the region has increasingly been settled
by urban escapees of all stripes, as well as by wine makers
appreciative of the soil and climate of this hidden valley. The
towns are tiny, ranging from Boonville (population 715) to the*

*handful of buildings which compose Navarro, but innkeepers
are gradually discovering the charms of the Anderson Valley
and playing host to a growing number of visitors.*

Places to Go, Sights to See

Horseback Riding. *The Sonoma Cattle Company* (tel. 707/996–8566) offers
guided one- and two-hour excursions at Jack London State Historic Park and
Sugarloaf Ridge State Park. Picnic and full-moon rides are also available.

Hot-Air Ballooning. *Sonoma Thunder* (4914 Snark Ave., Santa Rosa, tel.
707/538–7359 or 800/759–5638, fax 707/538–3782) operates hot-air balloons above
the vineyards and west along the Russian River, allowing visitors to view the
coastline. Other choices are *Once In a Lifetime* (tel. 707/578–0580) and *Air Flamboyant* (tel. 800/456–4711). In Napa, *Bonaventure Balloon Company* (tel.
707/944–2822), *Balloon Aviation* (tel. 800/367–6272), *Napa's Great Balloon
Escape* (tel. 707/253–0860), and *Napa Valley Balloons* (tel. 707/944–0228) take off
at dawn from different locations daily, depending on wind conditions.

Jack London State Historic Park (2400 London Ranch Rd., Glen Ellen, tel.
707/938–5216). Memorabilia from the life of the prolific author-sailor-farmer are displayed in a museum home. The remains of Wolf House, London's dream home that
burned down mysteriously in 1913, can be seen through a grove of redwood trees.

Luther Burbank Memorial Gardens (Santa Rosa and Sonoma Aves., Santa
Rosa, tel. 707/576–5115). The renowned horticulturist Luther Burbank chose this
area for his extensive plant-breeding experiments. He is remembered in this
well-maintained National Historic Landmark home, carriage house, and greenhouse, all of which can be seen on docent-guided tours.

Mud Baths. Nineteenth-century settlers discovered the health benefits of the
natural mineral waters and volcanic ash of Mt. St. Helena. Establishments on
Lincoln Avenue and elsewhere in Calistoga tout health regimens ranging from
immersion in mud baths to soaking in hot baths to full massage treatments.

The Petrified Forest (4 mi west of Hwy. 128, between Calistoga and Santa
Rosa, tel. 707/942–6667). Ancient trees, some more than 100 feet tall, were cov-
ered by volcanic ash 6 million years ago when nearby Mt. St. Helena erupted.
Also visible are petrified seashells, clams, and other remains of marine life.

Russian River (between Hwy. 101 and the Pacific Ocean along the Russian
River Rd., tel. 800/253–8800). Secluded beaches, angling spots, and boats,
canoes, and inner tubes for rent can all be found along the shady banks of this
popular resort area.

Sonoma State Historic Park (Sonoma, tel. 707/938–1578). Facing the plaza in
the center of the old city is *Mission San Francisco Solano* (1st St. and Spain St.
E), the site where the original flag of California was first flown in 1846. Barracks,
an old hotel, and other historic structures, including *La Casa Grande* (General
Mariano Vallejo's former home), are part of this complex.

Sugarloaf Ridge State Park (Hwy. 12, just outside Kenwood, tel. 707/833–5712). Some 25 miles of trails lead through grassy meadows and groves of redwood and laurel trees within this 2,500-acre park, where bird-watching, picnicking, camping, and horseback riding are popular.

Wineries

Choosing which of the 400 or so wineries to visit will be difficult, and the range of opportunities makes it tempting to make multiple stops. The wineries along the more frequented arteries of the Napa Valley tend to charge nominal fees for tasting, but in Sonoma County, where there is less tourist traffic, fees are rare. In Sonoma, you are more likely to run into a wine grower willing to engage in convivial conversation than you are along the main drag of the Napa Valley, where the waiter serving yards of bar has time to do little more than keep track of the rows of glasses.

One of California's earliest premier wineries, **Buena Vista Winery** (18000 Old Winery Rd., Sonoma, tel. 707/938–1266), was built in 1857 by Hungarian Count Agoston Harazthy, who enclosed his limestone caves within large stone buildings that still house barrels of wine. The Napa Valley cousin of France's Moët et Chandon label, **Domaine Chandon** (California Dr., Yountville, tel. 707/944–2280) offers a close-up of how sparkling wines are produced and bottled. **Hakusan Sake Gardens** (1 Executive Way, Napa, tel. 707/258–6160) is a refreshing change from winery tours; you can taste both warm and cold sake in the Japanese garden. **Husch Vineyards** (4400 Hwy. 128, Philo, tel. 707/895–3216) is the classic Anderson Valley winery, a place so unpretentious it could be mistaken for a toolshed, but one should never underestimate its Pinot Noir and Chardonnay. No tour of the Napa Valley would be complete without a visit to **Robert Mondavi** (7801 St. Helena Hwy., Oakville, tel. 707/963–9611), the winery owned by one of the most famous and admired wine makers in the United States. **Roederer Estates** (4501 Hwy. 128, Philo, tel. 707/895–2288), a French sparkling-wine maker, is one of very few wineries where visitors feel comfortable smoking—no doubt the French influence. Set atop a hill at the northern end of the Napa Valley, **Sterling Vineyards** (1111 Dunaweal La., Calistoga, tel. 707/942–5151) operates an aerial tramway that whisks visitors up to the winery. In 1990 Vicki and Sam Sebastiani opened the Tuscan-style **Viansa Winery** (Hwy. 12, Schellville, tel. 707/945–4747) overlooking the Sonoma Valley.

Restaurants

The Diner (tel. 707/944–2626) in Yountville is a homey American-Mexican diner specializing in hearty, simply prepared dishes that range from waffles or huevos rancheros at breakfast to seafood tostadas at dinner. North of Yountville is **Mustards Grill** (tel. 707/944–2424), an unpretentious roadside restaurant serving such fresh, flavorful fare as roast rabbit, grilled fish, and a long list of noteworthy appetizers. The restaurant at **Auberge de Soleil** (tel. 707/963–1211) is Rutherford's best. Mediterranean influences predominate at Jeremiah Tower's **Stars Oakville Café** (tel. 707/944–8905). Healdsburg's **Tre Scalini** (tel. 707/433–1772) offers a contemporary take on northern Italian cuisine; the café menu rotates daily at the town's lively, inexpensive **Samba Java** (tel. 707/433–5282). Lunch or dinner are superb at **All Seasons Café** (tel. 707/942–9111) in Calistoga, known for its fresh-baked breads, organic greens, and extensive wine list. Also in spa town, chef Jan Birnbaum's very fine **Catahoula** (tel. 707/942–2275) in the Mount View Hotel serves Southern-inspired American cuisine. In St. Helena, **Tra Vigne** (tel. 707/963–4444) has high ceilings, gilded moldings, and hearty Italian fare. In the El Dorado Hotel in Sonoma, **Ristorante Piatti** (tel. 707/996–2351), like its namesake in the Napa Valley, is known for its homemade pastas, calzones, and pizzas prepared in a wood-burning oven; grilled meats are another specialty. **Big 3** (tel. 707/938–9000) in Boyes Hot Springs is a casual restaurant at the Sonoma Mission Inn & Spa known for fresh local produce, poultry, and seafood. The breakfast and Sunday-brunch menus feature spa dishes as well as eggs, waffles, and Sonoma sausages. The menu is French country at the **Kenwood Restaurant & Bar** (tel. 707/833–6326) and at Geyserville's **Chateau Souverain Café** (tel. 707/433–3141). **John Ash & Co.** (tel. 707/527–7687) in Santa Rosa emphasizes regional meats and produce. **The Boonville Hotel** (tel. 707/895–2210) in the Anderson Valley specializes in California cuisine with Mexican and Italian flourishes, taking advantage of local products.

Tourist Information

Calistoga Chamber of Commerce (1458 Lincoln Ave., Calistoga, CA 94515, tel. 707/942–6333); **Healdsburg Chamber of Commerce** (217 Healdsburg Ave., tel. 707/433–6935 or 800/648–9922 in CA); **Napa Valley Visitors Bureau** (4260 Silverado Trail, Yountville, CA 94599, tel. 707/258–1957); **Sonoma County Visitors and Convention Bureau** (10 4th St., Santa Rosa, CA 95401, tel. 707/575–1191); **Sonoma Valley Visitors Bureau** (435 E. 1st St., Sonoma, CA 95476, tel. 707/996–1090). For information on Mendocino, contact the **Ukiah Chamber of Commerce** (495E E. Perkins St., Ukiah, CA 95482, tel. 707/462–4705) or the **Redwood Empire Association** (785 Market St., 15th Floor, San Francisco, CA 94103, tel. 415/543–8334).

Reservation Service

Bed & Breakfast Inns of Sonoma County (Box 51, Geyserville, CA 95476, tel. 707/433–4667).

Auberge du Soleil

Partially obscured by groves of gray-green olive trees, the "inn of the sun" is nestled into a hillside on the eastern edge of the Napa Valley. Claude Rouas, the French-born restaurateur who made San Francisco's L'Etoile the virtual headquarters of the society set, opened a restaurant on this site in 1981. "The restaurant took off immediately," recalls Rouas. "But I had always dreamed of opening an inn in the style of the country inns in Provence, like La Colombe d'Or. I wanted something with that Provence feeling but also something that would be fitting in the Napa Valley."

The guest accommodations also had to suit the existing restaurant, a stunning structure with light-colored walls and an extended balcony entwined with grapevines. To this end, Rouas went back to the original design team— architect Sandy Walker and designer Michael Taylor. Together they built nine maisons (each named for a French region) on the 33-acre site below the restaurant; two others were added in 1987. The result is a low-rise blend of southwestern French and adobe-style architecture.

Each room has its own entrance and a trellis-covered veranda facing the valley. The rooms have a fresh, streamlined look with smooth, hand-glazed terra-cotta tiles on the floors and framing the fireplaces. The walls are a soothing pale stucco, and tall double doors, covered with white wooden shutters, open onto the balcony. High ceilings and air-conditioning fight the summer heat; on winter nights, however, guests may want to pull the soft leather chairs close to the fireplace for warmth.

The Auberge du Soleil is eminently suited to honeymooners, who can remain sequestered, thanks to room service. But the inn also has ample public spaces where groups can gather. The restaurant, whose reputation suffered after the departure of the original chef, is now one of the valley's most popular. Although Rouas is often on the premises, the day-to-day business of management is left to George A. Goeggel, another European, who came to the inn from the Rosewood Hotel Group.

Address: *180 Rutherford Hill Rd., Rutherford, CA 94573, tel. 707/ 963–1211 or 800/348–5406, fax 707/ 963–8764.*
Accommodations: *31 rooms with baths, 19 suites.*
Amenities: *Air-conditioning; fireplace and refrigerator in rooms, whirlpool bath in 12 rooms; outdoor pool and whirlpool bath, tennis courts, tennis pro, massage room, restaurant, beauty salon, 24-hour room service, conference facilities.*
Rates: *$250–$345, suites $450–$650; Continental breakfast. AE, D, MC, V.*
Restrictions: *No smoking in some rooms, no pets, 2-night minimum.*

The Boonville Hotel

It's hard to miss the Boonville Hotel if you drive through the quiet Anderson Valley on Route 128. The white, two-story 19th-century hotel is right on the road, its entrance only a few yards and the width of the porch from the center divider. At first glance, it would seem more appropriate to arrive on horseback and simply tether your mount to the porch railing.

The property became famous in northern California in the early 1980s, when it was operated as a restaurant that gained a fanatical following of those devoted to fresh-from-the-garden cuisine. Fame turned to notoriety, however, when the former owners disappeared amid rumors of financial scandal. John Schmitt and his wife, Jeanne Eliades, took possession in 1988. Like its predecessor, the hotel's restaurant uses fresh herbs from the garden, but the menu is less elaborate and more in keeping with that of the restaurant Schmitt owned before taking over the Boonville Hotel.

After remodeling downstairs and gutting the upper floor, Schmitt and Eliades decided to redecorate the century-old hotel with handcrafted pieces from local artisans. An abundance of bare wood and contemporary Craftsman-style furnishings makes this one of the most distinctive hotel interiors anywhere in the wine country.

All the accommodations have wood-slatted window coverings, custom tilework in the baths, and pale beige Berber-weave carpeting. Many have four-paneled doors topped with transoms that flood the rooms with natural light. The suites are especially impressive, with their vaulted ceilings and white cotton curtains suspended from simple rods. Number 1 has a bed and an armoire made of ash, a wet bar, and a sofa, chair, and ottoman covered in mint-green fabric. French doors open onto the street-front porch shared with the adjacent suite, which is done in shades of mustard yellow and gray. Among the myriad details deserving of notice are the verdigris lamps and the highly idiosyncratic assortment of vases (including simple pitchers and small buckets) with fresh flower arrangements. All the guest accommodations are on the second floor, opening onto a central hallway. Despite the location, the rooms are quiet; there is very little traffic here except on Saturday morning or Sunday afternoon.

Address: *Hwy. 128 and Lambert Ln., Box 326, Boonville, CA 95415, tel. 707/895–2210.*
Accommodations: *6 double rooms with baths, 2 suites.*
Amenities: *Restaurant, off-street parking, proximity to brew pub and nearby wineries.*
Rates: *$70–$125, suites $150; Continental breakfast. MC, V.*
Restrictions: *No smoking, no pets.*

Camellia Inn

This graceful jewel is the real thing. Few California inns match the perfect appearance of this lovingly maintained Italianate Victorian set amid a garden of camellias on one side and, on the other, a tiny tiled pond in a shaded patio. Inside, it is replete with 12-foot ceilings, Oriental rugs, and a plethora of four-poster, queen-size canopy beds best entered via upholstered stepstool. The pale apricot-and-white ground-floor double parlor has twin marble fireplaces. High ceilings keep the rooms cool even during Healdsburg's warm summers, and a pool out back provides a good respite from the heat on superhot days.

The inn was built in 1869 by Ransome Powell, a tailor from Tennessee, and then appropriated as an infirmary by J.W. Seawell in 1892. Luther Burbank, a family friend of the Seawells, is responsible for many of the 50-odd varieties of camellia here. Remodeled in 1981, the inn was opened the following year by Ray and Del Lewand. Ray, who used to be in the insurance industry, oversees the property and, in his spare time, makes a limited supply of award-winning wines. Both he and Del, formerly the owner of a sportswear business, share guest-tending duties, except in the few months they spend at their Puerto Vallarta inn, when daughter Lucy (an antiques dealer) takes over.

Of the nine double rooms (most of them named for varieties of camellia), three are upstairs in the main house,

two in the rear, two in a separate building that once housed the dining room, and two in the former water tower, which was remodeled in 1989. Accessible via private entrance, Firelight has a carved oak mantel atop a gas-log fireplace and a Queen Anne–style bay window. Royalty, with a private entrance of its own, is equally impressive: It has a massive bed originally from a Scottish castle and three arched windows. Tiffany is done in Bradbury & Bradbury hand-silk-screened wallpaper, with a stained-glass window in the bath. Upstairs in the main house are Moonglow, Memento (which can be opened into a suite), and Demitasse, which features a double antique iron bedstead and an antique dresser inherited from Del's Michigan grandmother. In contrast to the other rooms, which are ornate, the latter two—Tower East and Tower West—are a refreshing vision of white-washed pine, with willow furnishings.

Address: *211 North St., Healdsburg, CA 95448, tel. 707/433–8182.*
Accommodations: *9 double rooms, some with baths, 1 suite.*
Amenities: *Pool, off-street parking, nearby shops and restaurants.*
Rates: *$85–$125; full breakfast. D, MC, V.*
Restrictions: *No smoking, no pets; 2-night minimum on weekends.*

Highland Ranch

The approach to the Highland Ranch is enough to make the nearby town of Philo look like an urban metropolis, but after 4 miles of narrow twists and turns, one arrives on a knoll overlooking a broad clearing. To one side, the 100-year-old ranch house is hidden in the shade of old oaks; to the left of the road, a handful of cabins look like little more than bunkhouses. Only slowly does the newcomer notice the strategically located ponds, the tennis court and small pool, the barn and riding ring in the back, and four hammocks strung beneath ancient redwood trees.

Highland Ranch didn't look this good in 1988, when George Gaines and his family took possession of what had become a rather run-down retreat. It took a mammoth effort to bury the electrical wires and perform the other feats of illusion that have resulted in a smooth-running operation. After a globe-trotting career as an international businessman, West Virginia–born Gaines came to California so that his wife, Mary Moore, could complete her studies to become an Episcopal priest. Depending on one's inclinations toward sociability, a sojourn here may be centered in the farmhouse, where guests gather in a well-worn living room lined with books, games, and memorabilia of the family's residences abroad, or in the privacy of one of the 11 cabins. These are homespun affairs, with good reading chairs and plenty of windows through which to watch deer and jack rabbits bound across the landscape.

This is not a turn-down-service, basket-of-amenities type of place but one where travelers can get some exercise and fresh air, good food, and a sense of peace so pervasive it might unnerve a big-city dweller. After breakfast, guests may take a short or an all-day horseback ride or hike, or go clay-pigeon shooting or fishing; at the end of the day, they may enjoy the sunset on their small private decks. Given the natural beauty of the setting, few visitors care that the walls of their cabin are fir plywood, the floors are Douglas-fir plank with only sparse carpeting, or that decoration consists of family collections of china or framed paintings—or even an old nonfunctioning camel horn that Gaines used to toot whenever he closed a particularly good deal.

Address: *Philo, CA 95466, tel. 707/ 895–3600, fax 707/895–3702.*
Accommodations: *11 cabins with baths.*
Amenities: *Fireplace, deck, phone in rooms, cribs available; pool, tennis court (racquets and balls provided), fishing, horseback riding, hiking, clay-pigeon shooting.*
Rates: *$175 per person, including all meals, beverages, and activities. No credit cards.*
Restrictions: *No pets; 2-night minimum.*

Kenwood Inn

erry and Roseann Grimm deserve an award for transforming a ramshackle antiques shop into a romantic Italian-style retreat facing the vineyards that lie on the hillsides across Highway 12. The two-lane road, in fact, is the biggest drawback to the Kenwood Inn, although there is little traffic noise after dark. This inn is separated from the road by a large flagstone patio, a swimming pool, and extensive grounds landscaped with dozens of rose bushes, as well as persimmon, fig, apple, and—most appropriately—olive trees.

In 1994, the inn embarked on a $1 million remodeling to add eight accommodations and a full-service spa on the premises. In addition, the pool area has been renovated to include a large stone deck shaded by trellises and grapevines. The new rooms are decorated in the same style as the original ones.

The owners have paid lavish attention to detail, from the down mattresses covered with Egyptian-cotton sheets to the aromatic sprigs of fresh-from-the-garden herbs used to garnish breakfast dishes. Although there is no regular food service beyond the morning meal, guests are welcome to make special requests, whether it's a late-afternoon platter of fruits and cheeses or a specially catered dinner for private parties. Advance notice for the latter is, of course, required.

Room Three, decorated in leafy green and lush burgundy, has a queen-size bed and a separate living room with paisley wallpaper and moss-color draperies. It also has a private patio and garden entrance and is separated from the other two ground-floor accommodations by a large living room furnished simply with glass-and-wrought-iron console tables along the walls, antique ebony straight-back chairs imported from Mozambique, and two overstuffed sofas, upholstered in Italian prints, flanking the fireplace. Room Six, located upstairs, claims the most privacy and the best view. A four-poster king-size bed is canopied in fabrics of mango, burgundy, and black.

Address: *10400 Sonoma Hwy., Kenwood, CA 95442, tel. 707/833–1293.*
Accommodations: *10 rooms with baths, 2 suites.*
Amenities: *Fireplaces, feather mattresses, down comforters and pillows; pool, sauna, steam bath, off-street parking.*
Rates: *$165–$225, suites $255; full breakfast, complimentary wine. MC, V.*
Restrictions: *No smoking, no pets; 2-night minimum on weekends.*

Larkmead

S et back in regal seclusion off a country lane, this 1919 inn could pass for a wine maker's residence. In fact, it was built as a farmhouse on the property that once encompassed the adjacent Hanns Kornell Sparkling Wines estate. In the 1880s, the winery was owned by Lillie Hitchcock Coit, the pioneer San Franciscan whose bequest to the city led to the erection of an observation tower on Telegraph Hill now known as Coit Tower. The property eventually came into the hands of the Italian-Swiss Salmina family, and the house was constructed by one of the Salmina sons for his bride. It was bought in 1978 by an East Bay couple, Gene and Joan Garbarino—he a dentist and she a former grade-school teacher—who transformed the place into a residential-style inn.

Larkmead has both Victorian and Palladian elements, the latter evident in such details as the second-floor window arranged directly above the entryway. One enters through an octagonal, wisteria-covered loggia flanked by two wings; the living quarters were established on the second floor, typical of structures built by Italian-Swiss families who wanted to enjoy afternoon breezes while gazing out over their surrounding vineyards.

The house is wonderfully quiet; even on busy summer weekends, traffic moves slowly on Larkmead Lane. Sheltered by magnolia, cypress, and sycamore trees, the inn has lawns for strolling outdoors, and Persian carpets and favorite family paintings in the living room. Joan, who tends to her guests on weekends (a manager takes over during the slower, midweek days), is a fastidious hostess who holds nothing back, not even the Imari china or the Grand Baroque silver used for breakfast in the formal dining room. In fact, the entire inn is somewhat stiff, in the manner of a favorite great-aunt's home, where the bedroom furnishings match almost too well. Four rooms, all named for Napa Valley varietals, have their idiosyncracies, however: Chenin Blanc is swathed in green-and-white floral fabric, right down to the wonderful chaise longue; Chablis has an enclosed porch; Chardonnay is evocative of the art-deco rage; and Beaujolais looks out over the loggia to the vineyards.

Address: *1102 Larkmead La., Calistoga, CA 94515, tel. 707/942-5360.*
Accommodations: *4 double rooms with baths.*
Amenities: *Air-conditioning, fireplace in living room; off-street parking.*
Rates: *$125–$138; Continental breakfast, afternoon wine and cheese. No credit cards.*
Restrictions: *No pets, but exceptions may be made for small dogs.*

Madrona Manor

A fraction of its former size, this estate dates from 1881, when San Franciscan John Paxton commissioned a mansion to be built on 240 acres on the outskirts of Healdsburg. To the Eastlake-style architecture he added gingerbread flourishes, steeply pitched dormers, gables, a mansard roof, and a wraparound porch. He filled it with massive furniture; many pieces, including a rosewood square grand piano, are still in use.

Today the estate comprises an 8-acre wooded knoll. In 1981 it was bought by Carol and John Muir, who had been living in Saudi Arabia. After redecorating the Carpenter Gothic carriage house, they added four third-floor guest rooms in the main house for a total of nine. Instead of duplicating the turn-of-the-century California decor of the lower floors, they chose Portuguese reproductions. Still, the newer rooms are more modern in tone than the original five. The bedroom suite in number 203 is American Victorian Renaissance, with circular mask crests on both the chest and the double bedstead. The only guests who might feel crowded are those in the first-floor room, where more than one visitor has reported seeing a ghost during the night.

Less successful are the accommodations in the outbuildings, which lack the elegance of the original rooms. The Meadow Wood Complex, with its very private bedroom and deck, is headquarters for travelers with children and dogs.

The Garden Suite is decorated with rattan furniture and a marble fireplace. Set in a secluded spot beyond the garden, it is third in popularity only to the veranda rooms. The carriage house, with its massive Nepalese hand-carved rosewood door, houses eight rooms, as well as the newer Suite 400, which has contemporary French furnishings and a Grecian marble bathroom. The whirlpool bath has shutters that open onto the sitting room, facing the fireplace.

Herbs and some vegetables from the inn's extensive gardens find their way to the dinner menu at Madrona Manor. Local fish, poultry, and game are often smoked on the premises, and the marmalade at breakfast is made from mandarin oranges picked from several trees on the property.

Address: *1001 Westside Rd., Healdsburg, CA 95448, tel. 707/433-4231 or 800/258-4003.*
Accommodations: *18 double rooms with baths, 3 suites.*
Amenities: *Air-conditioning, fireplace in 18 rooms, restaurant; pool.*
Rates: *$135-$225, suites $185-$225; full breakfast. AE, D, MC, V.*
Restrictions: *No smoking indoors.*

Beltane Ranch

Beltane Ranch is a century-old farmhouse that commands sweeping views of the Sonoma Valley vineyards. Innkeeper Rosemary Wood, whose family has owned the surrounding ranch for the past 55 years, converted the property into an inn back in 1981.

The two-story wraparound balcony, furnished with hammocks, a wooden swing, and plenty of chairs and tables, is an ideal spot for relaxing after a long day outdoors. Two of the three upstairs rooms extend the entire width of the building, with both front and back access to the porch. Ceiling fans, floral fabrics, comfortable reading chairs, and window shutters remain from the days when this was a cherished family retreat. Some furnishings, including a massive carved-wood mar-

ble-top dressing table, are antiques. The somewhat drab bathrooms are offset by cozy dressing areas. Despite a wood-burning stove and plenty of reading material, the public rooms are undistinguished. The inn's greatest glory is its gardens, which are occasionally the scene of various charity fund-raisers.

Address: *11775 Sonoma Hwy., Box 395, Glen Ellen, CA 95442, tel. 707/996–6501.*
Accommodations: *2 double rooms with baths, 2 suites.*
Amenities: *Private hiking trails, horseshoes, tennis court, off-street parking.*
Rates: *$95–$125, suites $115; full breakfast. No credit cards, but personal checks accepted.*
Restrictions: *No smoking indoors.*

Brannan Cottage Inn

The town of Calistoga grew up around Samuel Brannan's Calistoga Hot Spring Resort, and this is the last remaining cottage on the original site. Constructed in 1860, the main building has five arches, a wide wraparound porch, and scalloped ridge-cresting.

The four ground-floor rooms feature private entrances off the porch, which fronts a grassy garden. All the rooms have individual hand-painted floral stencil designs on the upper walls; the pastel colors are echoed in the decor, which includes simple pine tables and dressers, wicker chairs, ceiling fans, and lace curtains. The suites, located on the upper floor of a structure in the back, are cramped in comparison but are suitable for romantic getaways.

The white-and-green inn is owned and enthusiastically managed by Dieter Back, who gave up his career as a printer in southern California to take over the inn in 1993. Back hovers over guests, offering wine in the afternoon and dispensing his suggestions on the best places to go in town for spa treatments or dinner.

Address: *100 Wapoo Ave., Calistoga, CA 94515, tel. 707/942–4200.*
Accommodations: *4 double rooms with baths, 2 suites.*
Amenities: *Air-conditioning, ceiling fan in rooms, extra bed available; off-street parking.*
Rates: *$140; full breakfast, afternoon wine and cheese. MC, V.*
Restrictions: *No smoking indoors, no pets.*

Campbell Ranch Inn

Although this country property doesn't really feel like a ranch, the Campbell Ranch Inn does deliver all one might expect in terms of fresh air, expansive vistas, and open sky. The 35-acre property is headquartered at a 4,500-square-foot ranch house, built in the late 1960s in typical northern California style. It was bought in 1986 by Jerry and Mary Jane Campbell, who migrated west—separately—meeting in California, marrying in 1958, and raising a family. Now that the kids are grown, Mary Jane spends a lot of time putting up fruit and tending her impressive garden.

The residential-style rooms are nothing really special: clean and pastel with chenille bedcovers and lots of Jerry's excellent photographs prominently displayed. Three rooms are upstairs in the main house; a fourth, on a lower level, is more private. Located 4 miles from Lake Sonoma and 3 miles from the Russian River, the ranch is better suited to active people than to those who like to be in the thick of things.

Address: *1475 Canyon Rd., Geyserville, CA 95441, tel. 707/857–3476.*
Accommodations: *4 double rooms with baths, 1 suite.*
Amenities: *Fireplace in 2 rooms; off-street parking, pool, outdoor spa, tennis court, horseshoes, Ping-Pong, bicycles.*
Rates: *$100–$165; full breakfast. MC, V.*
Restrictions: *No smoking indoors; 2-night minimum on weekends.*

Cross Roads Inn

A better view of the area could be found only on a hot-air-balloon tour of the valley. It's no wonder that the most requested room at the Cross Roads Inn is the Puddle Duck, where from the corner whirlpool bath one can take in views of both the valley and the hillside in back. Named for Beatrix Potter characters, all the extra large rooms (such as the one with the king-size, pine four-poster bed Sam and Nancy Scott commissioned for the house) are decorated with pastel colors, lace tablecloths, delicate floral wallpaper, and mahogany, cherry, or pine furniture. The smallest and most private room is the Mrs. Ribby Room, the only guest room that's on the lower floor.

Breakfast can be taken privately or on the spacious decks. Guests can gather later in the living room, where a circular glass fireplace warms the room on chilly evenings.

Address: *6380 Silverado Trail, Yountville, CA 94558, tel. 707/944–0646.*
Accommodations: *3 double rooms with baths.*
Amenities: *Whirlpool bath, ceiling fan in 1 room; hiking trails.*
Rates: *$175–$200; full breakfast, afternoon and evening refreshments. MC, V.*
Restrictions: *No smoking; 2-night minimum on weekends and holidays.*

El Dorado Hotel

The pale stucco, white-trimmed adobe El Dorado was built in 1843 by Don Salvador Vallejo, a brother of the legendary Mexican general who laid out the historic Sonoma plaza, but the current interior of this landmark structure bears little resemblance to the original. There is nothing cozy about this inn, which is professionally run by the same company that owns Auberge du Soleil in the Napa Valley.

The open, airy feel of the ground floor—which houses an Italian restaurant and a clothing boutique—is unfortunately lost on the second floor, where most of the rooms are located. Though small, each has a little balcony overlooking either an inner courtyard or the historic town square. Rather than clutter the rooms with knickknacks,

the owners have made the most of the limited space by decorating with a light hand. A typical room, done in aqua and peach, has a simple, metal-frame four-poster bed flanked by matching verdigris reading lamps, woven rugs on bar Mexican paver floors, a large willow-framed mirror, and a couple of rattan chairs. The baths and closets are tiny.

Address: *405 1st St. W, Sonoma, CA 95476, tel. 707/996–3030, fax 707/ 996–3148.*
Accommodations: *27 double rooms with baths.*
Amenities: *Phone, TV, balcony in rooms; restaurant, pool.*
Rates: *$105–$145; Continental breakfast. AE, MC, V.*
Restrictions: *No smoking in rooms.*

The Gaige House

The Gaige House, built in 1890 for the local butcher, occupies one of the best sites of any Wine Country inn. Located near the town square of bucolic Glen Ellen, the beige-and-brown Italianate Queen Anne Victorian fits nicely into the village's tree-lined main street. Close to shops and restaurants, it's a short drive from Jack London State Historic Park, where the famous author made his home and farmed the sprawling ranch, now partly planted to grapes.

A 1.2-acre property that backs up against the forested Calabezas Creek, the Gaige House has the ambience of a private estate. Since Ardath Rouas took over in 1993, it has blossomed into a handsome, light-filled retreat. The owner's modern art pieces and hand-picked furnishings have brought to life

a place that had always suffered from a lack of identity. Rouas, part of the team that designed and decorated the luxurious Auberge du Soleil in the Napa Valley, has also added a downstairs room, which has a private entrance.

Address: *13540 Arnold Dr., Glen Ellen, CA 95442, tel. 707/935–0237.*
Accommodations: *10 double rooms with baths.*
Amenities: *Fireplace in 3 rooms; pool, bicycle rentals, off-street parking.*
Rates: *$120–$225; full breakfast, afternoon refreshments. AE, MC, V.*
Restrictions: *No smoking indoors; 2-night minimum Sat. and holidays.*

Harvest Inn

Harvests really do occur at this aptly named inn with a Mayacamas Mountains backdrop: 14 of its 24 acres are planted to cabernet sauvignon and merlot grapes. Impeccably landscaped grounds lend the property the feel of a private-school campus, so that despite its roadside location, the inn is surprisingly quiet.

The theme is English Tudor: steep-pitched roofs, lots of oak, acres of brick. Some of the rooms are a bit dark, but most are spacious with oak antiques and large stone fireplaces. They have cute names like the Dove, Robin and Marian, and the Duke of Daring; the latter is one of the best units, with plenty of light and a private patio. The main building houses an oak-paneled lobby, a wine bar, and a great room plus a stone fireplace large enough to roast an ox in.

Curving brick pathways meander throughout the beautiful gardens connecting the buildings. The Harvest Inn lacks the cachet of the big-name resorts, but does provide an excellent value.

Address: *One Main St., St. Helena, CA 94574, tel. 707/963–9463 or 800/950–8466.*
Accommodations: *54 rooms with baths.*
Amenities: *TV and radio in rooms, most have refrigerator, wet bar, and fireplace; 2 pools, 2 hot tubs; close to shops, restaurants, and wineries.*
Rates: *$98–$360; Continental breakfast. AE, D, MC, V.*
Restrictions: *No smoking in some rooms, no pets.*

Healdsburg Inn on the Plaza

Facing Healdsburg Plaza, a mini-version of Sonoma's historic square, the Inn on the Plaza occupies the two upper floors of a turn-of-the-century Victorian that once housed the local Wells Fargo Bank. Natural light streams in from vaulted skylights, delineating a multitude of arches, corbels, and turn-of-the-century chandeliers. In the second-floor all-weather solarium, guests can sip coffee and socialize in an indoor-garden setting. It's one of many idiosyncratic touches provided by innkeeper Ginny Jenkins, who divides her time between this inn and another in Napa.

The rooms, all of which open on to a large zigzag hallway, are larger than average but something of a hodge-podge. Four of them boast Eastlake Victorian antiques, oak rockers and settees, and claw-foot tubs with pedestal sinks in the baths. The color scheme is limited largely to pastels, white lace curtains, and, in some rooms, white iron-and-brass bed-steads. The most unusual room, Early Light, with a huge slanted window that substitutes for most of one wall on the east side, was originally Healds-burg's first photography studio.

Address: *110 Matheson St., Healdsburg, CA 95448, tel. 707/433–6991 or 800/431–8663.*
Accommodations: *7 double rooms with baths, 1 suite.*
Amenities: *Solarium.*
Rates: *$135–$175, suites $175; full breakfast. MC, V.*
Restrictions: *Smoking in roof garden only, no pets.*

Hope-Merrill House

The north Sonoma town of Geyserville has at least two things
going for it: location and this fas-
tidiously restored Eastlake Stick-style
manse. Rosalie Hope had been collect-
ing Victoriana long before she moved
here with her late husband Bob to
open a pair of inns—the 1904 Queen
Anne cottage (now the Hope-Bosworth
House) and the older house across the
street, named for J.P. Merrill, the original resident. The latter, built during
the 1880s, offered ample space, including a sitting room large enough to
accommodate a five-piece Eastlake
walnut parlor set.

In a building that has won recognition
from the National Trust for Historic
Preservation for outstanding restoration, it is not surprising to find the
original Lincrusta Walton wainscoting,

Bradbury & Bradbury silkscreen wallpapers, striped chaise longues, wicker
settees, and other Victorian features.
In collaboration with the nearby
Camellia Inn, the Hope-Merrill team
also operates a third inn near Puerto
Vallarta, Mexico.

Address: *21253 Geyserville Ave., Box
42, Geyserville, CA 95441, tel. 707/857–
3356 or 800/825–4233.*
Accommodations: *6 double rooms
with baths, 1 suite.*
Amenities: *Fireplace in 3 rooms,
whirlpool bath in 2 rooms; outdoor
pool, gazebo.*
Rates: *$95–$115, suite $125; full
breakfast. AE, MC, V.*
Restrictions: *No smoking indoors, no
pets; 2-night minimum on weekends,
3-night minimum on holidays
Apr.–Dec.*

Maison Fleurie

This three-part inn was built of
brick and fieldstone in 1873. Originally a hotel, it served as a bordello, a bastion of bootlegging, and a
4-H Club meeting place before being
restored during the late 1960s. The
Locken family ran it from 1977 until
late 1993, when it was purchased by
the Post family, which operates other
prestigious Four Sisters Inns in San
Francisco, Pacific Grove, and elsewhere.

When the inn, formerly the Magnolia
Hotel, reopened in 1994, it was unrec-
ognizable. The main building's rooms,
formerly dark and tiny, have been
totally revamped, their walls painted
in rich, lush colors with attractive plaid
accents. Other welcome touches
include bright, well-placed reading
lamps.

The rooms in the Garden Court and
Carriage House are even more spacious than those in the main building.
Provence, for example, has a huge bath
and doors on either side of the room,
one just steps away from the swimming pool and outdoor hot tub. It's
painted in a yellow glow reminiscent of
the vineyards in spring when the mustard blooms.

Address: *6529 Yount St., Drawer M,
Yountville, CA 94599, tel. 707/944–
2056.*
Accommodations: *13 double rooms
with baths.*
Amenities: *Air-conditioning, gas-log
fireplace in 5 rooms, wine cellar; pool,
hot tub, bicycles.*
Rates: *$109–$190; full breakfast. AE,
MC, V.*
Restrictions: *No smoking, no pets.*

Quail Mountain

T he private road off Highway 29 winds up, up, and up through a forest of redwood, Douglas fir, madrona, and oak trees to a site 300 feet above the valley floor. Wild quail scurry about, disappearing into wild lilac, ferns, berry bushes, and wildflowers. Don and Alma Swiers chose this 23-acre parcel in 1980 and opened their inn in 1984, after long careers in education and the oil industry, respectively.

The two smaller accommodations feature small semiprivate decks facing the forested slopes above the inn, but the best choice is the Fern Room, a minisuite with a small sun room facing the valley. The decor is unstudied country-style, with handmade quilts set atop white linen duvets. Furnishings are minimal: an attractive pine

bureau, two bedside tables, and a rocking chair.

Afternoon wine and cheese and morning meals are served in the brick-floored solarium. The enormous breakfasts can range from a dish of pureed rhubarb (home-grown) topped with crème fraîche to a colossal apple pancake.

Address: *4455 N. St. Helena Hwy., Calistoga, CA 94515, tel. 707/942–0315 or 707/942–0316.*
Accommodations: *3 double rooms with baths.*
Amenities: *Pool, hot tub.*
Rates: *$100–$125; full breakfast, afternoon wine. MC, V.*
Restrictions: *No smoking indoors; 2-night minimum on weekends.*

Sonoma Hotel

F ew American town squares evoke a sense of place and history as well as the plaza in the heart of old Sonoma. Flanked by old adobes and false-front buildings, the square was laid out in 1835 by General Mariano Vallejo. Many of the buildings have been restored and converted into restaurants, shops, and hotels, the most historic of which is the Sonoma Hotel.

An old-fashioned feeling pervades this three-story, century-old adobe structure (the high-gabled top floor was added around 1880). Only when you leave the hotel do you realize that you are in the 1990s, not the 1890s.

There are challenges to furnishing a hotel without a single reproduction— mattresses had to be custom-made to

fit the oddly shaped beds. Turn-of-the-century English and French bedroom sets furnish most of the accommodations; almost all have such quaint flourishes as lace curtains and chenille bedcovers. The ground-floor lounge is a favorite gathering spot for locals.

Address: *110 W. Spain St., Sonoma, CA 95476, tel. 707/996–2996.*
Accommodations: *16 rooms, 5 with baths, 1 suite.*
Amenities: *Restaurant, bar.*
Rates: *$75–$115, suite $120; Continental breakfast. AE, MC, V.*
Restrictions: *2-night minimum on holidays.*

Thistle Dew Inn

Steps away from historic Sonoma Square, this inn is actually two in one, with accommodations in both the main house, built in 1869, and in a 1905 cottage relocated to these grounds from three blocks away. Most of the Arts and Crafts–style furniture, original to the house, is a suitable match for the relatively simple design of the buildings. The six-leaf dining-room table and matching sideboards, for instance, are Gustav Stickley creations. There are also gallery-quality pieces of Mission furniture, such as the chest of drawers signed by Charles Limbert. In the cottage, where four rooms share a parlor, Navajo rugs and Amish quilts complement the early 1900s decor. The Rose Garden and the Cornflower rooms in the main house have walls that were sponge-painted in their namesake colors vividly enough to keep some guests awake at night.

After Larry and Norma Barnett bought the inn in 1990, Norma, a practicing psychologist, redecorated all of the guest rooms; Larry tends the kitchen and the English-style garden that borders the inn.

Address: *171 W. Spain St., Sonoma, CA 95476, tel. 707/938-2909.*
Accommodations: *6 double rooms with baths.*
Amenities: *Air-conditioning, Jacuzzi, bicycles, access to local health club.*
Rates: *$100–$140; full breakfast, afternoon refreshments. AE, MC, V.*
Restrictions: *No smoking indoors.*

Vintners Inn

In a few years, this 44-room country inn may acquire the patina of an established auberge in the south of France. When it opened in 1981, however, it stood out like a cactus in a vineyard. Surrounded by mostly open land, the Vintners Inn consists of four two-story Mediterranean-style villas, topped with red-tiled roofs and set off with arched windows, patios, walkways, and fountains. Clever landscaping makes the nearby freeway much less noticeable.

The decor consists of homey floral-print wallpapers and some antique furnishings, including turn-of-the-century pine chests, desks, and armoires in a French-country style. The suites are huge, and the upstairs corner rooms feature vaulted ceilings and windows on two sides. Instead of closets, there are hanging rods in the dressing room. Buffet breakfast is served in a casual dining room. California cuisine is available at the adjacent John Ash & Co., one of the county's top restaurants.

Address: *4250 Barnes Rd., Santa Rosa, CA 95403, tel. 707/575-7350 or 800/421-2584 in CA, fax 707/575-1426.*
Accommodations: *39 double rooms with baths, 5 suites.*
Amenities: *TV, radio, phone in rooms, fireplace in 18 rooms, refrigerator in suites, conference facilities; outdoor hot tub.*
Rates: *$128–$168, suite $195; buffet breakfast. DC, MC, V.*
Restrictions: *2-night minimum on weekends Mar. 15–Oct. 31.*

North Coast and Redwood Country

North Coast and Redwood Country
Including Mendocino and Eureka

The northwestern corner of California lies in splendid isolation. This land of scenic beauty and serene majesty— some 400 miles south to north, 50 east to west—has long lured the independent thinker, the artist, and occasionally the roadside entrepreneur.

California's magical Highway 1 hugs the coast until, about 50 miles north of Mendocino, it turns east, climbs over the Coast Range, connects with U.S. 101, and meanders through the redwoods to the Oregon border. Along the way it passes deep fern-filled gulches where streams and waterfalls flow, golden rolling hills dotted with oak trees, farms and sheep ranches, and the quaint fishing villages of Noyo, Albion, and Elk— century-old hole-in-the-wall ports where steamers navigated craggy inlets to pick up loads of lumber.

The redwoods, which once covered the hillsides, lured New Englanders here a century ago. The new settlers built houses just like the ones they had left back home, hence the clapboard architecture of most of the towns. They also brought the region a sense of community that's difficult to find in other, more urban parts of California. And now the fiercest protectors of the redwood forests are descendants of the immigrants who came to fell the trees.

It takes time to explore the North Coast, not only because the roads are narrow, twisty, and slow but also because so many sights require you to get out of your car and walk. But the region is worth exploring at leisure. Step up to a headland above a cove and watch the waves crash over the rocks. Take in the wildness of the ocean; maybe you'll be lucky enough to spot a whale in the distance, sounding and spouting. Take a walk among the redwoods and savor the silence, the scent of the flowers, the sweetness of the wood, the near-darkness created by the dense canopy of trees.

The shopkeepers, gallery owners, and restaurateurs along the North Coast are always ready to chat. Ask them what lured them to this isolated part of California, and most will tell you it's the stunning beauty of the coast and the freedom of the isolation, the chance to be part of a community that shares their values. The world they've created is rich for the visitor in both natural beauty and man-made luxuries. Good accommodations in historic bed-and-breakfast inns, outstanding cuisine made from superb local ingredients, and recreation and relaxation await you.

Places to Go, Sights to See

Eureka, population 27,000, is the North Coast's largest city. It's Old Town is one of the most outstanding Victorian-era commercial districts in California (*see below*). Eureka's diverse history is preserved at the *Clarke Museum* (tel. 707/443–1947); to sample the area's environmental splendors, consider a *Humboldt Bay Harbor Cruise* (tel. 707/445–1910).

Fort Bragg lies a few minutes' drive north of Mendocino, its logging and fishing-industry heritage still tangible in its unpretentious ambience and less-expensive shopping and dining options. A redwood boardwalk in *MacKerricher State Park* affords views of seasonal whale and seal migrations. *California Western Railroad's Skunk Trains* (tel. 707/964–6371) offer full- and half-day scenic excursions through the redwood forest. More adventuresome activities include the equestrian seaside rides offered by *Ricochet Ridge Ranch* (tel. 707/964–7669) or salmon and bottom-fishing boat trips provided by *Anchor Charters* (tel. 707/964–4550). Jazz buffs will enjoy hearing live combos while sampling local drafts at *North Coast Brewing Co.* (tel. 707/964–2739).

Fort Ross State Historic Park (12 mi north of Jenner on Hwy. 1, tel. 707/847–3286) is a reconstruction of the outpost founded in 1812 by Russian seal and otter hunters from Alaska. The visitor center has interpretive exhibits; there is also a Russian chapel, battlements, and picnic facilities.

Kruse Rhododendron State Reserve (10 mi north of Fort Ross on Hwy. 1, tel. 707/847–3221) provides 5 miles of hiking trails among 1,317 acres of wild pink flowering rhododendrons, redwood forest, and bridges over fern-filled canyons. The flowers are at their peak from April through June.

Mendocino, the largest of the villages along the coast, perches on headlands with spectacular ocean views. If the frame buildings of this former lumber port, dating from 1852, look familiar, it's because so many New England–set movies have been shot here. Now a thriving artists' colony, Mendocino hosts galleries, boutiques, and such unusual shops as Wind and Weather (weather instruments) and Out of this World (astronomical items). *The Kelley House Museum* (45007 Albion St., tel. 707/937–5791) exhibits historical artifacts and photographs depicting the town's logging days. The town sponsors a summer arts fair, a music festival, and two performing-arts companies. You get good views (and good picnicking) in Mendocino Headlands State Park, which surrounds the town.

Mendocino Coast Botanical Gardens (south of Fort Bragg, tel. 707/964-4352) covers 47 acres and includes heather, perennials, succulents, ivies, roses, camellias, wildflowers, and dwarf rhododendrons.

Point Arena Lighthouse and Museum (1 mi south of Point Arena, tel. 707/882-2777) is a former whaling station and lumber port. The lighthouse, built in 1870, has been automated; it now contains a museum of lighthouse history.

Redwoods. Redwoods once covered the hillsides above the Pacific from San Francisco all the way north to the Oregon border. Most of the trees have been logged, but a few outstanding groves remain preserved in state parks and in the Redwood National Park. *Armstrong Redwoods State Reserve* (tel. 707/869-2015), near Guerneville, is a 752-acre virgin-redwood grove with hiking trails and picnic facilities. *Humboldt Redwoods State Park* (tel. 707/946-2263), 45 miles south of Eureka on U.S. 101, contains the largest stand of virgin redwoods in the world; Avenue of the Giants, a 33-mile scenic highway; a visitor center and picnic areas; and the Founder's Trail in Rockefeller Forest, which leads to Founder's Tree, one of the tallest of the trees. *Richardson Grove State Park* (tel. 707/247-3318), south of Garberville on U.S. 101, is a 1,000-acre grove of big trees; the favorite scenic walks there are Lookout Trail and Tourney Trail.

Roadside attractions are part of the redwood experience. The *Drive-Thru Tree* at Myers Flat (tel. 707/943-3154) has a base with a diameter of 21 feet, wide enough for a car to drive through. Scotia is the home of *Pacific Lumber Company*, the world's largest redwood lumber mill; a museum displays tools, equipment, and photographs of early logging operations and provides free passes for a tour of the mill. At *Trees of Mystery* (tel. 707/482-5613), near Klamath, a giant statue of Paul Bunyan invites visitors to view unusual redwood formations, as well as a large collection of Native American artifacts, in a free museum.

State Parks. Much of the coast up through Sonoma and Mendocino counties belongs to California state parks. Two of the largest are *Sonoma Coast State Beach*, a 10-mile stretch from the mouth of the Russian River south to Bodega Bay, and *Salt Point State Park*, a 6,000-acre beach lover's paradise of wave-sculpted shoreline. Farther north, near Mendocino, *Russian Gulch State Park* offers redwoods, fern glens, and a waterfall; *Westport Union Landing Beach* has beautiful picnic sites.

Victoriana. In *Eureka's Old Town*—an ongoing project to preserve the city's many splendid Victorian buildings, the most striking of which is the Carson Mansion—visitors will find art galleries, boutiques, and antiques and specialty stores, as well as horse-drawn carriage rides. *Ferndale*, an architecturally authentic Victorian village, has been designated a state historic landmark. The town consists of colorful Victorians; the ones along Main Street have been converted into shops, restaurants, and inns. You can get a walking-tour map from the Chamber of Commerce (tel. 707/786-4477).

Restaurants

Several of the inns described here have exceptional restaurants. In addition, the following are recommended: **Cafe Beaujolais** (tel. 707/937–5614) in Mendocino may be the best restaurant in this part of California. Owner Margaret Fox's innovative breads and confections are famous. The restaurant at the **Hotel Carter** (tel. 707/445–1390) in Eureka has gained a reputation for sophisticated cuisine using many ingredients from the hotel's own gardens. The **Samoa Cookhouse** (tel. 707/442–1659), on the Samoa Peninsula, across Humboldt Bay from Eureka, is the last surviving lumber-camp cookhouse in the West and serves up hearty meals family-style at long tables. The two cozy Victorian dining rooms at **The Old Milano Hotel & Restaurant** (tel. 707/884–3256), just north of Gualala on the southern Mendocino coastline, offer creative California cuisine. The fare runs from game—baby pheasant and venison—to vegetarian dishes at **River's End Restaurant** (tel. 707/865–2484) in Jenner, where the food and ocean view are always first-rate, though the service can be erratic. Point Arena's **The Galley** (tel. 707/882–2189) is esteemed by locals for its dramatic ocean view and hearty, reasonably priced fresh-catch menu—some harvested by wetsuited divers you may see from the restaurant's tableside second-story windows. For similar fare in Eureka, try Old Town's **The Waterfront** (tel. 707/443–9190), whose handsome bar also provides "townies" with a popular nighttime gathering place. For on-the-road snacking, pick up some salmon jerky, readily available throughout the northernmost areas.

Tourist Information

Redwood Empire Association (785 Market St., San Francisco, CA 94103, tel. 415/543–8334); **Eureka/Humboldt County Convention and Visitors Bureau** (1034 2nd St., Eureka, CA 95501, tel. 800/346–3482, 800/338–7352 in CA); **Fort Bragg-Mendocino Coast Chamber of Commerce** (Box 1141, Fort Bragg, CA 95437, tel. 800/726–2780); **Russian River Visitors Information Center** (14034 Armstrong Woods Rd., Guerneville, CA 95446, tel. 707/869–9009).

Reservation Services

Bed and Breakfast International (Box 282910, San Francisco, CA 94128, tel. 800/872–4500, 415/696–1690 outside the U.S.); **Mendocino Coast Innkeepers Association** (Box 1141, Mendocino, CA 95460, tel. 707/964–0640 or 800/382–7244).

Applewood

Jay Gatsby would feel right at home at this country inn surrounded by forests of giant redwoods in the heart of the Russian River resort area. The creation of two refugees from the Bay Area, Jim Caron and Darryl Notter, Applewood occupies a designated landmark home built in 1922 by the flamboyant financier Ralph Belden. In late 1994, Jim and Darryl began construction—expected to be completed by summer 1995—on a new building in the same Mission Revival style as the original.

Jim and Darryl discovered the house while they were visiting the Russian River on vacation. "The area had long been a popular vacation spot for people from the Bay Area, including my family," Jim says. "But it had become run-down by the 1960s. One of our goals with Applewood is to restore the former elegance."

At the heart of the inn, on the main floor, are the three connecting common rooms. The former solarium, with windows on three sides and a full-width skylight, is now a dining room that seats 20. On cold afternoons a fireplace provides a crackling counterpoint to the room's garden ambience. The living room feels more subdued; with burgundy carpet, a heavy-beamed ceiling, and the back of the two-sided great stone fireplace, it evokes the feeling of a country lodge. Through a set of double doors lies a more formal dining room; from here, a pair of French doors open onto the pool area.

Guest rooms—located on the main floor, a lower level, and in the adjacent addition—are decorated in bright, clear jewel tones and furnished with comfort and understated elegance. They all boast sitting areas and plenty of light and are variously furnished with overstuffed love seats, boudoir chairs, chaise longues, and small desks.

The innkeepers pride themselves on their food. Both are accomplished cooks, Jim having learned "at my mother's knee" and Darryl at a cooking school in Bangkok. The fare tends more toward the hearty than the nouveau—eggs Florentine in the morning, steak or leg of lamb at dinner. Space allowing, seating at evening meals is open to non-guests.

Address: *13555 Hwy. 116 (near Guerneville), Pocket Canyon, CA 95446, tel. 707/869-9093.*
Accommodations: *16 double rooms with baths.*
Amenities: *Phone, hair dryers, and cable TV in rooms; fireplace, private balcony or patio, TV with VCR in 7 rooms; whirlpool bath in 2 rooms, shower for two in 5 rooms, heated swimming pool, outdoor hot tub.*
Rates: *$115–$225; full breakfast, dinner available (about $30). AE, D, MC, V.*
Restrictions: *No smoking, no pets; 2-night minimum on weekends.*

Gingerbread Mansion

The Gingerbread Mansion is a tourist attraction in and of itself; visitors are constantly making the detour from U.S. 101 to the Victorian village of Ferndale so they can take a picture of its bright-orange-and-yellow exterior and its flower-filled English gardens. The Gingerbread, with its spindle roof ridges and icicled eaves, its bay windows and shingled turret, must be one of the most photographed buildings in California. Pity those who never get inside to enjoy the whimsical fantasy rooms and the warm hospitality of innkeeper Ken Torbert and his staff.

The Gingerbread Mansion has served many different purposes in the years since 1899, when it was built as a doctor's residence. A 1920s expansion converted the Queen Anne–Eastlake mansion into a hospital. Over the years it turned into a rest home and later an American Legion hall; when Ken purchased it in 1981, it had become an apartment house. "Alice's experiences in Wonderland guided my renovating ideas," he says. The inn is full of surprises—pleasant ones, such as rooms with mirrors for people of all heights, and a pair of claw-foot tubs set toe to toe on a white-fenced platform.

The bathrooms are a special delight. The Fountain Suite bath has side-by-side claw-foot tubs facing a mirrored wall in which the flames in the newly added tiled fireplaces can be seen flickering. The claw-foot tub on a platform

in the Rose Suite bathroom is surrounded by floral wallpaper under a mirrored ceiling; bathing there gives you the feeling of being in a garden. The actual gardens are Ken's pride and joy. Narrow brick paths meander through sculptured boxwood and past blossoming rhododendrons, camellias, and azaleas in winter, and fancy fuchsias throughout the summer and fall.

There are thoughtful surprises, too. Rooms are straightened, the lamps and shades adjusted at turndown each evening. Umbrellas stay at the ready for protection when it rains. Morning coffee is prepared to order for each guest before breakfast, which is served at two large tables in the dining room. This is the time for conversation over a variety of home-baked breads, a selection of unusual local cheeses, and fruit.

Address: *400 Berding St., Box 40, Ferndale, CA 95536, tel. 707/786-4000.*
Accommodations: *9 double rooms with baths.*
Amenities: *Robes in rooms, fireplace in 3 rooms, guest refrigerator; bicycles.*
Rates: *$100–$185; full breakfast, afternoon high tea. AE, MC, V.*
Restrictions: *No smoking indoors, no pets; 2-night minimum on weekends and holidays.*

Harbor House

S ome of the guests who arrive at Harbor House never want to leave. Some don't: Innkeepers Helen and Dean Turner fell in love with Harbor House and purchased it in 1985.

Those who love the ever-changing character of the sea find themselves mesmerized by the view from this country inn perched right on the edge of the coast. If you have booked one of the inn's four red-and-white cottages, you'll be able to savor the view from your own furnished deck. In most of the rooms you can warm yourself by a fireplace while studying the sea. If you want to see the ocean close up, you need only descend the steep path to the inn's private beach; although swimming might be dangerous, this is a good place for a picnic.

Harbor House's magnificent setting is just one of its attractions. The rustic-elegant lodge dates from 1916, when it was built as an executive residence for the Goodyear Redwood Lumber Company, which shipped the lumber it logged out of the cove below. The main building—an enlarged version of the Home of Redwood, designed by Louis Christian Mullgardt for the 1915 Panama-Pacific International Exposition in San Francisco—was constructed entirely of virgin redwood.

The living room is a stunning example of the carpenter's craft. The floors, walls, and vaulted ceilings are made of old-growth redwood; they were

rubbed with beeswax, a natural preservative, to achieve the luster they still have today. This comfortable room beckons you to curl up on one of the overstuffed sofas flanking the enormous stone fireplace.

The guest rooms, also furnished with overstuffed chairs and sofas, are equally comfortable. The Cypress and Harbor rooms, occupying corners on the first and second floors respectively, are both large enough to hold two big beds plus two sitting areas. Both have sea views, as does the Lookout—the smallest room in the inn, on the second floor—which also has its own private deck. Its white cast-iron bed is spread with a wedding-ring quilt.

Breakfast and dinner are served in the dining room. Menus feature fresh local seafood and meats as well as organically grown vegetables.

Address: *5600 S. Hwy. 1, Box 369, Elk, CA 95432, tel. 707/877–3203.*
Accommodations: *6 double rooms with baths, 4 cottages.*
Amenities: *Fireplace in 9 rooms, restaurant; private beach.*
Rates: *$140–$250; MAP. No credit cards.*
Restrictions: *No smoking in restaurant, no pets; 2-night minimum on weekends, 3- or 4-night minimum on some holidays.*

Joshua Grindle Inn

L ike much of Mendocino, the Joshua Grindle Inn looks as if it were imported directly from New England and plunked down on the California coast. And in a way it was. Joshua Grindle, like many of the area's settlers, hailed from Maine. A raftsman for the Mendocino Lumber Company, he built the two-story redwood farmhouse for his bride in 1879; it stayed in the family until 1967.

The inn displays many of Mendocino's best qualities: functional New England architecture, a respect for the land, and a casual, relaxing ambience. It stands on a two-acre hilltop near the turnoff into town from Highway 1. The original farmhouse has five guest rooms, a parlor, and a dining room. Three bedrooms upstairs are bright and airy, with either ocean or treetop views. The guest room called the Library is particularly appealing. A small, cozy room, it has its own seating area, a four-poster queen-size bed, and floor-to-ceiling bookcases flanking a fireplace decorated with hand-painted tiles depicting Aesop's fables. In the late afternoon you'll find guests in the farmhouse parlor, reading or playing backgammon, sipping sherry, or fingering the antique pump organ.

There are two outbuildings. The weathered redwood Watertower has three rooms, including one on the second level with windows on four sides and, naturally, a splendid view of the ocean and town as well as the mountains to the east. The Cottage, which

has two rooms, is shaded by cypress trees that Joshua Grindle planted 100 years ago. Furnishings throughout the inn are simple but comfortable American antiques: Salem rockers, wing chairs, steamertrunk tables, painted pine beds.

Innkeepers Arlene and Jim Moorehead, who purchased the inn in 1989, came to innkeeping after careers with Bechtel in San Francisco. "It was a natural move," Jim said. "We love old houses, good food, and people." At breakfast guests gather around a long, 1830 pine harvest table. Although the table isn't big enough to accommodate everyone when the inn is full, no one seems to mind enjoying a prebreakfast cup of coffee on the veranda. After breakfast, guests frequently take the short walk into town to shop for antiques or explore the art galleries.

Address: *44800 Little Lake Rd., Box 647, Mendocino, CA 95460, tel. 707/937–4143.*
Accommodations: *10 double rooms with baths.*
Amenities: *Fireplace in 6 rooms, guest refrigerator.*
Rates: *$90–$155; full breakfast. MC, V.*
Restrictions: *No smoking indoors, no pets; 2-night minimum on weekends, 3-night minimum on holidays.*

St. Orres

This inn is the creation of a man who loves to build. With its copper-plated Russian-style onion domes, it's a landmark along the northern California coast. Eric Black, like many others, moved to Gualala to get back to the earth; he had been a Bay Area master carpenter. Eric purchased a run-down loggers' motel, razed it, and created a hotel that reflects the area's Russian heritage.

St. Orres offers three types of accommodations. The main hotel, which fronts the highway, has eight very small rooms upstairs, beautifully embellished with such woodwork touches as mitered redwood paneling and handcrafted doorless armoires with clothes hooks and shelves. Two groups of cottages offer more comfortable accommodations. The Meadows includes four cottages, ranging from rustic to elegant and offering elevated bedrooms, private decks through French doors, wood-burning stoves, and sun decks. The rustic Wildflower Cabin has an outdoor, but private and protected, shower. The seven Creekside cottages are more luxurious and—scattered on a wooded hillside away from the hotel—quite private. Pine Haven, the largest, has its own skylighted trio of onion domes, two enclosing bedrooms, the third a blue-and-white-tiled bathroom. These cottages share a complex with hot tub, sauna, and sun deck.

The dining room, filling an enormous domed corner of the hotel, has three-story-high leaded-glass windows and rough-hewn open beams. It's a first-class establishment, luring foodies all the way from San Francisco. Chef Rosemary Campiformio's fixed-price menu offers quail, rabbit, venison, wild boar, and occasionally wild turkey or raccoon potpie; accompaniments are equally exotic—cream of sorrel or cold strawberry soup, or pâté with sun-dried blueberries. Breakfast is served in the dining room to guests staying in the hotel rooms and delivered in a specially designed wooden box to cottage guests.

Gualala, an 1860s lumbering port, is a lively arts center with plenty of galleries. The Gualala River is a popular spot for swimming and steelhead fishing.

Address: *36601 S. Hwy. 1, Box 523, Gualala, CA 95445, tel. 707/884-3303.*
Accommodations: *Cottages: 11 double rooms with baths; lodge: 8 doubles share 3 baths.*
Amenities: *Fireplace in 3 rooms, wood-burning stove in 5 rooms, restaurant, spa complex in Creekside section with hot tub and sauna.*
Rates: *$50–$180; full breakfast. MC, V.*
Restrictions: *No smoking in restaurant, no pets; 2-night minimum on weekends, 3-night minimum on holidays.*

Timberhill Ranch

The two couples who created Timberhill Ranch were seeking a refuge from their harried, urban, corporate lives; they found it on 80 acres of rolling hills in Sonoma County—just a stone's throw from the coast, but worlds apart. Tarran McDaid and Michael Riordan and Barbara Farrell and Frank Watson admit that they created Timberhill mainly for their own pleasure. It has the kind of features they enjoy: privacy, expansive views of rolling hills (green in winter and spring and gold the rest of the year), tennis courts, a swimming pool, miles and miles of trails for quiet strolls in the woods, an excellent dining room, and outstanding and discreet service.

With 15 cottages tucked beneath trees on the hillside above a small pond, the focal point of the ranch is the quietly elegant lodge. The lodge contains an expansive living room with a Sonoma fieldstone fireplace and floor-to-ceiling windows with a view of the pool and the hills beyond.

The dining room is a point of pride. Candlelit and formal in the evenings, it's a marked contrast to the casual atmosphere of the rest of Timberhill. A six-course dinner featuring California cuisine is served nightly. A typical menu features such entrées as ahi tuna with a wasabi beurre blanc and pickled ginger, and New Zealand lamb with cabernet and blackcurrants. There's also a carefully selected wine list, including after-dinner port, sherry, and champagne.

The cottages are identical in design but differ in decor. Small log cabins built of sweet-scented cedar, they have tall windows and decks where many guests enjoy the Continental breakfasts the innkeepers deliver. The beds are dressed with handmade quilts, the walls tastefully decorated with original oils, and the fireplaces stocked up and ready to light. Timberhill provides terry-cloth bathrobes and huge fluffy towels.

This is a ranch, so there are animals: horses in the white-fenced paddock close by; ducks and geese cruising the pond in formation; a pair of llamas; and two dogs—Banger, an Australian shepherd, and Bridgette, a Shih Tzu—who trot behind the innkeepers as they make their daily rounds.

Address: *35755 Hauser Bridge Rd. (Timber Cove Post Office), Cazadero, CA 95421, tel. 707/847–3258, fax 707/847–3342.*
Accommodations: *15 double rooms with baths.*
Amenities: *Fireplace, minibar, refrigerator, and coffeemaker in rooms; swimming pool, outdoor hot tub, tennis courts, hiking trails.*
Rates: *$325–$375; MAP, picnic lunches ($15–$25). AE, MC, V.*
Restrictions: *No smoking in public areas, no pets.*

The Whale Watch Inn by the Sea

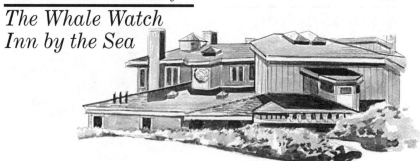

T he Whale Watch isn't really a bed-and-breakfast," says manager Joanna Wuelfing, "it's an illusion." Indeed, everything about this inn—from its location high on a cliff overlooking the Pacific to the attentive and efficient service and the quiet and airy rooms with their fresh flowers and dramatic ocean views—is designed to promote a sense of isolation in which guests can create their own realities.

Started in the mid-'70s, when original owners Irene and Enoch Stewart added a guest house to the original building to accommodate their frequent visitors, the Whale Watch has since added three more buildings, for a total of five. The luxurious modern rooms are decorated in light colors and feature high, angled, skylighted ceilings. Individualized furniture gives each room a different feeling, from Victorian to Asian. All rooms have a fireplace and a private deck, with most featuring an individual or two-person whirlpool bath. In some, large wall mirrors give one the impression of being surrounded by the ocean vistas; each has been carefully designed to preserve the sense of isolation. Four condo-like suites in the Sea Bounty building, equipped with full kitchens, are designed for longer stays.

After a delicious full breakfast served in their rooms, guests may brave the steep stairway down to the beach to explore tidal pools or watch wet-suited abalone fishermen heading out to sea in rubber boats. Other paths lead visitors on short strolls along the cliffs, through cypress groves and well-tended flower gardens. The Whale Watch building contains a large, comfortable common area with a sweeping view of the ocean and the annual migration of gray whales along the coast. The nearby town of Gualala has its share of restaurants and tourist attractions, and recreational facilities are within easy reach, but the Whale Watch seems designed less for activity than for relaxation, contemplation, and above all, privacy.

Address: *35100 Hwy. 1, Gualala, CA 95445, tel. 707/884–3667 or 800/942–5342.*
Accommodations: *11 double rooms with baths, 7 suites, 4 with full kitchens.*
Amenities: *Fireplace, whirlpool bath, icemaker in most rooms; private beach access.*
Rates: *$170–$255; full breakfast in room. AE, MC, V.*
Restrictions: *No smoking indoors, no pets; 2-night minimum on weekends, 3-night minimum on holiday weekends.*

Carter House

A deep-brown four-story Victorian, Carter House dominates Eureka's increasingly upscale Victorian Old Town. Though it may look old, Carter House is anything but. The creation of local builder turned innkeeper Mark Carter, the bed-and-breakfast was built in 1982 following a floor plan for a San Francisco mansion. Inside, the inn is as bright and airy as the exterior is dark and brooding. The inn doubles as a gallery for local artists.

The guest rooms on the top floor have the best views, while those on the basement level offer more privacy. The furnishings are simple, mostly antiques, with one dresser dating from the 18th century. There are beds with carved headboards, Victorian settees, and dormer windows with mountain views. Decorations include contemporary art and fresh flowers.

Breakfast is a four-course meal featuring local seafood, fruits, vegetables, and herbs.

Address: *1033 3rd St., Eureka, CA 95501, tel. and fax 707/445-1390.*
Accommodations: *3 double rooms with baths, 2 suites.*
Amenities: *Phone in rooms, fireplace and Jacuzzi in 1 suite, restaurant at adjacent Hotel Carter.*
Rates: *$125–$295; full breakfast, afternoon and evening refreshments. AE, D, DC, MC, V.*
Restrictions: *Smoking in parlors only, no pets.*

"An Elegant Victorian Mansion"

The 1888 Stick-style Eastlake "An Elegant Victorian Mansion" stands on a quiet street several blocks from downtown Eureka. Hosts Doug and Lily Vieyra, who welcome guests into their home with bright, warm smiles, are likely to be wearing turn-of-the-century costumes. Doug may invite you for a spin in one of his antique Fords, or start a croquet match on a lawn surrounded by flowers popular in Victorian-era gardens.

The four rooms upstairs are comfortably furnished with antiques; the Senator, for example, contains a bedroom set that Lily used as a child in her native Belgium. Common areas include an enormous double parlor furnished with family heirlooms from Belgium, a games room–library, and a family room with a TV with VCR and a stereo.

Lily, whose cooking has gained an excellent reputation locally, serves a breakfast that features French specialties in the formal dining room.

Address: *1406 C St., Eureka, CA 95501, tel. 707/444-3144 or 707/442-5594.*
Accommodations: *1 double room with bath, 2 doubles with detached private baths, 1 double with shared bath.*
Amenities: *Robes in rooms, fireplace in breakfast and living rooms, Swedish massage ($55 per hour), Finnish sauna, laundry service, bicycles.*
Rates: *$90–$125; full breakfast, afternoon ice-cream sodas. MC, V.*
Restrictions: *No smoking, no pets.*

Grey Whale Inn

From the outside, the boxy redwood Grey Whale Inn only hints at what it used to be: the Redwood Coast Hospital, in the heart of Fort Bragg's commercial district.

The rooms range from small to enormous; the largest contains enough space for two queen-size beds, a sitting area, and a minikitchen. A former delivery room still has the sink in which newborns were bathed. Large windows on all sides let in plenty of light and open out onto some stunning Pacific vistas. Rooms facing Main Street can be noisy early mornings.

Innkeepers Colette and John Bailey continue to spruce up the Grey Whale, which they opened in 1978. The freshly decorated rooms are definitely of the '90s, with soft, light colors, extensive redwood paneling, and bright, flowered quilts. The larger of the two penthouse rooms has a spacious outdoor deck and a big modern bathroom with a whirlpool tub; the other has a smaller deck and bathroom but a splendid ocean view.

Address: *615 N. Main St., Fort Bragg, CA 95437, tel. 707/964–0640 or 800/382–7244, fax 707/964–4408.*
Accommodations: *14 double rooms with baths.*
Amenities: *Phone in rooms, cable TV and kitchenette in some rooms, fireplace in 3 rooms.*
Rates: *$80–$160; full breakfast. AE, D, MC, V.*
Restrictions: *No smoking indoors, no pets; 2-night minimum on weekends, 3-night minimum on holidays.*

The Headlands Inn

Although the Headlands Inn offers the best ocean views in town, the hospitality of new owners David and Sharon Hyman is every bit as big a lure. Their three-story inn is an intriguing blend of New England saltbox with traditional California bay windows. "What we've done is lighten and brighten the inn since acquiring it," says David. They've also added feather mattresses and wood-burning stoves to each room.

The hosts greet their guests in a cheerful parlor furnished with antiques that include an Australian square piano from the 1860s. Two bedrooms open onto a comfortable parlor that's reserved for guests. Two rooms set into the third-floor gables have dormer windows; their bathrooms, though private, open onto a small parlor-landing. There's also a cottage (at one time it was a cookie bakery) behind the main house; it comes with a cannonball four-poster bed and a small refrigerator. The lavish breakfasts might include Florentine ham rolls, basil-seasoned baked eggs, or fruit- and mushroom-filled crepes.

Address: *Howard and Albion Sts., Box 132, Mendocino, CA 95460, tel. 707/937–4431.*
Accommodations: *5 double rooms with baths.*
Amenities: *Guest refrigerator.*
Rates: *$110–$180; full breakfast in room, afternoon refreshments. No credit cards.*
Restrictions: *No smoking indoors, no pets; 2-night minimum on weekends, 3- or 4-night minimum on holidays.*

Rachel's Inn

Although Rachel's Inn stands right on the highway, it's surrounded by more than 80 acres of parkland where you frequently see deer grazing. Rachel Binah greets her guests with an invitation to take a 20-minute stroll to the bluffs above the Pacific. "That way you'll know why I'm passionate about saving this coast from off-shore oil development," she says.

The inn consists of two buildings: a renovated 1860s farmhouse, the Main House, and the new Barn. The Main House has bedrooms on both floors and a guest parlor on the landing between. The Barn has two bedrooms and a parlor downstairs and two very bright suites upstairs. The furnishings throughout are simple—white wicker, French-country, contemporary, and a few antiques—with sunlight flowing in through the many large windows. A caterer by profession, Rachel serves a hearty full breakfast.

Address: *Hwy. 1 (2 mi south of Mendocino at Little River), Box 134, Mendocino, CA 95460, tel. 707/937–0088.*
Accommodations: *2 triple rooms, 5 double rooms with baths, 2 suites.*
Amenities: *Fireplace in 6 rooms, wet bar and refrigerator in suites; beach access.*
Rates: *$96–$180; full breakfast. No credit cards.*
Restrictions: *No pets; 2-night minimum on weekends, 3- or 4-night minimum on holidays.*

Scotia Inn

The Scotia Inn provides an inside look at the world's largest redwood-lumber mill operation. The hotel dates from 1923, when it replaced an earlier structure that had served stagecoach travelers to the Pacific Lumber Company. The inn still provides lodging for people who do business with the company, as well as for visitors who want to find out about the business side of the redwoods.

Although the inn (like the town) is owned by the Pacific Lumber Company, Gerald Carley took over the management of the hotel in 1985. The rooms are fairly Spartan (though the furnishings include carved and canopied beds and art-deco sofas). However, the exceptionally grand dining room and lobby demonstrate how truly beautiful polished redwood paneling, flooring, and woodwork can be. (Guest rooms on the second floor are reached via a gleaming redwood staircase.) The dining room is particularly pleasant, its tables set alongside closely spaced double-hung windows, with huge plants everywhere. Each month, Sunday specials focus on a different national cuisine.

Address: *Main and Mill Sts., Box 248, Scotia, CA 95565, tel. 707/764–5683.*
Accommodations: *10 double rooms with baths, 1 suite.*
Amenities: *Restaurant with banquet facilities, lounge.*
Rates: *$55–$150; Continental breakfast. MC, V.*
Restrictions: *Smoking in downstairs bar only, no pets.*

The Shaw House Inn

Built in 1854 by the founder of the Victorian town of Ferndale, the Shaw House is a spectacular gabled Carpenter Gothic inn listed in the National Register of Historic Places. A half-decade ago, Norma and Ken Bessingpas brought it back to life with their own antiques and a careful eye for old details, such as the original paint they've restored in some rooms and the gazebo in the garden.

Seth Shaw, a justice of the peace, performs small weddings in the parlor, which features an original marble-and-gilt fireplace from Gump's; the upstairs honeymoon suite, with its high coffered ceiling and private deck, is the perfect romantic retreat. The other five guest rooms, library, and parlor are filled with fresh flowers. Shaw House is rich in Victorian details, such as the flowered paper and vintage dresses adorning the walls. Gold-plated plumbing, claw-foot tubs in five of the bathrooms, and guest robes and slippers also help set an elegant but relaxing tone.

Address: *703 Main St., Box 1125, Ferndale, CA 95536, tel. 707/786–9958.*
Accommodations: *5 double rooms with baths, 1 suite.*
Amenities: *Fireplace in library and parlor, guest phone; croquet and bicycles available.*
Rates: *$75–$125; full breakfast. MC, V.*
Restrictions: *No smoking indoors; 2-night minimum on some holiday weekends.*

The Stanford Inn by the Sea

Innkeepers Joan and Jeff Stanford have presented their guests with only one problem: keeping up with everything that's going on at the Stanford Inn by the Sea. In addition to running the inn itself, they raise llamas and black swans; operate Big River Nurseries, a California-certified organic garden; rent canoes to visitors who want to explore the nearby Big River estuary; and provide mountain and road bikes for tours of the area's scenic biking trails. A spacious indoor swimming pool completes the recreational package.

The comfortable paneled rooms have decks with ocean views, traditional furnishings with four-poster or sleigh beds, fireplaces or wood stoves, and an appealing selection of paintings by local artists. The tourist attractions of Mendocino are only a short walk away.

Address: *Coast Hwy. and Comptche-Ukiah Rd., Box 487, Mendocino, CA 95460, tel. 707/937–5615 or 800/331–8884.*
Accommodations: *23 double rooms with baths, 3 suites.*
Amenities: *Fireplace, refrigerator, phone, TV with VCR, CD player in rooms, indoor swimming pool; canoes and bicycles available.*
Rates: *$160–$230; Continental breakfast. AE, D, DC, MC, V.*
Restrictions: *No smoking indoors; 2-night minimum on weekends, 3-night minimum on holidays.*

Sacramento and the Central Valley

Sacramento and the Central Valley
Including the Sierra Foothills

Sacramento is rarely the first city that leaps to mind when California is mentioned. So it's reasonable to ask why this pleasant if self-effacing metropolis, about 90 miles inland from San Francisco, is the capital of one of the largest and showiest states in the land.

The answer is obvious to anyone familiar with California history: The saga of the state's earliest days is very much the story of Sacramento. In 1848, gold was discovered in the foothills of Coloma, just 30 miles away. Though little more than a modest settlement of farmers and fur trappers then, Sacramento quickly became the jumping-off spot for argonauts seeking their fortune in the nearby hills and a bustling supply center.

As the Gold Rush boomed, Sacramento bloomed. After statehood in 1850, Sacramento survived a lively competition— in which the seat of government was moved six times—to become the state capital in 1853. A logical choice because of its (then) central location and proximity to the state's vast river system, Sacramento saw several communication and transportation firsts. The first transcontinental telegraph message was sent from here in 1861. It was the western end of the Pony Express. The deal that created the first continental railroad was forged in Sacramento, which is where the Big Four train moguls put the first station.

This history is worth noting because, aside from rich farmland and an admirable collection of rivers and lakes, history is largely what Sacramento and the tree-lined towns of the vast central valley have to offer these days. Its rip-roaring past is also what makes the area's relative anonymity and laid-back pace so seductive. If Sacramento, an artless metropolitan sprawl with nearly 1.5 million people—and almost as many cars—is a big city now, under its patina of sophistication it remains a small town. People ride bicycles on its busiest streets. Huge trees shade its many parks. Even the big-time business of running this enormous state seems a little slower, a little less impenetrable than it might were it based in Los Angeles, say, or San Francisco.

A short drive to the north or south are the tomato and asparagus farms and the thousands of acres of fruit and nut orchards that have long been the backbone of central California's economy. (This is, after all, some of the richest farmland in the world.) And though the classic valley towns, like Lodi, Yuba City, and Chico are not obvious destinations for visitors, they can surprise and delight in subtle ways. Most have a street or two of handsome Victorian houses, nicely restored. This is also superb motoring country if you enjoy a cruise past tranquil acres of cherry trees, grape vines, and almond groves. Best of all, you don't just have to look. Farmer's markets are everywhere, and their offerings, sensibly priced, are inevitably the freshest, sweetest, and juiciest imaginable.

Places to Go, Sights to See

Arco Arena (1 Sports Parkway, Sacramento, tel. 916/928–8499), a $40 million state-of-the-art multipurpose complex, is home to the Kings, Sacramento's NBA franchise, and regularly hosts music, entertainment, and sports events.

Bidwell Mansion (525 The Esplanade, Chico, tel. 916/895–6144) was built in 1865 by Chico's founder, General John Bidwell, who was on the first wagon train to cross the mountains. Restored and fully furnished in grand Victorian style, it's open for tours daily.

California State Capitol (10th and L Sts., Sacramento, tel. 916/324–0333) was completely gutted in 1976 and rebuilt to look as it did at the turn of the century. The enormous white, gold-domed building in downtown Sacramento houses the governor's offices, both divisions of the California State Legislature, and a museum, with re-creations of early 20th-century government offices. The Senate chamber, where visitors can watch debates from the gallery, is particularly flamboyant, with gilded columns, massive crystal chandeliers, and a magnificent crenelated ceiling.

California State Fair. Held each August in Sacramento, this enormous fair covers 350 acres and offers dancing horses, nightly fireworks, and livestock exhibitions, including a national pot belly pig show.

California State Railroad Museum/Central Pacific Railroad Station (2nd and I Sts., Sacramento, tel. 916/448–4466) is widely regarded as the finest interpretive railroad museum in the United States. It has a collection of more than two dozen vintage engines and cars, which visitors can walk through and inspect. The Sonoma, a late-19th-century high-tech masterpiece, is a standout restoration of an American Standard locomotive. The Gold Coast private car, with its marble fireplace and swagged curtains, offers a glimpse of how passengers traveled in high style, circa 1895.

Crocker Art Museum (216 O St., Sacramento, tel. 916/264–5423) houses an appealing, if uneven, collection of European and American art in a richly restored Italianate Victorian mansion. The collection is particularly strong in Old Master prints and drawings and in California paintings from the late 19th century and the post-1945 period.

Lake Oroville (tel. 916/533–2542) is situated behind 770-foot-high Oroville Dam, the highest earth-filled dam in the United States. With 167 miles of shoreline, the lake is one of the biggest (and least used) in the state. Boating, swimming, fishing, and waterskiing, all from Bidwell Canyon Marina, are among the attractions here.

Leland Stanford Mansion (802 N St., Sacramento, tel. 916/324–0575), built in 1856 by the founder of Stanford University, is the oldest house in Sacramento and is currently being refurbished top to toe. Tours, which are offered on a limited basis, show what's involved in a major historical restoration.

Governor's Mansion of California (1526 H St., Sacramento, tel. 916/323–3047), an opulent white Victorian (and one of the first homes in California to have indoor plumbing), was home to the state's governors and their families until 1966, when Ronald Reagan requested a newer residence. The eclectic furnishings include a handsome four-poster bed that was extended to 7 feet to accommodate Governor Earl Warren's height, and an old-fashioned claw-foot bathtub with red fingernail polish on its toenails.

Micke Grove. This handsome, 65-acre grove of oaks trees, located between Stockton and Lodi, is a fine place for picnics, baseball, swimming, and other outdoor activities. The exquisitely maintained two-acre Japanese Garden is graced by waterfalls, arched bridges, and artfully arranged plants and stonework. In addition, the zoo has a strong collection of cats, birds, California sea lions, and primates, including the endangered golden lion tamarin, a rare little monkey from Brazil. The nearby *San Joaquin Historical Society and Museum* (11793 Micke Grove Rd., Lodi, tel. 209/463–4119), which specializes in agricultural history, features a tractor from 1917, a one-room schoolhouse from 1866, and the largest collection of hand- and foot-powered tools in the West (4,000 in all).

Old Sacramento. Once a derelict slum, this historic area of Sacramento was transformed in the mid-1960s into a living museum of the gold-rush era, complete with cobbled streets, raised wooden sidewalks, and gaslights. Its frontier-style buildings house more than 100 restaurants, theaters, and shops, as well as the fine *Sacramento History Museum* (101 I St., tel. 916/264–7057) and the *Towe Ford Museum* (2200 Front St., tel. 916/442–6802), with a collection of over 150 vintage Fords.

Sutter's Fort (2701 L St., Sacramento, tel. 916/445–4422), built in 1839, provided free shelter and supplies for pioneers, including surviving members of the ill-fated Donner Party in 1846.

Restaurants

Sacramento's best restaurants are a pleasing blend of sophistication and health consciousness. Two of the finest serve adventurous northern Italian food: **Capitol Grill** (tel. 916/736–0744) and **Biba** (tel. 916/455–BIBA), the latter owned by cookbook author Biba Caggiano. The seafood, tortellini, and cheesecake are the draws at popular **Harlow's** (tel. 916/441–4693), where the California-Italian dishes are as lively as the crowd. **Chanterelle** (tel. 916/442–0451), a California French restaurant, is a popular place for catching state legislators tucking into duckling with pear schnapps or quail with truffle sauce. **California Fats** (tel. 916/441–7966) in Old Town serves up big portions of seafood tacos, herb roasted chicken, and drunk steak. For a quick and inexpensive lunch or dinner (or weekend breakfast), drop by Mexican **Ernesto's** (tel. 916/441–5850), whose specialties include fajitas and margaritas. If touring Sacramento leaves you sagging, drop in for a caffeine pick-me-up at one of the eight **Java City** (tel. 641–1330) locations in town. **Zephyrs Restaurant** (tel. 916/895–1328), in Chico, offers a selection of surprisingly well-prepared contemporary entrées.

Tourist Information

Greater Chico Chamber of Commerce (500 Main St., Chico, CA 95927, tel. 916/891–5556); **Lodi District Chamber of Commerce** (1330 S. Ham La., Lodi, CA 95241, tel. 209/367–7840); **Old Sacramento Visitor Information Center** (1104 Front St., Old Sacramento, CA 95814, tel. 916/442–7644); **Stockton and San Joaquin County Convention and Visitors Bureau** (46 W. Fremont St., Stockton, CA 95202, tel. 209/943–1987).

Reservation Services

B&B International (Box 282910, San Francisco, CA 94128, tel. 415/696–1690 or 800/872–4500, fax 415/696–1699); **Eye Openers B&B Reservations** (Box 694, Altadena, CA 91003, tel. 213/684–4428 or 818/797–2055, fax 818/798–3640).

Abigail's

There's no Abigail, but Susanne Ventura, who owns this light-filled 1912 Colonial Revival house with her husband, Ken, is as warm and welcoming as a favorite aunt. She leaves her guests homemade cookies on a carved wooden sideboard at night, and the dining-room breakfast table is set with sterling silver flatware and draped with a lacy cloth.

Susanne first visited Abigail's as a paying guest in 1985. A year later, she quit her job with an insurance company and bought the place, situated on a tree-lined street in what was once one of Sacramento's toniest neighborhoods. By the 1960s, many of the area's big, boxy mansions had become rundown; Abigail's, renovated in the early 1980s, was one of the first gentrified houses in this now eclectic community, a few blocks from corner coffee houses, antiques shops, and art galleries.

Abigail's five rooms, named for Susanne's and Ken's relatives, include Margaret, with a king-size verdigris bed with an ever-changing canopy: winter white, springtime roses, hearts and flowers for Valentine's Day. Keeping a watchful eye over the proceedings is Ken's Aunt Margaret, depicted in all her flapperish glory in a large photograph on the wall. Uncle Albert boasts Victorian wallpaper and a queen-size bed. Breezy Aunt Rose is feminine and flowered with yellow wallpaper and a bouquet of flowers hanging from the headboard of the queen-size brass bed.

Abigail's has two big welcoming parlors. The more formal has two sofas and a wingback chair facing a cheery fireplace and a big '20s Art-Deco light fixture from the Alhambra, a much-missed Sacramento movie palace. The sitting room across the hall reflects Susanne's interest in the arts; it contains an upright piano and a bulletin board listing the latest gallery openings and who's playing at the concert hall.

A fine cook whose recipes have been published widely and won prizes, Susanne continues to innovate in the kitchen. Lately, she's been developing delicious but healthy recipes that are low in fat, sugar, and cholesterol.

Address: *2120 G St., Sacramento, CA 95816, tel. 916/441–5007 or 800/858–1568, fax 916/441–0621.*
Accommodations: *5 double rooms with baths.*
Amenities: *Air-conditioning, robes, radio, and phone in rooms, Jacuzzi in 1 room, TV available, games in living room; garden hot tub, gift baskets available for special occasions, off-street parking.*
Rates: *$95–$155; full breakfast, afternoon refreshments, evening snacks. AE, D, DC, MC, V.*
Restrictions: *No smoking, no pets; 2-night minimum some weekends, 3-night minimum some holiday weekends.*

Amber House

Michael Richardson admits it isn't always easy to run a bed-and-breakfast inn. "It's like having your mother-in-law for Christmas dinner every day of the year," he says. Still, Michael and his wife, Jane Ramey, former southern California residents, have no regrets about their decision to move to Sacramento in 1986 to become proprietors of Amber House, a meticulously restored Craftsman home from 1905. Jane, a former merchandise manager for Marriott hotels, redecorated the original house's five guest rooms, haunting estate sales for antiques and fashioning each room around a poet. Michael, formerly in real estate, set about buying and restoring the 1913 Mediterranean-style house next door, which now hosts an enormous sitting room with a fireplace and four guest rooms, all under the spell of French Impressionist color schemes.

Though situated on a boring block not far from the State Capitol, Amber House is atmospheric, with lots of nooks and crannies. The main sitting room, with its hardwood floor and wood-beamed ceiling, has plenty of comfortable chairs. In the late afternoons, guests snack here on cookies, coffee, and mineral water, or retreat to the smaller, front sitting room, with glass-fronted bookshelves and a window seat. Classical music wafts through all the public rooms.

The nine guest rooms are floral and romantic. They range from snug (Chaucer) to gloriously spacious (Renoir). The latter has leaded glass windows, a king-size bed, a sofa, and a bathtub built for two. The sunny yellow Van Gogh is arguably the most glamorous; it's dominated by a sybaritic greenhouse bathroom with a corner Jacuzzi and white wicker chaise longue.

Breakfast is served at a large wood table in the dining room or at little tables in each guest room. Since guests often stay more than one night, it's never the same two days in a row. Quiche and potatoes with bell peppers is an Amber House specialty, as are waffles and strawberries. As a prelude to the meal, Michael sets early morning coffee or tea on a tiny table outside each room.

Address: *1315 22nd St., Sacramento, CA 95816, tel. 916/444–8085 or 800/755–6526, fax 916/447–1548.*
Accommodations: *9 double rooms with baths.*
Amenities: *Air-conditioning, cassette player and clock radio in rooms, phone, cable TV with VCR, robes in 6 rooms, Jacuzzis in 5 rooms; bicycles.*
Rates: *$85–$195; full breakfast, afternoon refreshments. AE, DC, D, MC, V.*
Restrictions: *No smoking indoors, no pets.*

Hartley House

Boulevard Park is one of Sacramento's less heralded historic treasures. Not far from the State Capitol, the area boasts several blocks of magnificent turn-of-the-century houses. The six little parks in the middle of 21st and 22nd streets form the district's centerpiece; each is a large, grassy, tree-shaded oval. In the early 1900s, the streets formed a genteel race course; residents in the large houses looked on and cheered as horses ran around the greens.

The original owners of Hartley House, a rambling white 1906 Colonial Revival home, had one of the best views. It's easy to imagine them seated on the expansive front porch, holding cool drinks and watching the races. Guests still sit on the porch, often on the big porch swing, and sip fresh lemonade delivered by innkeeper Randy Hartley.

A fourth-generation Sacramentan, Randy purchased this one-time boarding house in 1986 and brought new life into it. He restored the hardwood floors and stained-glass windows in the public rooms to their former glory and outfitted the five guest rooms with a cozy, chintz-free mix of antiques and amenities that evoke the crisp comforts of an Edwardian townhouse.

Brighton, set in what was once the sun porch, is arguably the prettiest and certainly the lightest guest room, with three walls of windows, a white wrought-iron bed, ceiling fan, and small TV. Dover flaunts the house's original bathroom fixtures, including a ball-footed tub.

Randy runs a comfortable, down-to-earth inn. The enormous white kitchen, the house's only blatantly 1990s touch, is outfitted with tall stools, where visitors nibble home-made cookies and chat with Randy until he shoos them out. Breakfast—omelets, blintzes, Belgian waffles—is served in the spacious dining room or, in good weather, in the courtyard.

Games are piled high on the sitting room shelves and the chess board is always set up on the polished-wood coffee table. But the sitting room is mainly a relaxing place to peruse a good book or the *Sacramento Bee.*

Address: *700 22nd St., Sacramento, CA 95816, tel. 916/447–7829 or 800/831–5806, fax 916/447–1820.*
Accommodations: *5 double rooms with baths.*
Amenities: *Air-conditioning, cable TV, clock radio, robes, phone in rooms; patio.*
Rates: *$95–$135; full breakfast, after-noon refreshments. AE, D, DC, MC, V.*
Restrictions: *No smoking indoors, no pets.*

Johnson's Country Inn

Countryish Chico, where agriculture is the main industry, would seem an unlikely spot to find a romantic Victorian bed-and-breakfast inn. But here is Johnson's, a big, bright-pink farmhouse with wraparound veranda situated amid ten acres of almond trees. Although a mere two miles from downtown Chico and the city's state university campus, the inn retains a feeling of quiet country elegance. There's even a lacy white gazebo tucked in among the trees, and the scent of roses fills the air.

Johnson's is the creation of David and Joan Johnson, incurable romantics who escaped the urban tangle of Los Angeles in 1992 for a quiet life in the country. They built the inn from the ground up using ideas from San Francisco's famed "painted ladies" and Petaluma's Victorians. While common rooms—parlor, dining room, sunny garden room—display the Victorian theme, guest rooms reflect the lives and interests of the innkeepers.

Two of the most interesting rooms contain artifacts of David's family history. The Jarrett, a corner room in the front of the house, is dedicated to the work and art of David's uncle, prominent 1930s illustrator Charles Dixie Jarrett. An art deco–style bed with red sheets and shiny crimson spread dominates the room. Original drawings and poster art by Charles Jarrett grace the walls. Across the hall, the Harrison is dedicated to President Benjamin Harrison, who was David's great-great-grandfather. An 1860s Eastlake bed captures immediate attention in this room, which has black-and-pink paisley wallpaper and interesting mementos of the 23rd U.S. president. Icart, done in burgundy and black, reflects the art noveau period; a big double shower in the bathroom makes this room wheelchair-accessible.

Guests awake to a bedroom cup of coffee. As one might expect in farm country, breakfast, served in a room overlooking the almond grove, is full—and then some. A typical menu includes fruit salad, a selection of scones and muffins, and zucchini quiche accompanied by Canadian bacon.

Address: *3935 Morehead Ave., Chico, CA 95928, tel. and fax 916/345-7829.*
Accommodations: *4 double rooms with baths.*
Amenities: *Air-conditioning, robes, Jacuzzi and fireplace in 1 room, fireplace in parlor, guest phone; horseshoes, lawn games.*
Rates: *$70–$125; full breakfast, afternoon refreshments, after-dinner dessert. No credit cards.*
Restrictions: *No smoking, no pets; 2-night minimum on holiday weekends and for graduation.*

Wine & Roses Country Inn

I n her high-necked white lace blouse, Kris Cromwell, the personable owner of Wine & Roses Country Inn, looks as though she stepped straight out of *Victoria* magazine. It's no surprise, then, that her inn on three acres of rich farmland in Lodi, a grape-growing, wine-making community a half-hour south of Sacramento, is unabashedly romantic. The curtains are of white lace, a fire crackles in the sitting room, and fresh, fragrant flowers are everywhere. Ribbons and bows are ubiquitous, too.

Kris's Victorian touches nicely complement this rambling two-story country house, built in 1903. The sitting room is large and airy, with two walls of windows, rose-colored carpeting, and cushiony sofas. A treadle sewing machine stands in a corner, and family photographs grace the mantel.

Wine & Roses, which opened in 1988, is very much a family affair. Kris, a former real estate agent, runs the place with her son, Del Smith, and his wife, Sherri, whom he met when she was hired as the inn's chef. Sherri, now a mother of two and the executive chef, supervises the inn's food service.

Comfort, coziness, and strong colors seem to have been Kris's priorities while decorating the 10 guest rooms. Eidelweiss, which overlooks the garden, is typical, with deep green walls, pale mauve carpeting, and a green and white floral print duvet on the big brass bed. The bathroom has a claw-foot tub with a shower. A clock radio awakens you if the chickens don't. Brides love the attic suite with its cathedral ceilings, French doors, rooftop deck, and sitting room furnished with two velvet wingback chairs.

Breakfast, Sunday brunch, lunch (Tues.–Fri.), and dinner (Wed.–Sat.) are served in the mauve dining room, overlooking the rosebushes. On warm days and nights, guests can eat outside on big round tables. Or you can sip coffee or wine in the sitting room with Kris, who likes to chat with her guests.

Address: *2505 West Turner Rd., Lodi, CA 95242, tel. 209/334–6988, fax 209/334–6570.*
Accommodations: *9 double rooms with baths, 1 suite.*
Amenities: *Air-conditioning, TV, phone, clock radio in rooms; restaurant, croquet, badminton, horseshoes, free use of health club off-site.*
Rates: *$99 weekdays, $110 weekends, suite $145; full breakfast, afternoon and evening refreshments. AE, MC, V.*
Restrictions: *No smoking, no pets.*

Harkey House

This classic Stick-style Victorian was built in 1864 by Sheriff William Harkey, who wanted to live near where he worked, the Sutter County courthouse in Yuba City. The big cream-colored house with blue-and-red trim is still a temporary home to many with business at the courthouse.

Harkey House rooms boast an eclectic clutter of Victoriana: quilts, ruffles, Oriental rugs, floral wreaths, brass beds—even an antique kimono mounted on the wall in the stylish Empress Room. Three upstairs rooms, including a suite, are reached via a steep staircase. There are two parlors, one containing an antique piano rumored to have come around the Horn. Breakfast is served in the sunny solarium, which innkeeper Bob Jones

says was originally a screened-in porch. Bob and his wife, Lee, have lived in the area for more than 30 years and readily provide information on what to see and do in their small city.

Address: *212 C St., Yuba City, CA 95991, tel. 916/674–1942.*
Accommodations: *3 double rooms with baths, 1 suite.*
Amenities: *Air-conditioning, robes, cable TV, phone, clock radio in rooms, fireplace in 2 rooms; outdoor hot tub.*
Rates: *$75–$100; Continental breakfast, afternoon refreshments. AE, MC, V.*
Restrictions: *No smoking indoors, no pets.*

Lake Oroville Bed & Breakfast

This big, yellow Victorian farmhouse, perched on a knoll east of Lake Oroville, is the perfect place for those seeking solitude. Ron and Cheryl Damberger's inn is located about 15 miles east of the historic gold-rush town of Oroville; the last mile and a half is a graded gravel road through a forest of pine and oak trees. Forty of the thousands of acres of surrounding woodland belong to the inn.

Accommodations include large, airy guest rooms that have private entrances from a broad, covered veranda. The decor differs from room to room, but most have botanical accents and either sylvan or lake views. On a clear day you can see across the Central Valley all the way to the Coast Range.

Three common rooms are available for guests: a parlor with sweeping view, where breakfast is served; the small sun room, which has the best sunset view; and the billiard room, where Ron displays his collection of baseball cards.

Address: *240 Sunday Dr., Berry Creek, CA 95916, tel. 916/589–0700 or 800/455–5253.*
Accommodations: *6 double rooms with baths.*
Amenities: *Phone, clock radio in rooms, whirlpool tub in 5 rooms, cable TV in parlor, stocked guest refrigerator, billiard room; outdoor barbeque, hiking trails.*
Rates: *$65–$110; full breakfast, afternoon refreshments. AE, D, MC, V.*
Restrictions: *No smoking indoors, no pets; 2-night minimum on holiday weekends.*

The Sterling Hotel

I t's a nice surprise to find that this classic California Victorian house, with turrets, bay windows, and a graceful, sloping lawn, is actually a small hotel. The California-French offerings of its restaurant, Chanterelle, regularly attract state senators and other politicos from the nearby State Capitol building.

The Sterling Hotel, which opened in 1988, has the size and scale of a bed-and-breakfast without the intimacy— or the complimentary meals. Sparsely furnished rooms are spacious and often amusingly shaped, with a few pieces of reproduction Queen Anne and Empire furnishings, pale pink carpets, potted palms, and rich, raspberry-color bed-spreads. Bathrooms are a feast of pale pink marble, with ample tubs, whirl-pool baths, and pedestal sinks. The

hotel has an attractive lobby with abundant marble, Oriental rugs, and comfortable chairs, but it's sometimes rented out to groups and not available to guests.

Address: *1300 H St., Sacramento, CA 95814, tel. 916/448–1300 or 800/365–7660, fax 916/448–8066.*
Accommodations: *12 double rooms with baths.*
Amenities: *Whirlpool bath, air-condi-tioning, cable TV, phone, clock radio in rooms, ornamental fireplace in 3 rooms, laundry service, room service, restaurant, meeting facilities.*
Rates: *$95–$225. AE, DC, MC, V.*
Restrictions: *No smoking, no pets.*

Victorian Manor

A sweet little time-warp town 14 miles north of Sacramento, Newcastle had its heyday at the turn of the century, when Newcas-tle pears were highly prized in Chicago and New York. These days the town's primary attractions are its sleepy pace, tree-shaded square, and a fine collec-tion of rambling Victorian homes, including Victorian Manor, a proud, white two-story house with ginger-bread trim and a garden filled with camellias.

Ed and Cordy Sander, who bought the house in 1984, have tried hard to infuse it with the furnishings, styles, and even sounds of a bygone era. The sit-ting room features a 90-year-old Edi-phone, a scratchy precursor of the phonograph, that Ed cranks up for vis-itors. And Cordy spent hours poring

over history books before making the ruffled pillow shams, fringed lamp shades, and quilts that fill the four carefully furnished guest rooms. (Each has an elaborately carved antique bed.) She also created a vast collection of turn-of-the-century costumes for guests who want to play dress up and have their pictures taken.

Address: *482 Main St., Newcastle, CA 95658, tel. 916/663–3009.*
Accommodations: *1 double room with bath, 3 doubles share 2 baths.*
Amenities: *Air-conditioning; garden, gazebo, off-street parking.*
Rates: *$60–$65; Continental breakfast. AE, MC, V.*
Restrictions: *No smoking indoors, no pets.*

Gold Country

Gold Country
Along Highway 49

*The reason California is called the Golden State is found right
here, on a long, narrow expanse of land about 150 miles
inland from San Francisco, stretching from Mariposa in the
south to Sierra City in the north. The hills in these parts are
often the color of spun gold, but it was the riches hidden inside
that set off the biggest gold rush in history, endowed California
with its buoyant economy—and earned the state its 18-karat
nickname.*

*When gold was discovered on January 24, 1848, at John
Sutter's Sawmill in Coloma, this sleepy town on the banks of
the American River was overrun by frenzied prospectors. By
the next year, some 80,000 treasure seekers had poured in from
every direction to set up mining camps throughout the western
foothills of the Sierra Nevada mountains. Boomtowns rose up
on the sites of big strikes—and were abandoned as quickly
when the gold ran out.*

*Today the colorful towns along the aptly named Highway 49 (a
reference to the year that prospectors flooded the area) still
reflect much of the character of the gold-rush days, though
they are quite different from one another. Nevada City and
Sutter Creek, for example, have become trendy getaways for
city folk, while Columbia and Coloma have been carefully
restored, with wooden sidewalks, blacksmith shops, and horse-
drawn carriages evoking their heyday.*

*Another tradition has recently been revived here. The roots of
wine making in the region go back to the gold-rush days, but
the population decline after the closing of the mines, the
devastating phylloxera vine disease, and Prohibition all
caused the wineries to be abandoned over the years. In the past
couple of decades, however, more than two dozen wineries have
sprung up across these rolling Sierra foothills, producing
zinfandels and cabernets as robust as the region from which*

they hail. Although the Gold Country is becoming an increasingly popular destination for wine lovers, here—in contrast with commercialized Napa Valley—you're still likely to be greeted in the tasting rooms by the wine makers themselves.

The Gold Country is one of the few parts of California that hasn't had a population explosion in recent years. The locals like it that way. Up in the foothills of the Mother Lode, Jackson, with around 4,000 inhabitants, is considered big. And although visitors pour into these tiny townlets on hot summer weekends, this is still a splendid place for fleeing the crowds.

The Mother Lode is also a magnificent backdrop for motoring. Driving along Highway 49, you'll see gently rolling hills, sheep and cows, lazy streams—and just when you need some relief from the bucolic, up pops a gold-rush town, such as Drytown, Volcano, or Jackass Hill. Each is outfitted with old wooden buildings, a rustic spot for a picnic, and a pretty little creek. And if that's not enough, the names alone should keep you amused.

Places to Go, Sights to See

Amador County Museum (225 Church St., Jackson, tel. 209/223–6386) offers a glimpse of mining history with a large-scale reconstruction of the famous headframe-hoisting equipment, stamp mill, and wheels used during the 1920s at Jackson's Kennedy Mine, the largest gold mine from the turn of the century until it closed in 1942.

Apple Hill (Apple Hill Visitor Center, 4103 Carson Rd., Camino, tel. 916/644–7692). Orchards of apples, pears, peaches, cherries, plums, persimmons, and pumpkins thrive in the fertile Sierra foothills east of Placerville. Families flock here for events such as the month-long Apple Festival in October, the West Coast Cherry Pit Spitting Championship in June, and outdoor music at the orchards. There are also several good wineries in the vicinity.

Coloma. The gold rush, and all the fuss, started on January 24, 1848, in this unassuming town. *Marshall Gold Discovery State Historic Park* (Hwy. 49, tel. 916/622–3470) immortalizes the big event. The town also has a pleasing collection of reconstructed buildings, including an 1850s Chinese store.

Columbia State Park (off Hwy. 49, tel. 209/532–0150). Dozens of the Mother Lode's boomtowns are now ghost towns, but Columbia never became deserted. In

1945, the state of California turned this tiny hamlet into a historic state park where only horses, stagecoaches, and pedestrians are allowed on the unpaved streets. Bartenders and shopkeepers don Wild West attire. And visitors who tire of scouring Main Street's museums and candy stores can try panning for gold at the nearby creek. There's also an excellent nature trail, and the Fallon Theater puts on polished theatrical productions.

Daffodil Hill. In mid-March this 4-acre ranch just north of the tiny town of Volcano, near Jackson, becomes a vibrant display of color with more than 500,000 spring blooms, including, of course, daffodils.

Frog Jumping Jubilee. Held the third weekend in May at the Calaveras County fairgrounds just south of Angels Camp, this much-touted international competition inspired by Mark Twain's story "The Celebrated Jumping Frog of Calaveras County" allows visitors to "rent a frog."

Moaning Cavern (off Rte. 4, on Parrot's Ferry Rd., Vallecito, tel. 209/736–2708) is California's largest public cavern. In addition to taking a guided tour of the main chamber, adorned with minerals and prehistoric bones, visitors who don't mind descending by rope can explore deeper chambers.

Murphys. Known as the Queen of the Sierras, this picturesque gold-rush town has a tree-shaded Main Street lined with rustic wooden buildings. *Murphys Hotel* (457 Main St., tel. 209/728–3444) has a guest book signed by Mark Twain, Black Bart, and Ulysses S. Grant. Upstairs is a reconstruction of the room where Grant stayed in 1880. A few blocks away is *Mercer Caverns* (Sheepranch Rd., tel. 209/728–2101), a collection of unusual natural crystalline formations in wildly varied sizes and textures. Several nearby wineries are open to the public, including the beautiful new *Kautz Ironstone Vineyards* (Six Mile Rd., tel. 209/728–1251), where wines age in caverns cut 200 feet deep into the hillsides, *Stevenot Winery* (2690 San Domingo Rd., tel. 209/728–3436), and *Milliaire Winery* (276 Main St., tel. 209/728–1658).

Nevada City. This lovely gold-rush town ringed by pine-covered hills is a weekend mecca for city folk looking for R&R, including some top-notch window-shopping, dining, and entertainment. The entire downtown area has been registered as a National Historic Landmark. California's oldest theater, *The Nevada Theatre* (401 Broad St., tel. 916/265–6161), once hosted such illustrious patrons as Jack London and Samuel Clemens. *The National Hotel* (211 Broad St., tel. 916/265–4551) is the state's oldest continuously operating hotel. *Firehouse No. 1* (214 Main St., tel. 916/265–5468), often photographed for its Victorian bell tower and gingerbread trim, is now a museum devoted to the Indian and Chinese influence in the area.

Placerville. Nicknamed Hangtown during the gold rush for the punishment given to a gang of gold-thirsty criminals, Placerville is today the pleasant, bustling seat of El Dorado County. A few bargains can still be found in the antiques shops along narrow Main Street. The *El Dorado County Historical Museum* (100 Placerville Dr., tel. 916/626–2250) displays an elegant stagecoach, Indian artifacts, and a Pelton wheel turbine that was used to power a mine. At *Gold Bug Park* (about 1 mile north of downtown on Bedford Ave.) you can take a self-guided tour of a gold mine.

Sutter Creek. The Mother Lode's classiest little town, this is an ideal place to survey the wooden buildings, narrow streets, and rolling hills that make the Gold Country so appealing. Main Street and Hanford Street boast some of the area's most intriguing antiques and gift shops. The *Stoneridge Winery* (13862 Ridge Rd., tel. 209/223–1761) is also nearby.

Restaurants

In Nevada City, **Cirino's** (tel. 916/265–2246) is a favorite among locals for its unusual pizzas and other Italian specialties. Coloma's **Vineyard House** (tel. 916/622–2217) serves classic American fare, including chicken and dumplings and bread pudding, in several opulent dining rooms. Just east of Placerville on a quiet country road, **Zachary Jacques** (tel. 916/626–8045) offers hearty French-country cuisine. The **Imperial Hotel** in Amador City (tel. 209/267–9172) has a well-earned reputation for its elegant American-style food. But it's getting competition from **Ballads** (tel. 209/267–5403), its next-door neighbor. In nearby Sutter Creek, **Pelargonium** (tel. 209/267–5008) changes its specials, including a vegetarian entrée, nightly. **Teresa's** (tel. 209/223–1786) in Jackson has local color and good standard Italian fare. An impressive wine cellar and dishes featuring local produce are trademarks of the restaurant at the **City Hotel** (tel. 209/532–1479) in Columbia. In Sonora, **Alfredo's** (tel. 209/532–8332) is known for its authentic Mexican cuisine, while **Coyote Creek Café & Grill** (tel. 209/532–9115) serves everything from Spanish tapas to grilled steak.

Tourist Information

Amador County Chamber of Commerce (Box 596, Jackson, CA 95642, tel. 209/223–0350 or 800/649–4988); **Auburn Area Chamber of Commerce** (801 Lincoln Way, Auburn CA 95603, tel. 916/885–5616 or 800/427–6463); **Calaveras Lodging and Visitors Association** (Box 637, Angels Camp, CA 95222, tel. 209/736–0049 or 800/225–3764); **El Dorado County Chamber of Commerce** (542 Main St., Placerville, CA 95667, tel. 916/621–5885 or 800/457–6279); **Nevada County Chamber of Commerce** (248 Mill St., Grass Valley, CA 95945, tel. 916/273–4667 or 800/655–4667); **Tuolumne County Visitors Bureau** (55 W. Stockton Rd., Sonora, CA 95370, tel. 209/533–4420 or 800/446–1333).

Reservation Services

B&B International (Box 282910, San Francisco, CA 94128–2910, tel. 415/696–1690 or 800/872–4500, fax 415/696–1699); **Eye Openers B&B Reservations** (Box 694, Altadena, CA 91003, tel. 213/684–4428 or 818/797–2055, fax 818/798–3640); **Amador County Innkeepers Association** (tel. 209/296–7778 or 800/726–4667); **Gold Country Inns of Tuolumne County** (tel. 209/533–1845).

City Hotel

I n 1856, when Columbia was all
ablaze with gold fever, George Morgan built the City Hotel in the heart
of town. Intended as a lodging for gen-
tlemen, this two-story brick storefront
was refurbished by the state in 1975
and now welcomes all.

The City Hotel, located inside
Columbia State Historic Park, is part
of a living museum. The restoration
and furnishings accurately reflect the
gold-rush era, with only a nod to contemporary conveniences. Most furnishings predate 1875. The oldest is an
antique writing desk from the 1820s.

While 14-foot ceilings make all rooms
feel spacious, the best and largest are
those that open onto the parlor. The
two rooms across the front of the hotel
are the most desirable of these; they
have small balconies from which one
can watch the Wells Fargo stagecoach
pass by on the street below.

All rooms contain massive, carved
wooden beds, marble-topped dressers,
Oriental rugs, and Victorian-style floral wallpapers. Each room has a half-
bath equipped with a wicker basket of
"necessary items"—robe, disposable
slippers, towels, et cetera—for the
walk to the shower down the hall. A
central sitting parlor scattered with
Oriental rugs has a felt-topped poker
table, books, magazines, and games.

The hotel, which serves as a training
center for hospitality students at
nearby Columbia College, routinely
schedules Victorian-themed special
events. Most popular is the annual Victorian Christmas Pageant, a typical
holiday celebration of the 1860s, complete with costumed revelers.

The clubby restaurant at the City
Hotel has long been considered among
the best in the Gold Country. The prix-
fixe menu includes an array of classic
French and California selections. The
What Cheer Saloon next door may look
like a knock-off of a western movie set,
but as with everything else about
Columbia, it's an accurate reflection of
gold-rush era watering holes.

Address: *Main St., Columbia State
Historic Park, Box 1870, Columbia,
CA 95310, tel. 209/532–1479 or 800/
446–1333, ext. 1280, fax 209/532–7027.*
Accommodations: *10 double rooms
with half-baths share 2 showers.*
Amenities: *Air-conditioning, robes
and slippers in rooms, lobby phone,
restaurant, saloon, theater–dinner
packages; off-street parking.*
Rates: *$70–$90; expanded Continental
breakfast, afternoon refreshments.
AE, MC, V.*
Restrictions: *No smoking, no pets.*

The Coloma Country Inn

It was in Coloma that California's gold-rush fever first erupted in 1848 with the discovery of gold at Sutter's Sawmill. Among the few remaining structures from that period, the Coloma Country Inn, a pretty farmhouse with a wraparound porch and gray shiplap siding, sits behind a long, white-picket fence in the verdant, 300-acre Gold Discovery State Park.

Cindy and Alan Ehrgott first came to now-tranquil Coloma (population 250) in 1983 with the intention of expanding their Los Angeles–based adventure travel business but ended up becoming innkeepers. They still offer rafting trips and hot-air-balloon rides, the latter complete with a full champagne breakfast.

Coloma's history is represented by old photographs along the staircase on the inn's hand-stenciled walls, but the treasures in the house are not restricted to California's gold-rush era: Cindy has a fabulous collection of quilts from the 1880s to 1920s. Equally impressive is her collection of English and German blue-and-white delftware storage jars. An assortment of antique bric-a-brac is displayed in the living room, where you can relax in wingback chairs in front of the fireplace.

The guest-room furnishings are also eclectic, and each room is bright and tasteful. Rose has lots of windows, a private patio, and a bed and dresser made of New Mexico fruitwood. Eastlake boasts an oak Eastlake set with bed, dresser, and washstand. The Geranium suite, a private hideaway popular with honeymooners, has its own trellised garden. The roomy, dreamy Cottage has delphinium-blue walls and sage-green trim, as well as a white Jenny Lind–style bed with turned spools. The lovely grounds include a gazebo, crabapple trees, a small pond, and a formal rose garden.

Guests are wont to gaze out at the pond over breakfast while listening to the ancient strains of Celtic music. Although Coloma is rather isolated, you can have a good dinner at the nearby Vineyard House.

Address: *345 High St., Box 502, Coloma, CA 95613, tel. 916/622–6919.*
Accommodations: *3 double rooms with baths, 2 doubles share bath, 1 suite, 1 double suite.*
Amenities: *Air-conditioning, kitchens in suites, guest phone; bicycles, canoe, hot-air-balloon and whitewater-rafting packages.*
Rates: *$89–$155; expanded Continental breakfast, afternoon refreshments. No credit cards.*
Restrictions: *No smoking indoors, no pets; advance notice for children under 10.*

The Foxes Bed and Breakfast Inn

The simple, pale gray two-story structure that houses the Foxes Bed and Breakfast Inn in Sutter Creek was built during the gold rush, but while its 19th-century origins are intriguing, this elegant seven-room inn owes its chief appeal to the late-20th-century pampering of guests. Min Fox, who has owned the inn with her husband, Pete, since 1980, sits down with guests each evening and discusses the next day's breakfast. (There's an airy French toast made with apple juice and egg white for the cholesterol-conscious.) Breakfast is served in your room on an antique wooden table or at a private table in the garden shaded by a pink dogwood tree. An ornate silver pot holds coffee or tea. The place mats are crocheted, as is the little round doily that is slipped over the base of the stemmed orange-juice glass.

For years Pete and Min ran an antiques shop that specialized in Victorian pieces. When they decided to turn the house into an inn, they rearranged the unsold tables, armoires, and carved beds (one headboard is nine feet tall) and—*voilà*—the place was practically furnished. Guest rooms have grown increasingly romantic over the years, particularly the three newer rooms in the carriage house out back.

The big Blue Room, with ice-blue floral-print wallpaper, has a large bed with a carved headboard. A wooden half-tester canopy with pale blue curtains is suspended overhead. The armoire, which looks French-country,

was actually made in Argentina more than a century ago. A print of a red fox in winter repose hangs on one the walls. (Every room here has a foxy touch, such as a fox-head pillow or print.) Appealing in a different way, the Anniversary Room in the front of the main house is tucked into a gable with light-filled windows on three sides; it has an elaborately carved 12-foot-tall armoire facing the bed.

The house also has a peach-colored front parlor, with a spool-based table and a couple of Rococo Revival sofas for curling up with a good book or flipping through Min and Pete's menu collection. Or you may prefer to sit in the gazebo out back and admire the lush garden, particularly enticing in the spring when the big pink dogwood is in bloom.

Address: *77 Main St., Sutter Creek, CA 95685, tel. 209/267–5882, fax 209/267–0712.*
Accommodations: *5 double rooms with baths, 2 suites.*
Amenities: *Air-conditioning; robes, radio, and tape deck in rooms; fireplace, TV in 4 rooms; off-street parking.*
Rates: *$95–$135; full breakfast. D, MC, V.*
Restrictions: *No smoking, no pets; 2-night minimum on weekends.*

Groveland Hotel

Of all the gold-rush towns, Groveland wears its past most easily. Not a deserted ghost town like nearby Chinese Camp, or gentrified and upscale like Sutter Creek, Groveland remains what it always has been: commercial center, home to miners and workers who built the Hetch Hetchy Dam, and a short drive from Yosemite National Park. The Iron Door Saloon here claims to be the oldest in the state still operating. And one of the two buildings that comprise the Groveland Hotel, an adobe built in 1849, is considered to be one of California's oldest and largest. Always a hotel, during the gold rush the adobe had a reputation among the miners as being the "best house on the hill, offering all the pleasures a man could want."

When Peggy Mosley discovered that the adobe and adjacent Queen Anne Victorian were for sale and slated for demolition in 1990, she rescued them and began the renovations that would make them inviting to 20th-century guests without compromising their 19th-century history. Thus the adobe still displays its original facade, wraparound verandas, casement windows, and central staircase. Likewise the Victorian has gingerbread and bay windows. Peggy looked to the past in decorating, installing floral wallpapers, antique French beds, wicker furnishings, and English armoires.

The three suites are the nicest accommodations; each occupies a pair of the original hotel rooms. Lilly Langtry on the second floor, a popular choice with honeymooners, is the prettiest of the suites, with feminine floral wallpaper. It has a sofa opposite the fireplace and a spa tub in the bathroom. Two of the four upstairs rooms in the original adobe have stenciled decorations on the walls and French doors providing direct access to the veranda; they all open onto the guest lounge, where there's a TV available and a selection of books and magazines.

The restaurant at the Groveland Hotel, open for dinner and Sunday brunch, is noteworthy for an eclectic contemporary menu, casual ambience, and good service.

Operating the Groveland Hotel is a new career for Peggy, a spunky woman who spent more than 40 years in the aerospace industry and even now flies her own airplane. Highlights of her life, she says, include knowing Elvis Presley and flying in the Powder Puff Derby.

Address: *18767 Main St., Groveland, CA 95331, tel. 209/962-4000 or 800/273-3314, fax 209/962-6674.*
Accommodations: *14 double rooms with baths, 3 suites.*
Amenities: *Air-conditioning; radio, phone, robes in rooms, fireplace and whirlpool tub in suites, restaurant, saloon.*
Rates: *$75–$155; Continental breakfast. AE, D, DC, MC, V.*
Restrictions: *No smoking indoors.*

Red Castle Inn

Dubbed the Castle as it rose on Prospect Hill in 1857, this four-story, brick Gothic Revival house still looks majestic. Set in a grove of cedars, chestnuts, and walnuts, the Red Castle Inn has a classic pitched gable roof dripping with icicle-shaped gingerbread and a broad veranda shaded by white sail-canvas curtains tied back with red sashes.

Conley and Mary Louise Weaver, who bought the house in 1985, were the perfect inheritors of this Sierra-foothills treasure: He was an architect in San Francisco, and her specialty was interior design and historic preservation. Between them, the Weavers have transformed the inn into a virtual Vatican of Victoriana. The elegant parlor, its tall French doors draped in lace and framed by satin valances, contains volumes on period furniture and architecture.

Modern baths were installed in the former trunk-storage areas, but the guest rooms are all original to the house. On the first floor, one level below the main entrance, a private door leads to Forest View, where a large mahogany bed has a lighted canopy. On the main floor, the Garden Room's dramatic display of "Victorian clutter" includes a Renaissance Revival hall tree complete with a carved deer's head and real antlers and a reproduction Chinese Chippendale canopy bed. Down the hall in the Gold Room, rust-and-gold drapes hang from a faux-burled cornice. Two diminutive suites on the third floor, formerly the

children's quarters, have seven-foot ceilings. Garret East and West, separated by a parlor with a commanding view of the town, feature Gothic arched windows and mid-19th-century sleigh beds.

Gardens covering an acre and a half of hillside are cool and inviting on a warm summer day. Chairs, benches, and a porch swing hide in secluded corners amid the camellias and azaleas.

Mary Louise and Conley's breakfasts, served buffet-style on a sideboard in the main foyer, often include traditional American dishes such as Indian pudding or Dutch babies. Guests can eat in the parlor, outdoors in the terraced garden, or in the seclusion of their private sitting areas and verandas. On Saturday morning, you can hire a horse-drawn carriage to tour the town's historic district.

Address: *109 Prospect St., Nevada City, CA 95959, tel. 916/265-5135.*
Accommodations: *4 double rooms with baths, 2 suites, 1 double suite.*
Amenities: *Air-conditioning in suites.*
Rates: *$70–$140, double suites $140 ($70 each half); full breakfast, afternoon refreshments. MC, V.*
Restrictions: *No smoking indoors, no pets; 2-night minimum on weekends Apr.–Dec. and holiday weekends.*

Camino Hotel

Built at the turn of the century as a boardinghouse for loggers, the Camino Hotel, on the Carson Migrant Wagon Trail, was restored in 1990 by Paula Norbert and John Eddy. There's still a lumber mill in town, but the trail now winds through orchards and wineries.

Because the guests are no longer loggers, the hotel has been gussied up with antiques, most of them local. Paula's hand-sewn curtains complement the rooms' quilts, and such details as a wicker birdcage at the foot of a bed or a hanging sunbonnet with trailing dried flowers help set a country tone, as do the showcase antique sewing machines and quilt stands in the hall. The covered storm porch and large parlor are good spots for reading or chatting with other guests.

After serving a hearty breakfast, Paula and John will point you toward an orchard bakeshop that sells fabulous apple cheesecake and to a hiking trail where you can work it off.

Address: *4103 Carson Rd., Box 1197, Camino, CA 95709, tel. 916/644–7740 or 800/200–7740.*
Accommodations: *3 double rooms with baths, 6 doubles share 2 baths, 1 suite.*
Amenities: *Guest phone in hall.*
Rates: *$65–$85; full breakfast, afternoon refreshments. AE, D, MC, V.*
Restrictions: *No smoking indoors, no pets.*

The Chichester–McKee House

Doreen Thornhill is filled with historic lore about the 1892 Queen Anne that she and her husband, Bill, bought in 1990: It was the first house in Placerville with built-in plumbing; an entrance to a gold mine lies underneath the dining-room table; and the fireplace in the parlor came from San Francisco's Barbary Coast Hotel. Built on a hillside (and accessed by a flight of steep stairs) by lumber baron D. W. Chichester, the house makes lavish use of redwood inside and out, with a decorative cherry-wood fretwork in the library and parlor. It also has a wonderful tin-floored conservatory.

Rooms are furnished with a mix of antiques and reproductions; each has an armoire draped with an amusing piece of Victorian lingerie. A window

seat as well as an Amish oak bed with a handmade fishnet canopy make Yellow Rose the most appealing room, despite the faint traffic sounds.

After Doreen's hearty breakfast, guests can walk a few blocks to downtown Placerville or drive to nearby Apple Hill for a wine tasting.

Address: *800 Spring St., Placerville, CA 95667, tel. 916/626–1882 or 800/831–4008.*
Accommodations: *3 double rooms with half-baths share bath.*
Amenities: *Air-conditioning, robes in rooms, guest phone.*
Rates: *$75–$85; full breakfast, afternoon refreshments. AE, D, MC, V.*
Restrictions: *No smoking indoors, no pets.*

Combellack-Blair House

This textbook 1895 Queen Anne, with gingerbread, two-story bay windows, stained glass, and even a cupola, stands pink and proud behind twin palm trees and a white picket fence, one block from busy Main Street Placerville.

Victorianaholics will not be disappointed by the Combellack-Blair House's interior. The front parlor is hung with heavy drapes and has a crystal chandelier. Off the kitchen, the romantic Mazzuchi guest room has a lace bedspread, a claw-foot tub, and French doors opening onto a large porch. Smaller Blair is breathtaking, with its wooden canopy bed inlaid with flowers and burl, window seat, and trompe l'oeil wallpaper.

Hosts Al and Rosalie McConnell, who acquired the inn in 1991 after running a home for foster children in Gilroy, have enthusiastically entered into the Victorian spirit, serving their guests breakfast by candlelight or, in good weather, outside on the shaded deck.

Address: *3059 Cedar Ravine, Placerville, CA 95667, tel. 916/622-3764.*
Accommodations: *2 double rooms with baths, 1 double shares bath.*
Amenities: *Air-conditioning in 1 room, cable TV in rooms, phone in 1 room.*
Rates: *$89–$99; full breakfast. MC, V.*
Restrictions: *No smoking indoors, no pets.*

Cooper House

In 1865, Mark Twain came to Angels Camp and immortalized the food served there: "Beans and dishwater for breakfast, dishwater and beans for dinner, and both articles warmed over for supper." Twain's spirit still resonates through this tiny mining town, but, fortunately, the food's improved. Each morning owners Tom and Kathy Reese produce a prodigious breakfast fit for miners: eggs, sausage, potatoes, onions, muffins.

A simple Craftsman cottage on the outside, the inn boasts many striking decorative details inside: an expansive vaulted ceiling; custom woodwork in its wainscoting, beams, and moldings; unique doors that angle across a corner; a few fine examples of Arts-and-Crafts furniture; a selection of original art on the walls; and a dining table

with carved legs originally owned by Archie Stevenot, an early developer of the area. The guest rooms, which are furnished simply, have private verandas and great garden views.

Address: *1184 Church St., Box 1388, Angels Camp, CA 95222, tel. 209/736-2145.*
Accommodations: *1 double room with bath, 2 suites.*
Amenities: *Air-conditioning; off-street parking.*
Rates: *$90; full breakfast, afternoon refreshments. AE, D, MC, V.*
Restrictions: *No smoking indoors, no pets; 2-night minimum holiday weekends and 3rd weekend in May.*

The Court Street Inn

The offbeat collectibles—ornate brass cash registers, shoe-shine chair, industrial-size coffee grinder—that Janet and Lee Hammond gathered to decorate the old-fashioned general store they once planned to open are well showcased in the Court Street Inn, which they bought with their daughter and son-in-law, Gia and Scott Anderson. The 1872 yellow clapboard house, with embossed tin ceilings, is a short stroll from downtown Jackson.

The most enchanting guest room is the bright Blair suite upstairs. Its highlights include an ivy-and-violet theme, two-person whirlpool tub in a bedroom-size bath, and wood-burning stove. The Indian House, a two-bedroom cottage overlooking a small rose garden, has a wood-burning stove, a piano, and a huge bath with a claw-foot tub. Guests gather in the formal dining room for a breakfast that may include eggs Benedict with spiced apples. Hors d'oeuvres and dessert are served in the evening.

Address: *215 Court St., Jackson, CA 95642, tel. 209/223-0416 or 800/200-0416.*
Accommodations: *3 double rooms with baths, 2 doubles share bath, 1 suite, 1 double suite in cottage.*
Amenities: *Radio, tape player, robes in rooms, fireplace in 2 rooms, guest phone, TV available, massage available; outdoor whirlpool, off-street parking.*
Rates: *$90–$130; double suite $125 (one couple), $180 (two couples); full breakfast. AE, MC, V.*
Restrictions: *No smoking indoors, no pets.*

Dunbar House, 1880

From the jar of marshmallows by the parlor fireplace to the bedtime chocolates and complimentary bottle of wine, innkeepers Barbara and Bob Costa are devoted to details. They have furnished the guest rooms of this 1880 Italianate house with comfortable, newly reupholstered antiques, as well as floral floor-length drapes and matching spreads, wood stoves, down comforters, and antique-replica radios.

This is a great place to perfect the art of lounging: in the spacious parlor, on the wraparound porch, in the garden hammock, or in the comfortable rooms. The Cedar's sun porch has a view of the white-flowering almond tree; in Sequoia, you can soak in a bubble bath in front of the wood stove while gazing at the garden.

Breakfast is an elegant affair. The Costas whip up dishes they've discovered while attending professional food shows, and Barbara's mother bakes fresh bread and cookies.

Address: *271 Jones St., Box 1375, Murphys, CA 95247, tel. 209/728-2897 or 800/225-3764, ext. 321, fax 209/728-1451.*
Accommodations: *2 double rooms with baths, 2 suites.*
Amenities: *Air-conditioning, refrigerator, phone, TV with VCR in rooms; hair dryer, towel warmer, 2-person whirlpool tub in suite; video library.*
Rates: *$105–$155; full breakfast, evening refreshments. AE, MC, V.*
Restrictions: *No smoking indoors, no pets; 2-night minimum on weekends.*

Fallon Hotel

From 1850 to 1858, Columbia was a boomtown, with $87 million in gold discovered in its hills. Back then, Owen Fallon's hotel was *the* place to stay. Things calmed down once the gold disappeared.

These days, Columbia is a booming state park, and the state-owned Fallon, sensitively restored to its 1890 appearance, is its shiniest showpiece. Many of the antiques and furnishings are original to the hotel. The front guest rooms are huge, with reproduction Victorian wallpapers, velvet drapes, and headboards in carved oak or brass from the 1890s. The smaller rooms are painted instead of papered. The elegant lobby features curvy Victorian settees, ornate wallpapers, and fussy lamp shades.

Guests at the hotel can take advantage of theater and dinner packages that include performances at the historic Fallon Theatre next door and dinner at the City Hotel restaurant (*see above*).

Address: *Washington St., Columbia State Park, Box 1870, Columbia, CA 95310, tel. 209/532–1470.*
Accommodations: *1 double room with wheelchair-accessible bath, 13 doubles with half-baths share 5 showers.*
Amenities: *Air-conditioning, robes and slippers, ice cream parlor; off-street parking.*
Rates: *$55–$90; Continental breakfast. AE, MC, V.*
Restrictions: *No smoking, no pets. Closed Mon.–Wed. 2nd week in Jan.–3rd week in Mar.*

Flume's End

This is a cool, relaxing spot, with the tranquil tones of tumbling water echoing continuously in the background. Like a waterfall, this historic inn cascades down a hillside into all-year Gold Run Creek, replete with ponds, pools, and rivulets. The flume for which the inn is named spans the creek; it was built in 1854 to carry water from Nevada City to the town of Rough and Ready, 16 miles away.

Gregarious innkeepers Steve Wilson and Terrianne Straw (who always has seeing-eye dog Rowanna at her side) have created an inn that is casually comfortable, rather than a showplace, with one surprise after another: a great view, a ghost story, perhaps some flecks of gold sparkling in the creek bottom. In addition to balconies off guest rooms, there are secluded

spots throughout the three acres where one can curl up with a good book and dream of days gone by.

Terrianne puts out a generous buffet breakfast featuring egg entrées, sausage, potatoes, and curried fruit.

Address: *317 S. Pine St., Nevada City, CA 95959, tel. 916/265–9665.*
Accommodations: *6 double rooms with baths.*
Amenities: *Private deck outside 4 rooms, Jacuzzi in 2 rooms, sitting room with wet bar shared by 2 rooms, wood-burning stove in 1 room, stocked guest refrigerator, guest phone.*
Rates: *$75–$135; full breakfast. MC, V.*
Restrictions: *No smoking indoors, no pets; 2-night minimum on weekends Apr.–Dec.*

Grandmère's

Doug and Geri Boka left Los Angeles, where he was a police sergeant and she worked for the school district, to run this 1856 Colonial Revival inn near downtown Nevada City. Avid history buffs, they'll tell you all about such colorful past inhabitants of this house as Aaron August Sargent, a forty-niner from Massachusetts who supported women's rights.

Grandmère's is as quaint as its name, with manicured public areas and prim American-country rooms, all of which are unusually large. Similar in decor, they have quilts or floral bedspreads, hand-painted chests at the foot of the beds, and gleaming baths with pedestal sinks and brass fixtures. The Master suite has an outside entrance and displays Geri's collection of antique dolls.

You'll be drawn to the colorful back garden, with its stone benches, birdbaths, and footpaths leading through violets, daffodils, and camellias. But sitting on the front veranda, munching Geri's cookies and people-watching, is equally appealing.

Address: *449 Broad St., Nevada City, CA 95959, tel. 916/265-4660.*
Accommodations: *5 double rooms with baths, 2 suites.*
Amenities: *Air-conditioning, phone in hall, soft drinks and cookies available, guest refrigerator; off-street covered parking.*
Rates: *$100-$150; full breakfast. MC, V.*
Restrictions: *No smoking indoors, no pets.*

Grey Gables

British transplants Roger and Sue Garlick renovated and enlarged a late-1870s building that had previously been a store and a restaurant into an inn with the feel of an English country manor. This welcome and exceptionally attractive addition to the Gold Country bed-and-breakfast scene opened in 1994.

An inviting parlor has polished wood floors, a fireplace, two bay windows, a reproduction Duncan Fife table, and wingback chairs. Brilliant bouquets of roses stay continuously in bloom on the wallpaper in dining room, where tables for two or four are set in front of a fireplace.

Sue's excellent eye for color is particularly in evidence in the bedrooms, which are decorated in rich hues like

raspberry and hunter green. Named for poets—Browning, Shelley, Byron, and others—the rooms are spacious and equipped with modern bathrooms. Many have views of the inn's colorful garden.

Address: *161 Hanford St., Box 1687, Sutter Creek, CA 95685, tel. 209/267-1039 or 800/473-9422.*
Accommodations: *8 double rooms with baths.*
Amenities: *Air-conditioning, fireplace in rooms, guest phone.*
Rates: *$95-$125; full breakfast, afternoon tea, evening hors d'oeuvres. MC, V.*
Restrictions: *No smoking indoors, no pets; 2-night minimum on weekends.*

The Heirloom

You don't see a lot of homes reminiscent of the Old South in California's Gold Country. But the Heirloom in Ione, a one-street foothills mining town, occupies a gracious two-story house built for a Virginia farmer in about 1863. It's got columns atop columns, a two-story veranda, wisteria and magnolia—the antebellum works.

The Heirloom is peaceful and old-fashioned. The dining room, where owners Patricia Cross and Melisande Hubbs serve breakfast, is decorated with china plates and copper kettles. The front parlor includes a handsome grand piano once owned by Lola Montez, the Madonna (as in the singer) of the gold-rush era. Guest rooms in the main house are snug, with tall windows, lace curtains, and quilts. The biggest has a fireplace, a four-poster bed, and a balcony. Out back, a rustic, sod-roofed adobe cottage has two guest rooms with wood-burning stoves and fragrant cedar, redwood, and pine beams.

Address: *214 Shakeley La., Ione, CA 95640, tel. 209/274-4468.*
Accommodations: *4 double rooms with baths, 2 doubles share bath.*
Amenities: *Air-conditioning in rooms, fireplace in 1 room, wood-burning stove in 2 rooms; croquet.*
Rates: *$60–$92; full breakfast, afternoon refreshments. AE, MC, V.*
Restrictions: *No smoking, no pets; 2-night minimum on weekends.*

Imperial Hotel

A hotel since the 1880s, the Imperial has been all dolled-up and decorated for the 1990s. With its selection of huge, brilliantly colored paintings, murals, and whimsical touches—riotous floral patterns, 1990s interpolations of art-deco and folk-art female nudes and the like—by local artists John Johannsen and Moreno Larose, this is not your ordinary Victorian.

Soft-spoken innkeeper Bruce Sherrill, who has lived in the Gold Country most of his life, owned the red-brick building for some time before opening the hotel and restaurant in 1988. Rooms have brass and white-iron beds, wicker chairs and settees, art-deco appointments—and those highly whimsical touches. Out back there's a colorful garden with tables and chairs that is used by both inn and restaurant guests.

The hotel has earned a good reputation for its restaurant, which specializes in contemporary cuisine. The menu includes several heart-smart options.

Address: *Hwy. 49, Box 195, Amador City, CA 95601, tel. 209/267-9172 or 800/242-5594.*
Accommodations: *7 double rooms with baths.*
Amenities: *Air-conditioning, hair dryer and towel warmer in rooms, balcony off 2 rooms, TV in 1 room; guest phone, restaurant and saloon, room service.*
Rates: *$60–$90; full breakfast. AE, D, MC, V.*
Restrictions: *Smoking on patio only, no pets; 2-night minimum on weekends.*

Indian Creek

Built by Hollywood producer Arthur Hamburger as a weekend residence in 1932, Indian Creek is set on a hillside surrounded by 10 acres of meadow, replete with creek and frog pond. From its design it's clear that this was intended to be a party house, and local legend has it that Hamburger entertained wildly here. It's easy to imagine John Wayne, who was a regular visitor, sitting in front of the enormous stone fireplace of this two-story log-walled cabin, his voice echoing from the 25-foot cathedral ceiling.

The public rooms boast an international look: wooden Adirondack chairs and an 1872 Belgian chamber piano in the living room, Mexican rugs in the reading nook. The guest rooms are just as eclectic: trendy rag-rolled walls and a Civil War–era "sword chair" in one, white-draped ceiling and Sterno fireplace in another.

Breakfast might include cream cheese–tarragon French toast or German puff pancakes, which you can devour on the deck overlooking the Japanese garden.

Address: *21950 Hwy. 49, Plymouth, CA 95669, tel. 209/245–4648 or 800/242–7335.*
Accommodations: *4 double rooms with baths.*
Amenities: *Balcony and fireplace in 2 rooms, guest phone; pool, hot tub.*
Rates: *$70–$95; full breakfast, evening refreshments. D, MC, V.*
Restrictions: *No smoking indoors, no pets.*

Power's Mansion Inn

Gold-rush history is very much alive at this inn, which has been decorated to reflect the elegant showplace it once was. There are two light-filled parlors with gleaming oak floors, ornate Victorian chairs and settees. Photo displays on the walls reveal the story of the gold fortune that built the mansion.

The second story, where guest rooms are located, is a maze of narrow corridors leading to blind corners. Rooms are nicely decorated, if in need of some sprucing up, with brass and pencil-post beds covered with shiny satin spreads. Some bathrooms have whimsical tubs: a heart-shaped Jacuzzi or a claw-footed tub equipped with whirlpool jets.

Resident managers Tony and Tina Verhaart serve a breakfast with entrées like eggs Benedict and French toast.

Address: *146 Cleveland Ave., Auburn, CA 95603, tel. 916/885–1166, fax 916/ 885–1386.*
Accommodations: *11 double rooms with baths.*
Amenities: *Air-conditioning; phone, robes in rooms, fireplace in 1 room, whirlpool tub in 2 rooms, cable TV in parlor; German, Chinese, Dutch spoken.*
Rates: *$79–$149; full breakfast, afternoon refreshments. AE, MC, V.*
Restrictions: *No smoking indoors, no pets.*

The Ryan House

I t is said that the Ryan for whom this pale blue Victorian is named fled Ireland in 1855 to escape the potato famine, coming to Sonora to seek his fortune. Later treasure seekers—of natural beauty rather than wealth—Nancy and Guy Hoffman pulled up their corporate roots in the nearby San Francisco Bay Area in 1987 and bought the Ryan House.

This B&B is more modest than some of the flamboyant Gold Country inns, but guests will appreciate the Hoffmans' gentle manner, the few well-chosen antiques, the formal rose garden, and Nancy's zeal for baking (scones and sourdough waffles are her specialty). The most appealing room is the attic suite, which has its own parlor with four blue velvet Eastlake chairs; a large pink and burgundy bathroom with a deep, double soaking tub; and brass bed boasting a blue and pink star quilt. Guests gather for afternoon tea in front of the wood stove in the library, with its carved grape-pattern Victorian love seat and dusty-rose walls.

Address: *153 S. Shepherd St., Sonora, CA 95370, tel. 209/533–3445 or 800/831–4897.*
Accommodations: *3 double rooms with baths, 1 suite.*
Amenities: *Air-conditioning, robes, 3 guest parlors, TV in pantry, dinner–theater packages; off-street parking.*
Rates: *$85–$150; full breakfast, afternoon refreshments. AE, MC, V.*
Restrictions: *No smoking indoors, no pets; 2-night minimum on holiday weekends.*

Serenity, A Bed & Breakfast Inn

A ptly named, this brand new Victorian farmhouse surrounded by six wooded acres is tranquillity itself. From the big veranda, you can glimpse the deep azure sky through tall ponderosa pines, sniff the incense of cedar, and hear birds chirping by day and frogs croaking by night.

Serenity was designed and built by innkeepers Fred and Charlotte Hoover, who moved here from the San Diego area. The inn has two guest sitting areas—a parlor downstairs furnished with a pair of overstuffed sofas and a small, book-filled library upstairs. Airy rooms with modern bathrooms and other contemporary comforts occupy the corners on first and second floors. Decorated in bright colors with simple furnishings, each showcases a quilt handmade by Charlotte. You can admire her work throughout the inn: an afghan, hand-crocheted lace edging on linens, and a wall of needlepoint samplers.

Breakfast, served in the formal dining room, is as carefully crafted as the quilts.

Address: *15305 Bear Cub Dr., Sonora, CA 95370, tel. 209/533–1441 or 800/426–1441.*
Accommodations: *4 double rooms with baths.*
Amenities: *Air conditioning, fireplace in 2 rooms, guest parlor with books and games.*
Rates: *$85–$125; full breakfast, afternoon refreshments. AE, MC, V.*
Restrictions: *No smoking indoors, no pets; 2-night minimum on holiday weekends.*

High Sierra

High Sierra
Including Yosemite, Lake Tahoe, and Western Nevada

"The Range of Light" is the name the naturalist John Muir applied to the Sierra Nevada, the massive granite mountains that form two-thirds of California's eastern border. Stretching from Lassen Peak in the north past Yosemite, Kings Canyon, and Sequoia (the site of 14,494-foot Mt. Whitney) national parks to the Tehachapi range in the south, the Sierra Nevada encompasses 450 miles of snowcapped peaks encircling alpine lakes, flower-filled meadows, towering waterfalls (including Yosemite Falls, which drops nearly a half mile), and endless forests, including the giant sequoias.

The mountains have played a significant role in the state's history. Initially, they formed an all but impenetrable barrier to explorers and pioneers. (The tragic story of the Donner party—trapped in the brutal Sierra winter of 1846–47 and driven by starvation to madness and cannibalism—became engraved in American legend.) To this day some high passes are closed during the winter, and snow and ice force others to close intermittently. And the railroad tracks across Donner Summit still pass through a series of snowsheds so that the trains can run through the winter.

Despite the rough terrain, the thirst for gold and land compelled the 49ers and emigrants to confront the Sierra, which they crossed on a handful of trails blazed by explorers— the same routes that the cross-mountain roads follow today. California gold was mined mainly on the lower elevations of the gentle western slope; the edge of the sheer eastern escarpment yielded the extraordinary silver riches of Nevada's Comstock Lode, for which hordes of hopefuls backtracked over the Sierra, taming it further. Mountain timber shored up the mine shafts, braced the hillsides, and tied together tracks when the railroad finally conquered the mighty range.

Today, vacationers, sightseers, and outdoor enthusiasts are lured by the gorgeous scenery and endless recreation. In the southern portion, the scenic splendor of the three national parks draws millions of visitors each year. Yosemite is the most famous, with its glacier-carved canyon, giant granite monoliths, thundering waterfalls, and pristine acres of alpine wilderness. The Ahwanhee Hotel, with its cathedral ceilings, great stone hearth, and richly decorated Indian rugs, stands in a choice spot, with a stunning view of Half Dome. Sequoia, a strip of rugged natural beauty at 8,000 feet, gets its name from the world's largest living thing, the giant sequoia tree. This park and the adjacent Kings Canyon National Park offer more than 1,000 miles of high-country trails.

Lake Tahoe—at 12 by 22 miles (and with an average depth of nearly 1,000 feet)—is itself a scenic wonder: The largest alpine lake in North America has water so pure that you can spot a dinner plate 75 feet beneath the surface. Lake Tahoe is a two-season paradise. Winter brings 300–500 inches of snow to the upper elevations, along with some of the finest skiing in the West and some of the best facilities: cross-country trails, snowmobile trails, snow-play areas, and more than 200 lifts and tows. During the summer, the recreation shifts to boating, fishing, and waterskiing, along with biking and hiking.

North of Lake Tahoe is a largely undiscovered portion of the High Sierra, which includes the Lakes Basin Recreation Area, a gentle wilderness of pristine lakes, trails, and peaks. Historically this is gold country; today it's timber country. Visitors will discover a sparse population and several well-placed bed-and-breakfast inns amid mile upon mile of tranquil, scenic beauty.

Places to Go, Sights to See

Bodie (off Hwy. 395, 7 mi south of Bridgeport, CA, tel. 619/647–6445), an eerily beautiful, noncommercial ghost town, grew to more than 10,000 residents by 1881 during the gold rush and was completely deserted by the 1940s.

Cross-country Ski Centers. *Sorensen's* (Hope Valley, CA, tel. 916/694–2203) provides 20 kilometers of groomed trails and 100 kilometers of marked, unimproved trails, rentals, lessons, and day tours. *Spooner Lake Cross-Country Ski Area* (Glenbrook, NV, tel. 702/749–5349) divides 101 kilometers among 21 groomed trails and offers rentals, lessons, and moonlight tours. *Tahoe Nordic Center* (Hwy. 28, Tahoe City, CA, tel. 916/583–9858) provides 65 kilometers of groomed trails as well as rentals, lessons, races, and full-moon tours. *Royal Gorge Cross-Country Ski Resort* (off I–80 at Donner Summit, Soda Springs, CA, tel. 916/426–3871) has 317 kilometers of groomed track, 77 trails, as well as rentals, lessons, warming huts, trailside cafés, and a ski patrol. *Tahoe Donner Cross-Country* (3½ mi off I–80 at Donner State Park exit, tel. 916/587–9484) has 65 kilometers of track, 32 trails, and offers rentals, lessons, and night skiing (Wed.–Sat.). *Tamarack Cross-Country Ski Center* (Tamarack Lodge, Mammoth Lakes, CA, tel. 619/934–2442 or 800/237–6879) has more than 40 kilometers of groomed trails. *Yosemite Cross-Country Ski School* (Badger Pass, 6 mi east of Chinquapin Junction at Hwy. 41, Yosemite, CA, tel. 209/372–1244) offers 35 kilometers of groomed trails and 80 kilometers of marked trails.

Donner Memorial State Park and Museum (Donner Pass Rd., 2 mi west of Truckee, tel. 916/582–7892) lies beneath the granite wall of Donner Summit, where 22 feet of snow trapped the Donner party during the winter of 1846–47. The *Emigrant Trail Museum* contains exhibits recounting their tragedy and illustrating the history of the Central Pacific Railroad. *Donner Lake*, with 7½ miles of alpine shoreline, offers swimming, fishing, sailing, sunbathing, horseback rentals, and hiking trails.

Genoa, Nevada (Foothill Rd., off Hwy. 207), the first settlement in the state, retains its historic flavor; the town's Victorian Gothic homes are of particular interest. The *Carson Valley Chamber of Commerce and Visitors Authority* (1524 Hwy. 395, Suite 1, Gardnerville, NV 89410, tel. 702/782–8144) offers tourist information.

Lake Tahoe Cruises. Several companies offer cruises on the lake. The *Tahoe Queen* (Box 14292, South Lake Tahoe, CA 96151, tel. 800/238–2463) is a glass-bottom stern-wheeler that departs on a variety of excursions from Emerald Bay and includes lunch and sunset dinner-dance cruises. *North Tahoe Cruises* (700 N. Lake Blvd., Tahoe City, CA 96145, tel. 916/583–0141) takes visitors on champagne Continental-breakfast cruises, shoreline cruises, and sunset cocktail cruises. *Woodwind Sailing Cruises* (Box 1375, Zephyr Cove, NV 89448, tel. 702/588–3000) operates a 41-foot trimaran on regular excursions (daily Apr. 1–Oct. 31). M.S. *Dixie II* (Box 1667, Zephyr Cove, NV 89448, tel. 702/588–3508) offers daily breakfast and dinner cruises to the south and east shores of Emerald Bay in a brand new sternwheeler.

Lake Tahoe 72-Mile Shoreline Drive (guide from Lake Tahoe Visitors Authority, *see* Tourist Information, *below*) is a stunning scenic drive with views of many of Tahoe's high points: deep-green Emerald Bay, the 38-room Scandinavian castle called Vikingsholm, the beautiful beaches at Meeks Bay and D. L. Bliss State Park, and the early 19th-century homes at the Tallac Historic Site.

Laws Railroad Museum and Historical Site (on Rte. 6 off Hwy. 395 at north end of Bishop, CA, tel. 619/873–5950) is a re-creation of a small frontier community, built at the site of the old Laws Railroad Station. *The Slim Princess*, the last narrow-gauge locomotive operating as a public carrier in the West, rests here after 70 years of service. There are also excellent minimuseums displaying rock collections, old bottles, and Indian artifacts.

Mammoth Mountain Bike Park (Mammoth Lakes Mountain Biking Association, Box 7142, Mammoth Lakes, CA, tel. 619/934–0606) has 50 miles of mostly single-track trails for advanced-beginner to advanced riders. Ask about the 62 newly marked miles of trails in surrounding areas.

Plumas-Eureka State Park (5 mi west of Blairsden on Hwy. A–14, tel. 916/836–2380), which summons up the gold-mining era in California, contains Johnsville, which verges on being a ghost town, a partially restored stamp mill, and a museum illuminating hard-rock mining and early pioneer life.

Portola Railroad Museum (Box 608, Portola, CA, tel. 916/832–4131) illustrates the history of the Western Pacific Railroad with 25 diesel locomotives as well as freight cars and track and maintenance equipment. You can even drive the train here; one-hour lessons are available.

Sierra County Historical Park and Museum at the Kentucky Mine (Hwy. 49, 1 mi east of Sierra City, CA, tel. 916/862–1310). The mine operated on and off from the 1850s until 1953. The museum contains a collection of local mining memorabilia; tours include a restored stamp mill, tunnel, blacksmith shop, and trestle. Concerts of all kinds are held here on Friday evening in July and August.

Ski Areas. North Lake Tahoe alone has 108 lifts serving 16,500 skiable acres in 12 alpine ski areas. Most areas are served by a single lift ticket, the Ski Tahoe North Interchangeable Lift Ticket. A brief sampling includes *Alpine Meadows* (2600 Alpine Rd., off Hwy. 89, outside Tahoe City, CA, tel. 916/583–4232); *Diamond Peak* (Incline Village, NV, tel. 702/832–1177); *Homewood* (West Shore, Lake Tahoe, CA, tel. 916/525–7256); *Mount Rose* (Mt. Rose Hwy., outside Reno, NV, tel. 702/849–0704); *Northstar-at-Tahoe* (off Hwy. 267, 6 mi from Lake Tahoe, CA, tel. 916/562–1010 or 800/533–6787); and *Squaw Valley USA* (1960 Squaw Valley Rd., off Hwy. 89, Olympic Valley, CA, tel. 916/583–6985). The major resort in South Lake Tahoe is *Heavenly Valley* (½-mile off Hwy. 50, South Lake Tahoe, CA, tel. 916/541–1330 or 800/243–2836). Yosemite's skiers resort is *Badger Pass* (6 mi east of Chinquapin Junction at Hwy. 41, Yosemite, CA, tel. 209/372–1330); *Mammoth Mountain* (off Hwy. 395 in Mammoth Lakes, CA, tel. 619/934–2571) is closer to southern California.

Sleigh rides are popular during the winter. Contact *Borges Carriage and Sleigh Rides* (Hwy. 50 and Parkway at Lake Tahoe, NV, tel. 916/541–2953); *Camp Richardson Corral* (Hwy. 89 at Camp Richardson, CA, tel. 916/541–3113); *Kirkwood Ski Resort* (Hwy. 88, 7 mi west of Carson Pass, CA, tel. 209/258–RIDE), or *Northstar* (Hwy. 267 between Truckee and Lake Tahoe, CA, tel. 916/562–1010).

Tahoe Trailways is a network of bicycling and walking paths edging the lake. The trail extends north from Tahoe City along Highway 89 toward Truckee, then east as far as Dollar Point and south along the West Shore to Meeks Bay. Bicycles can be rented from *Olympic Bike Shop* (620 N. Lake Blvd., Tahoe City, CA, tel. 916/581–2500) and *Tahoe Gear* (5095 W. Lake Blvd., Homewood, CA, tel. 916/525–5233).

Virginia City, Nevada (Hwy. 341, off Hwy. 50 east of Carson City, tel. 702/847–0311), site of the Comstock Lode, is the nation's most famous mining boomtown. Retaining its century-old rustic flavor, the town contains old-time saloons, Piper's Opera House, a frontier cemetery, shops, museums, mine and mansion tours, gambling, and the offices of the *Territorial Enterprise*, where Mark Twain once worked.

Restaurants

Two of the inns listed below, **Sorensen's** in Hope Valley and **The Alpenhaus** in Tahoma, have restaurants. **Le Bistro** (tel. 702/831–0800) in Incline Village has a reasonably priced set menu of rustic French-California dishes. In Tahoe City, **Le Petit Pier** (tel. 916/546–4494) offers lakeside dining and is one of the best French restaurants in the area. **Sunnyside** (tel. 916/583–7200), just south of Tahoe City, has a lakeside dining room with a charming old-boating atmosphere and serves seafood and prime rib. **O.B.'s Pub and Restaurant** (tel. 916/587–4164), in Truckee, is popular for its old-fashioned lace curtains, stained glass, and old-time atmosphere, and for its California cuisine. The restaurant at the elegant **Ahwahnee Hotel** (Yosemite Valley, tel. 209/372–1489) serves California cuisine in its 135-foot-long dining room, where no jeans or tennis shoes are allowed. Reserve at least two weeks in advance. In Mammoth Lakes, **Anything Goes** (tel. 619/934–2424) offers fresh-baked breads and creative California cuisine in hearty portions.

Tourist Information

Bishop Chamber of Commerce and Visitor Center (690 N. Main St., Bishop, CA 93514, tel. 619/873–8405); **California Highway Information** (tel. 800/427–7623); **Lake Tahoe Visitors Authority** (Box 16299, South Lake Tahoe, CA 96151, tel. 916/544–5050, 800/288–2463 for lodging information, or 900/776–5050 for local entertainment and events information at a $1-per-minute rate); **Mammoth Lakes Visitors Bureau** (Village Center Mall, Main Street, Box 48, Mammoth Lakes, CA 93546, tel. 619/934–8006 or 800/367–6572); **Nevada Highway Information** (tel. 702/289–0250); **North Lake Tahoe Chamber of Commerce** (Box 884, Tahoe City, CA 96145, tel. 916/583–2371); **Plumas County Chamber of Commerce** (500 Jackson St., Box 11018, Quincy, CA 95971, tel. 916/283–6345 or 800/326–2247); **South Lake Tahoe Chamber of Commerce** (3066 Lake Tahoe Blvd., South Lake Tahoe, CA 96150, tel. 916/541–5255); **Yosemite National Park** (Box 577, CA 95389, tel. 209/372–0265).

Reservation Service

B&B International (Box 282910, San Francisco, CA 94128, tel. 415/696–1690 or 800/872–4500, fax 415/696–1699).

The Cain House

nnkeeping is in Marachal Gohlich's blood. In 1972, when she was 10, her family fled the Orange County smog to open the Walker River Lodge in Bridgeport. Seventeen years later, Marachal came back to Bridgeport from southern California, where she had worked as a hotel operations director, and bought the Cain House, which she runs with her husband Chris, a schoolteacher. A new addition to the family, Cavanagh, probably has innkeeping in her blood, too.

In the late 1920s the descendants of James Stuart Cain, the principal landowner in what was once the boomtown of Bodie, built this clean-lined two-story structure, painted burnt-red and white with a gray slate roof and cedar siding. It's two doors north of Bridgeport's landmark 1880 courthouse, whose bell tower plays oldies and show tunes on the hour. In remodeling the house, Marachal not only replaced the plumbing and electricity, she also devoted a great deal of attention to stylish detail. The rock fireplace, moldings, and the bathroom of the Candelaria room, decorated with swirly green wall tiles and a large peach-colored sink, are all original to the house. The rest of the furnishings are recent acquisitions, and the seven guest rooms, parlor, and dining room are beautifully color coordinated.

Roomy Aurora, all peaches and pinks, boasts whitewashed pine furniture. Silverado's pale greens are a cool complement to its white wicker bedroom set. The deep-blue Masonic, the largest room in the house, has two queen-size brass beds and a library set that belonged to Marachal's grandmother. The Cain Room is arresting, with its four-poster cherry-wood bedframe, dark red-and-green paisley wallpaper and quilt, and dark green carpet.

The dining room is decorated with Swiss posters, an Okaw woodstove, and a large built-in china cabinet; French doors lead to the side porch. At romantic tables for two, you can savor such delights as shrimp-and-brie scrambled eggs or lemon-and-raspberry pancakes. After breakfast, take the rugged road out to Bodie, which has been a ghost town since the 1940s.

Address: *340 Main St., Box 454, Bridgeport, CA 93517, tel. 619/932–7040 or 800/433–CAIN, fax 619/932–7419.*
Accommodations: *7 double rooms with baths.*
Amenities: *Cable TV in rooms; badminton, croquet, off-street parking.*
Rates: *$80–$135; full breakfast, evening refreshments. AE, D, DC, MC, V.*
Restrictions: *No smoking indoors, no pets; 2-night minimum last weekend in June and 4th of July weekend; closed Nov. 1–Apr. 14.*

The Feather Bed

Bob and Jan Janowski escaped the corporate world of the San Francisco Bay Area and took over the Feather Bed in 1992. Their 1893 Queen Anne–style house, with such Greek Revival touches as Corinthian columns, is a pale peach charmer with turquoise and brick-red trim. Located across from the historic courthouse in downtown Quincy, the inn is within walking distance of Main Street dining, shopping, and entertainment.

The large front porch of the main house is a quiet setting for reading, conversation, or relaxation. The pleasant atmosphere continues at the large antique table in the dining room, where the Janowskis serve up enticing breakfasts that start with the inn's trademark smoothie, made from homegrown blackberries. Dining on the flower-bedecked front porch in summer is a real treat.

The Janowskis have decorated their spacious rooms with vintage wallpapers and a few well-chosen Victorian antiques. The front guest room on the second floor overlooks the courthouse, while the Barrett room, well-suited for business travelers, features an oak drop-leaf desk with leather inlay and an antique fireplace mantel used as a headboard.

Behind the house, the secluded Sweetheart Cottage, as romantic as its name, has a brass and white-iron bed, delicate floral wallpaper, and a claw-foot tub in the carpeted bathroom; French doors open onto a private garden. The new guest house next to the main house combines elegance and ruggedness with its romantic gas fireplace and rustic pheasant borders.

The gardens at the Feather Bed are spectacular in spring. Tulips, daffodils, Oriental poppies, and phlox surround the stone fountain in the formal Victorian garden. The Janowskis are planning to expand the gardens between the inn and the Sweetheart Cottage; one will provide a private eating area. A cheerful border of plants and a lush green lawn complete the idyllic picture.

Guests often find themselves chatting with the gregarious innkeepers on the porch or in the parlor. Bob or Jan will direct you to such local sights as the Plumas County Museum, devoted to gold rush–era history, or to Plumas–Eureka State Park (an hour's drive away), with its ghost town, stamp mill, and pioneer museum.

Address: *542 Jackson St., Box 3200, Quincy, CA 95971, tel. 916/283–0102.*
Accommodations: *4 double rooms with baths, 1 suite, 2 separate guest houses.*
Amenities: *Phone, radio in rooms, air-conditioning in 5 rooms, TV in sitting room; bicycles, airport pickup, off-street parking.*
Rates: *$70–$100; full breakfast, afternoon refreshments. AE, DC, MC, V.*
Restrictions: *No smoking indoors, no pets.*

High Country Inn

When you first drive up to the High Country Inn, you become aware of the ranch-like grounds, but are still not prepared for the well-kept secret that awaits you. The craggy Sierra Buttes in the background provide one of the most stunning views in all of the Sierra. More than 30 jewel-like lakes nestle against those jagged mountains in the remote Lakes Basin Recreation Area.

Owner Cal Cartwright, whose roots in this region date from the 1850s, wanted to settle here upon retirement. When he and his wife Marlene found a ranch-style mountain house on a 2½-acre corner, they snapped it up.

The house was built in 1961; a new section, added in 1981, offers the best room, the second-floor Sierra Buttes Suite. Tall cathedral windows across one wall frame the buttes; you can laze in bed and watch the morning sun creep down them and listen to the river that rushes through the property. A wood-burning stove occupies one corner. The modern bath–dressing room boasts a 6½-foot antique tub.

The furnishings reflect Cal and Marlene's families' histories. The cane-seat chairs in the Golden Pond Room came from the East with Calvin's family in 1852. Marlene has decorated the inn with antiques and quilts hand sewn by her mother.

The heart of the inn is a big, open living room, dining room, and kitchen.

Guests can curl up in front of the large stone fireplace with a book from the Cartwrights' library (which focuses on local history) or simply admire the view.

The inn has a special brand of entertainment in its trout pond. Marlene invites guests to feed the fish—more than 300 nibblers come right up to the grassy shore to catch a bite.

Marlene sets up breakfast places at a long table fronting the window wall; in good weather she serves on the deck. You can expect such delights as corn bread and quiche spiced southwestern-style, or zucchini-walnut waffles. A 7 AM wakeup tray of coffee, fruit, and homemade nut breads gets guests going in the morning.

Address: *100 Green Rd. (at Bassets, HCR 2, Box 7, Sierra City, CA 96125, tel. 916/862–1530 or 800/862–1530.*
Accommodations: *2 double rooms with baths, 2 doubles share bath.*
Amenities: *TV with VCR in living room; trout pond, river.*
Rates: *$80–$125; full breakfast. MC, V.*
Restrictions: *No smoking indoors, no pets; 2-night minimum on holiday weekends.*

New England Ranch

A beautiful drive three miles outside of Quincy brings you to 88 acres of pasture land and a white house that, as its name suggests, looks like a Vermont cottage. Built in the 1850s, the New England Ranch had fallen into disrepair by the time Barbara Scott purchased it in the late 1980s. Scott spent three years restoring it, and in 1991 opened this striking, intimate inn, furnished with beautiful family heirloom antiques and polished wood floors.

Sunlight floods both upstairs guest rooms, which have an expansive view of the countryside. The pale apricot Vincent, with a lace-covered, brass step-up bed, shares a cozy sitting room with Chandler, which has a chenille bedspread and delicately patterned wallpaper. The bathrooms are especially cheery, with white-painted wood floors and bright floral wallpaper; one has an old English commode with a built-in sink, and the other features a large pedestal sink and claw-foot tub. The downstairs room is the largest and most deluxe, with a king-size bed.

The exquisite pair of gold-leaf Czechoslovakian plates on the dining table are just for show, but Barbara does bring out her china and silver to serve the fresh ranch eggs, blintzes, and scones that she cooks on the house's original wood stove. The fresh herbs, vegetables, and fruits are all from her newly planted garden. In winter, if you're not up for nearby skiing or snowmobiling, you can retire after breakfast to the dusty-rose parlor and look out the bay window or into a blazing fire.

But in fine weather, you'll want to go out and explore the grounds. The outbuildings include an old creamery, which Barbara has converted into a country store. Some of the land is leased to neighboring ranchers, so cattle and horses graze the grounds. You can ride out into the rolling green hills on one of Barbara's mountain bikes or take a dip in one of the creeks on the property. Ask Barbara to introduce you to her pet llama Pierre and his sidekick-donkey Jose, who might nibble carrots or alfalfa from your hand.

Address: *2571 Quincy Junction Rd., Quincy, CA 95971, tel. 916/283-2223.*
Accommodations: *3 double rooms with baths.*
Amenities: *Portable phone; creeks, mountain bicycles, horse stables and corrals, off-street parking, airport pickup.*
Rates: *$70–$95; full breakfast. MC, V.*
Restrictions: *No smoking indoors, no pets (horses allowed).*

Sorensen's

Those seeking a bona fide High Sierra atmosphere in rustic surroundings amid Tanglewood, Douglas fir, pinon, and ponderosa, will want to consider this historic mountain resort alongside the Carson River at the 7,000-foot level. Sorensen's, just east of Carson Pass, is open year-round. It offers access to 600 square miles of public land. Hiking, fishing, cross-country skiing, star-gazing—you name it, you'll find it here.

The inn provides comfortable accommodations, ranging from the rudimentary to the classy, in bed-and-breakfast units and housekeeping cabins. One of the latter is a replica of a 13th-century Norwegian summer home shipped to Hope Valley piece by piece by Sorensen's former owner. Another, the Chapel, is a honeymooners' favorite. The log cabin has a steeple, church doors, vaulted ceilings, and a spiral staircase to heaven—well, to the bedroom, anyway.

Some of the cabins date from the turn of the century, when Martin Sorensen, an immigrant Danish shepherd, and his wife, Irene, began camping here. For more than 50 years, the place was primarily a hangout for family and friends, travelers, and wilderness folk. In 1970, the family sold the inn, which began a decade of decline; Sorensen's came to be known locally as the "Last Resort."

Then John and Patty Brissenden, community activists from Santa Cruz, purchased the place for 1,000 ounces of gold and set about to revitalize it, renovating some of the cabins and building others from scratch. The result is an eclectic collection of accommodations connected by a network of trails. Most of the cabins have kitchens; many have sitting areas and lofts. All cabins are offered on a housekeeping basis (breakfast not included), but small, simply furnished bed-and-breakfast rooms are available as well. Guests select breakfast from the menu at the Country Café, housed in a log cabin and open for all three meals.

John and Patty enhance your appreciation of the surroundings with classes in astrology, fly fishing, nature, art, and other subjects. Guests can also hike along the historic Emigrant Trail (which passes through the property), study the stars, and cross-country ski throughout the winter.

Address: *14255 Hwy. 88, Hope Valley, CA 96120, tel. 916/694–2203 or 800/ 423–9949.*
Accommodations: *1 double room with bath, 2 doubles share bath, 28 housekeeping cabins, each accommodating 2–6 persons.*
Amenities: *Restaurant, wood-burning stove in 18 rooms, pets permitted in 3 cabins; convenience store, sauna, trout pond, picnic tables, barbecues, children's play area.*
Rates: *$60–$110, cabins $55–$300; full breakfast (for B&B guests). MC, V.*
Restrictions: *No smoking; 2-night minimum on weekends, 3- or 4-night minimum on holidays.*

White Sulphur Springs

This big white farmhouse has welcomed travelers since the 1850s, when it was built as an overnight lodge for the Quincy Mohawk Stage Line. A tranquil charm surrounds the inn now; it's hard to imagine that thousands of prospectors once ranged over these tree-covered hillsides and gentle valleys. But if the magnificent view of Mohawk Valley, the airy elegance of the main house, the seclusion of the cottages, and the warmth of the innkeepers don't remind you that you've left the madding crowds far behind, the sounds of bullfrogs, cows, and distant coyotes surely will.

The ambience of the inn remains much the way it was when George McLear operated it as a stagecoach stop. Many of the furnishings are original to the inn: a pump organ in the parlor, an antique piano, brocade-covered Victorian settees, a pine bedroom set handcrafted by McLear himself. The inn also contains the original wood stove that the town of Clio (pronounced "Cl–EYE–oh") was named after. The attic has been converted to a museum where visitors can enjoy collectibles from the stage coach days.

There are guest rooms in the main house and in two cottages, the Dairy House and the Hen House (the original chicken coop). All have expansive views of meadows and mountains; a balcony across the front of the main house extends the view for guests on the second floor. The Victorian furnishings include a fainting couch, antique washstands, dry sinks, and rocking chairs.

Guests are served an elaborate ranch-style breakfast in the formal dining room. Breakfast is likely to consist of sausage-spinach frittata, homestyle potatoes, homemade bread, and fruit.

The inn has a warm, spring-fed, Olympic-size swimming pool. With four championship courses in the area, golf is popular with visitors, as are hiking, fishing, and cross-country skiing. Downhill skiing and snowmobiling are nearby at Johnsville.

Address: *Hwy. 89, Box 136, Clio, CA 96106, tel. 916/836–2387 or 800/854–1797.*

Accommodations: *1 double room with bath, 5 doubles share 2 baths, 1 housekeeping cottage, 1 double housekeeping with kitchen.*

Amenities: *Robes; outdoor pool, picnic area, barbecue.*

Rates: *$89–$140; full breakfast. D, MC, V.*

Restrictions: *No smoking indoors, no pets; 2-night minimum on summer and holiday weekends.*

The Alpenhaus

With its dormer windows and long balcony, the Alpenhaus still looks—from the outside, at least—like the 1944 Swiss chalet that until recently was known as the Captain's Alpenhaus. Inside, however, new innkeepers Al and Patty Mulken, who left Australia to open a Tahoe B&B, have enhanced the knotty-pine-paneling, Old Tahoe-country motif with lacy curtains, floral patterns, and frilly fabric. They've also renovated the mountain cottages, each of which has two double rooms upstairs. The 100-year-old Amy's Cottage is the Alpenhaus's honeymoon hideaway. The Mulkens, who have two small children of their own, welcome families to stay at the Alpenhaus.

The rustic dining room occupies the center of the lodge, surrounding a large stone fireplace. Hearty American breakfasts include eggs Benedict with ranch potatoes and all the fixings.

Address: *6941 W. Lake Blvd., Box 262, Tahoma, CA 96142, tel. 916/525–5000, fax 916/525–6266.*
Accommodations: *5 double rooms with baths, 2 doubles share bath, 2 suites, 4 double housekeeping cottages, 1 honeymoon cottage.*
Amenities: *Phone in rooms, TV in some rooms, fireplace in cottages, restaurant, beer bar; pool, spa, badminton, volleyball, horseshoes, Ping-Pong.*
Rates: *$75–$160; full breakfast (except for cottages). AE, D, MC, V.*
Restrictions: *No smoking indoors, pets in cottages only; 3-night minimum on holiday weekends, 2-night minimum on weekends in cottages.*

Busch and Heringlake Country Inn

Don't be fooled by the exterior of this historic inn. Once you walk inside, you'll be amazed at what owner Carlo Giuffre has done with the place. Like many other High Sierra and Gold Country hostelries, the Busch and Heringlake Country Inn was originally a stagecoach stop. Guests will find reminders of the building's history in the brick facade, old boiler, and antique safe—and especially in the saloon—complete with brass boot-rests and an exposed-stone wall behind the bar.

Upstairs, however, the accommodations are thoroughly modern, with four guest rooms comfortably furnished to reflect an earlier era: brass and four-poster beds, exposed woodwork, and original art on the walls. Carlo, who bought and renovated the property in 1986, is full of information about the exploits of local adventurers and offers plenty of advice on where to see what they discovered.

Carlo serves up a hearty mountain breakfast, complete with ranch eggs, vegetable-loaded potatoes, fruit, and extras.

Address: *Main St., Box 68, Sierra City, CA 96125, tel. 916/862–1501.*
Accommodations: *4 double rooms with baths.*
Amenities: *Whirlpool tub in 2 rooms, fireplace in 1 room; bar (seasonal).*
Rates: *$85–$110; full breakfast. MC, V.*
Restrictions: *No smoking, no pets.*

Chalfant House

This quasi-Victorian wood house in the heart of Bishop was built in 1898 by P. A. Chalfant, publisher of the first Owens Valley newspaper. The house was converted in the 1940s into a hotel. When Sally and Fred Manecke acquired it in 1989, they painstakingly revitalized major structural elements—the water pressure is outrageous!—but also the finer details, such as the etched glass in the doorway transoms. A few antique pieces are complemented by new country-style furnishings. Historical black-and-white photographs of the Chalfants and early Bishop grace the hall walls.

Guests climb to the second-floor door of the Loft Room, then down six stairs to the bedroom. One suite is in the front dormer; it has an A-shaped parlor and separate bedroom. Around back is the deluxe suite, which has a full kitchen—and an antiques shop below.

The dining room has a fireplace and bay window. Here, the Maneckes serve a breakfast that might include Dutch babies, homemade bread, and homemade grape juice.

Address: *213 Academy St., Bishop, CA 93514, tel. 619/872-1790.*
Accommodations: *7 double rooms with baths, 3 suites.*
Amenities: *Air-conditioning, TV in parlor and suites, guest phone; off-street parking, airport pickup, antiques shop.*
Rates: *$60–$90; full breakfast, evening ice-cream sundaes. AE, MC, V.*
Restrictions: *No smoking indoors, no pets.*

Clover Valley Mill House

The Clover Valley Mill House is intimately connected with the history of the tiny sawmill town of Loyalton, abutted by the Tahoe National Forest on one side and the flat Sierra Valley on the other. A cream-colored Colonial Revival structure that sits on an acre of manicured lawn, it was built for the town's mill owner in 1906. Leslie Hernandez bought it in 1986 from the mill's last supervisor.

Leslie has lavished the house with antiques and family heirlooms. In the sprawling living room, a beautiful oak sideboard displays a collection of Waterford crystal. The Sugarpine suite is the most alluring of the four lovely guest rooms, with a lacy daybed in the sitting room and, in the bedroom, a four-poster pine bed and matching armoire on a sky-blue dhurrie rug. After breakfast in the sunny dining nook or on the deck, you can play lawn games or just relax on the porch.

Address: *Railroad Ave. and S. Mill St., Box 928, Loyalton, CA 96118, tel. 916/993-4819.*
Accommodations: *3 double rooms (1 with half-bath) share 1 full bath; 1 suite.*
Amenities: *Phone in rooms, TV with VCR in living room; horseshoes, volleyball, tetherball.*
Rates: *$75–$105; full breakfast. MC, V.*
Restrictions: *No smoking indoors, no pets.*

Deer Run Ranch

David and Muffy Vhay searched the West for the perfect spot to build their bed-and-breakfast, and they found it—right on the Washoe Valley ranch where Muffy grew up. The Deer Run, which has been in her family for more than 60 years, is a working alfalfa ranch nestled against the Virginia Range (of Virginia City fame), with a view across the valley of the Sierra and Washoe Lake. On the grounds are a pond (used for skating in the winter, ice-skates supplied), swimming pool, horseshoe pit, sled run, garden, small orchard, and a potter's studio where Muffy turns out all the plates and containers used at the ranch. There's hardly enough time to take advantage of all the activities this amenities-packed B&B makes available.

The two guest rooms have handmade quilts, wall-to-wall window seats with built-in magazine racks, and ranching decor. Breakfast—specialty eggs, homebaked bread, fruits and vegetables from the grounds—is served in the guest sitting room, which has a fireplace, kitchenette, and library.

Address: *5440 Eastlake Blvd., Washoe Valley, NV 89704, tel. 702/882-3643.*
Accommodations: *2 double rooms with baths.*
Amenities: *TV with VCR available; skating, swimming, sledding, barbecue.*
Rates: *$75-$85; full breakfast, refreshments. AE, MC, V.*
Restrictions: *No smoking indoors; 2-night minimum on holiday weekends.*

Genoa House Inn

Genoa is the oldest town in Nevada, its location chosen by Church of Jesus Christ of Latter-Day Saints settlers in 1851 for its scenery—it's right at the bottom of the Sierra's eastern scarp—and agricultural and commercial potential. The Genoa House Inn, which was erected in 1872, is one of the oldest houses in the state. It's a compact two-story Victorian, owned since 1986 by congenial Linda and Bob Sanfilippo.

One of the previous owners tore off the second story and replaced it with a cross-gable two-bedroom addition, full of angles and corners, nooks and crannies. One guest room upstairs has mahogany antiques and a Jacuzzi; the other has 100-year-old stained-glass windows, an antique fainting couch, and a bi-level shower stall. The new

guest room downstairs has a private entrance; the bath features a 1906 Wolf tank toilet.

A coffee tray at the door greets guests in the morning. Breakfast, served in a small dining room, is usually coddled eggs, cinnamon rolls, and fruit. Use of the facilities at Walley's Hot Springs nearby (mineral baths, heated swimming pool, sauna, and exercise equipment) is included in the rates.

Address: *180 Nixon St., Box 141, Genoa, NV 89411, tel. 702/782-7075.*
Accommodations: *3 rooms with baths.*
Amenities: *Off-street parking.*
Rates: *$99-$120; full breakfast, refreshments. AE, MC, V.*
Restrictions: *No smoking indoors, no pets. 2-night minimum on holiday weekends.*

Gold Hill Hotel

Gold was discovered on Gold Hill in 1859, in what was still the far western edge of Utah territory. Though its sister town, Virginia City, is far more famous, Gold Hill was there first. Its hotel hearkens back to the early Comstock Lode days—making it the oldest operating inn, and one of the oldest buildings, in Nevada.

There's a noticeable tilt to the floors in the hotel's 135-year-old wing. The original Great Room is now the lounge, with a stone floor and fireplace, stucco walls with exposed brick, and period furniture. The cozy bar was added in 1960; the restaurant opened in 1984.

The four guest rooms in the old stone structure are small and a bit porous. Of the seven rooms in the new wing, built in 1987, four are suite sized and feature stone fireplaces, wet bars, balconies, and large, modern baths. The all-wood Guest House across the road holds two one-bedroom suites with full kitchens.

Address: *Hwy. 342 Gold Hill, NV (mailing address: Box 304, Virginia City, CA 89440), tel. 702/847–0111.*
Accommodations: *4 rooms (2 with baths) in original wing, 7 rooms with baths in newer wing, 2 one-bedroom suites.*
Amenities: *Clock radio, phone in rooms, TV in newer wing rooms, 4 rooms with fireplace.*
Rates: *$35–$115; Continental breakfast. AE, MC, V.*
Restrictions: *2-day minimum weekends and holidays, with reservations more than 2 weeks in advance.*

Haus Bavaria

The first bed-and-breakfast in Incline Village, built by a German couple in 1980, the two-level, stucco-and-wood Haus Bavaria is still the only B&B at the north end of the lake. It's now owned by cheerful Bick Hewitt, who left an airline job in San Diego to run the inn in 1990. Haus Bavaria is a good alternative to the impersonal condos and cacophonous casinos of the east-lake resort towns.

After a strenuous day on the slopes—or a lazy one on the beach—guests can relax on the leather sling-chairs in the living room, where a wood stove waits ready to be fired up when needed. The simple guest rooms have Danish-style dressers and headboards and sliding glass doors that open onto private decks.

Breakfast, served in the knotty-pine dining room, might include the terrific cornmeal pancakes that Bick makes from his Texan grandmother's recipe. Guests are provided passes to Incline's private beaches and recreation center.

Address: *593 N. Dyer Circle, Box 3308, Incline Village, NV 89450, tel. 702/831–6122 or 800/731–6222.*
Accommodations: *5 double rooms with baths.*
Amenities: *TV in living room, guest phone, mudroom; off-street parking, hot tub.*
Rates: *$90–$110; full breakfast. AE, D, MC, V.*
Restrictions: *No smoking indoors, no pets.*

The Matlick House

About 50 yards off Highway 395 and sheltered by a row of towering trees, the Matlick House is a good stopover for those touring the eastern side of the Sierras. This stately, gray-and-pink house with a double veranda, the only three-story house in Bishop, was built in 1906 by Alan Matlick, an Owens Valley pioneer. It took two years for friendly Nanette Robidart to restore the mansion, which she opened as a B&B in 1987.

The dark woods with which Nanette has furnished the spacious parlor—an impressive claw-foot settee with massive curved arms, an antique recliner, and a European burled-wood armoire—complement the original cherry-wood fireplace. Nanette and her mother made the quilts in all of the bedrooms. The prettiest room, Lenna,

has a white-iron bed, an Eastlake chair, and a pink quilted settee. A traditional American breakfast of scrambled eggs, bacon, and homemade biscuits is served in the cheery dining room.

Address: *1313 Rowan La., Bishop, CA 93514, tel. 619/873-3133.*
Accommodations: *5 double rooms with baths.*
Amenities: *Air-conditioning in rooms, TV in common area; off-street parking.*
Rates: *$75-$85; full breakfast, afternoon refreshments. No credit cards.*
Restrictions: *No smoking indoors, no pets.*

Nenzel Mansion

The Nenzel family is the latest in a long line of owners since this mansion was built in 1910. The three-story, 8,000-square-foot house faces downtown Gardnerville and the Sierra Nevada beyond; Carson Valley ranch land surrounds it on the other three sides.

The large foyer's 85-year-old wallpaper has been lovingly restored, and the four archways retain their original, custom-rounded double doors. The Great Room parlor seats 100 comfortably for wedding ceremonies, or 40 for sit-down dinner. Twelve-foot ceilings enhance the open, airy ambience.

Upstairs, the Honeymoon Suite is done up in white-and-blue florals; the bath has a bidet and 60-year-old raspberry-colored tiles. The other three rooms

come in wicker, brass, and antique themes.

Egg soufflés, Texas toast, biscuits, and fruit are served in the formal dining room, under a massive 20-bulb crystal chandelier, by innkeepers Chris and Virginia Nenzel.

Address: *1431 Ezell St., Gardnerville, NV 89410, tel. 702/782-7644.*
Accommodations: *1 room with bath, 2 rooms share bath, 1 suite.*
Amenities: *Coffee for early risers, laundry facilities; off-street parking, tree swing.*
Rates: *$70-$100; full breakfast. AE, MC, V.*
Restrictions: *No smoking indoors, no pets.*

Rainbow Tarns

This rustic 1920s log house is tucked up against a hillside of enormous granite boulders that seem to defy gravity; it's fronted by three tranquil ponds where trout from nearby Crowley Lake come to spawn. In 1988, Lois Miles, a tanned and hospitable outdoorswoman with a long white braid, bought the 3-acre property, halfway between Bishop and Mammoth Lakes at 7,000 feet, and opened a bed-and-breakfast. She renovated it in 1992, adding skylights, two of the brightest bathrooms you'll ever see, a new kitchen, and a loft for herself.

Everywhere you rest your eyes in this relaxing house there is an interesting artifact with a long story behind it, which Lois delights in relating: local crafts and photographs, bricks for the kitchen, family-made furniture, antiques.

Lois's breakfast feasts usually include eggs from her chicken coop and Costa Rican coffee. Once you're good and fed, all you have to do is step outside, where all this beautiful country is yours to enjoy.

Address: *Rainbow Tarns Dr. (off Crowley Lake Dr.), Rte. 1, Box 1097, Crowley Lake, CA 93546, tel. 619/ 935-4556.*
Accommodations: *3 double rooms with baths.*
Amenities: *Whirlpool bath in 2 rooms, trout ponds, horse stables and corral (for guests' horses).*
Rates: *$95–$125; full breakfast, afternoon refreshments. No credit cards.*
Restrictions: *No smoking indoors, no pets (except horses); 2-night minimum on weekends, 3-night minimum on holiday weekends.*

Rockwood Lodge

Be prepared to remove your shoes upon entering this quietly elegant inn; shoeless, you'll save *and* savor the plush white carpet. Innkeepers Lou Reinkens and Connie Stevens are clearly proud of their luxurious, antiques-filled inn on the west shore of Lake Tahoe—one of the last to be constructed in the Old Tahoe style, with knotty-pine paneling, brass fixtures, feather beds, tile baths, large front patio with stone fireplace, and a lake view.

The lodge was built in 1939 by Bay Area–dairyman Carlos Rookwood with winnings from the Irish Sweepstakes. Its adornments are as striking as the architecture: original Dalí and Boulanger prints, an 18th-century cobbler's bench in the Rubicon Bay Room, and a 7-foot soaking tub and

shower for two in the shared bathroom.

The inn makes a good headquarters for a Tahoe visit. It's located across the street from a public beach and marina, where you can rent boats, and is a short distance from ski lifts and bike and cross-country trails.

Address: *5295 W. Lake Blvd., Box 226, Homewood, CA 96141, tel. 916/525-5273 or 800/538-2463, fax 916/525-5949.*
Accommodations: *3 double rooms with baths, 2 doubles share bath.*
Amenities: *Robes; mudroom with ski storage, barbecue.*
Rates: *$100–$200; full breakfast, afternoon refreshments. No credit cards.*
Restrictions: *No smoking indoors, no pets; 2-night minimum on weekends, 3-night minimum on holidays.*

White Horse Inn

When interior designer Diann Lloyd and her builder husband, Russ, moved from Palm Desert to open a B&B in Mammoth Lake, they bought a rather nondescript 1970s ski house. But Diann drew on the acquisitions of her extensive travels to decorate the guest rooms in a delightfully fanciful style.

The most dramatic room evokes Mammoth's Chinese Quarter from the gold-rush days: It has a Chinese wedding bed with a carved canopy, an intricately carved desk, a green dragon urn, lacquered chests, and eye-popping emerald-green carpeting and walls. Everything in the Blizzard Room is white: the snow-textured walls, the English featherbed, and the moire swag drapery. The Tribal Room features a twin bed draped with an old

Amish buggy blanket and walls covered in camel suede. Guests meet on contemporary American territory in the rumpus room, where they gather around the pool table, fireplace, kitchen, or VCR. Hostess Lynn Criss dishes up a big breakfast of soufflés, quiche, homemade breads and baked goods, and fruit.

Address: *2180 Old Mammoth Rd., Box 2326, Mammoth Lakes, CA 93546, tel. 619/924-3656.*
Accommodations: *4 double rooms with baths.*
Amenities: *Laundry facilities, pool table, fireplace, TV with VCR, mudroom.*
Rates: *$75-$150; full breakfast, afternoon refreshments. AE, D, DC, MC, V.*
Restrictions: *No smoking indoors, no pets.*

The Yosemite Peregrine

Finding a place to spend the night in Yosemite can seem as difficult as climbing the face of Half Dome, and if you do manage to get lodging in the valley, you've got to contend with crowds and auto fumes. A much better option has been provided since 1993 by Yosemite's federal magistrate Don Pitts and his artist wife, Kay, who opened a bed-and-breakfast just inside the southern edge of the national park near the intersection of Hwy. 41 and the road to Badger Pass at 6,200 feet.

Picture windows afford stunning long views of the Sierra and short views of the plentiful local birdlife. Fireplaces made of local rock in each guest room are subtly patterned to reflect the room's theme. Kay has painted murals for two of the rooms and put up attractive hand-painted curtains in all of them.

Breakfast is served in the cathedral-ceilinged dining area on a big redwood burl table, or out on the deck. If you're itching to head outdoors, Don and Kay will send you off for a nearby hike or a cross-country ski trip with breakfast packed to go.

Address: *7509 Henness Circle, Box 306, Yosemite, CA 95389, tel. 209/372-8517 or 800/396-3639.*
Accommodations: *3 double rooms with baths.*
Amenities: *Fireplace and refrigerators in rooms, spa in 1 room, TV room; outdoor hot tub, off-street parking.*
Rates: *$100-$150; full breakfast, evening hors d'oeuvres. MC, V.*
Restrictions: *No smoking indoors, no pets.*

Directory 1
Alphabetical

A

Abigail's 170
The Alamo Square Inn 105
Albion House Inn 105
The Alpenhaus 207
Amber House 171
Anaheim Country Inn 42
Apple Lane Inn 75
Apples Bed & Breakfast Inn 22
Applewood 154
Archbishops Mansion 96
Auberge du Soleil 135

B

Babbling Brook Inn 76
Ballard Inn 61
Bancroft Hotel 123
Bath Street Inn 61
Bayberry Inn 62
Bayview Hotel 85
The Beach House 62
The Bed and Breakfast Inn 106
Bed and Breakfast Inn at La Jolla 12
Bella Maggiore Inn 63
Beltane Ranch 142
Blackthorne Inn 123
Blue Lantern Inn 34
Blue Quail Inn 51
Blue Spruce Inn 85
The Blue Whale Inn 52
Bock's Bed and Breakfast 106
The Boonville Hotel 136
Brannan Cottage Inn 142
Brookside Farm 7
Busch and Heringlake Country Inn 207

C

The Cain House 201
Camellia Inn 137
Camino Hotel 187
Campbell Ranch Inn 143
Carriage House 42
The Carriage House 24
Carter House 161
Casa del Mar 118
Casa Madrona Hotel 119
Casa Tropicana 35
The Centrella 86
Chalfant House 208
Channel Road Inn 36
Chateau Du Lac 23
Chateau Tivoli 97
The Cheshire Cat 53
The Chichester-McKee House 187
Christmas House 37
City Hotel 182
Cliff Crest Bed and Breakfast Inn 86
Clover Valley Mill House 208
The Coloma Country Inn 183
Combellack-Blair House 188
Cooper House 188
The Cottage 12
Country Rose Inn 87
The Court Street Inn 189
Cowper Inn 124
Cross Roads Inn 143

D

Deer Run Ranch 209
Dunbar House, 1880 189

E

The Eagle Inn 63
Eagle's Nest 24
East Brother Light Station 124
Eiler's Inn 43
El Dorado Hotel 144
El Encanto 54
"An Elegant Victorian Mansion" 161

F

Fallon Hotel 190
The Feather Bed 202
Flume's End 190
The Foxes Bed and Breakfast Inn 184

G

The Gaige House 144
Garden Street Inn 64
Gatehouse Inn 87
Genoa House Inn 209
Gingerbread Mansion 155
Glenborough Inn 64
Gold Hill Hotel 210
Gold Mountain Manor 25
Golden Gate Hotel 107
Gosby House 88
Gramma's Inn 125
Grandmère's 191
Green Gables Inn 77
Grey Gables 191
Grey Whale Inn 162
Groveland Hotel 185

H

Happy Landing Inn 88
Harbor House 156

Harkey House *175*
Hartley House *172*
Harvest Inn *145*
Haus Bavaria *210*
The Headlands Inn *162*
Healdsburg Inn on the Plaza *145*
The Heirloom *192*
The Hensley House *125*
Heritage Park Bed & Breakfast Inn *8*
High Country Inn *203*
Highland Ranch *138*
Hope-Merrill House *146*
Hotel Griffon *107*
Hotel Triton *98*

I

Imperial Hotel *192*
Indian Creek *193*
Ingleside Inn *13*
Inn at Depot Hill *78*
The Inn at Fawnskin *25*
Inn at Laguna Beach *43*
Inn on Mt. Ada *38*
Inn at the Opera *99*
Inn at Rancho Santa Fe *9*
Inn San Francisco *108*
Inn at 657 *44*
Inn at Summer Hill *65*
Inn at Union Square *108*

J

J. Patrick House *65*
The Jabberwock *79*
Jackson Court *109*
James Court Hotel *109*
Johnson's Country Inn *173*
Joshua Grindle Inn *157*
Julian Hotel *13*

K

Kenwood Inn *139*
Korakia Pensione *14*

L

La Mer *66*
Lake Oroville Bed & Breakfast *175*
Larkmead *140*
Loma Vista Bed and Breakfast *10*
Lord Mayor's Inn *39*
Los Olivos Grand Hotel *55*

M

Madrona Manor *141*
Maison Fleurie *146*
Malibu Beach Inn *40*
Mangels House *80*
Mansion Inn *44*
The Mansions Hotel *100*
Martine Inn *81*
The Matlick House *211*
The Mill Rose Inn *120*
Mill Valley Inn *126*
The Monte Cristo *110*
Montecito Inn *66*
Mountain Home Inn *126*

N

Nenzel Mansion *211*
New England Ranch *204*

O

Olallieberry Inn *67*
Old Monterey Inn *82*
Old Thyme Inn *127*
Old Turner Inn *45*
Old Yacht Club Inn *56*
The Olive House *67*
Orchard Hill Country Inn *14*

P

The Parsonage *57*
Pelican Cove Inn *15*

The Pelican Inn *121*
Petite Auberge *110*
Pickford House *68*
Pillar Point Inn *127*
Portofino Beach Hotel *45*
Post Ranch Inn *83*
Power's Mansion Inn *193*

Q

Quail Mountain *147*
The Queen Anne *101*

R

Rachel's Inn *163*
Rainbow Tarns *212*
Rancho Valencia Resort *11*
Red Castle Inn *186*
Rockwood Lodge *212*
The Romantique Lakeview Lodge *26*
Roundstone Farm *128*
The Ryan House *194*

S

St. Orres *158*
Salisbury House *46*
San Ysidro Ranch *58*
Sandpiper Inn *89*
Savoy Hotel *111*
Scotia Inn *163*
Scripps Inn *15*
Sea View Inn *89*
Seal Beach Inn and Gardens *41*
Serenity, A Bed & Breakfast Inn *194*
Seven Gables Inn *90*
The Shaw House Inn *164*
The Sherman House *102*
Simpson House Inn *59*
Sonoma Hotel *147*
Sorensen's *205*
Spencer House *111*
The Squibb House *68*

The Stanford Inn by
the Sea *164*
The Sterling Hotel
176
Stonehouse Inn *90*
Stonepine *84*
Summerland Inn *69*
Switzerland Haus *26*

T

Ten Inverness Way *128*
Thistle Dew Inn *148*
Tiffany Inn *69*
Timberhill Ranch *159*
Tres Palmas Bed and
Breakfast *16*

U

Union Gardens *122*
Union Hotel/Victorian
Mansion *60*
Union Street Inn *112*
The Upham *70*

V

Venice Beach House *46*
Victorian Inn on the
Park *103*
Victorian Manor *176*
Villa Rosa *70*
Villa Royale *16*
Vintners Inn *148*

W

Washington Square Inn
112
The Whale Watch Inn
by the Sea *160*
White Horse Inn *213*
White Sulphur Springs
206
White Swan Inn *104*
Wine & Roses Country
Inn *174*

Y

The Yosemite
Peregrine *213*

Directory 2
Geographical

A

Amador City
Imperial Hotel *192*
Anaheim
Anaheim Country Inn *42*
Angels Camp
Cooper House *188*
Aptos
Apple Lane Inn *75*
Bayview Hotel *85*
Mangels House *80*
Auburn
Power's Mansion Inn *193*
Avalon
Inn on Mt. Ada *38*
Old Turner Inn *45*

B

Ballard
Ballard Inn *61*
Benicia
Union Gardens *122*
Berkeley
Bancroft Hotel *123*
Gramma's Inn *125*
Berry Creek
Lake Oroville Bed & Breakfast *175*
Big Bear City
Gold Mountain Manor *25*
Big Bear Lake
Apples Bed & Breakfast Inn *22*
Eagle's Nest *24*
Switzerland Haus *26*
Big Sur
Post Ranch Inn *83*
Bishop
Chalfant House *208*
The Matlick House *211*
Boonville
The Boonville Hotel *136*

Bridgeport
The Cain House *201*

C

Calistoga
Brannan Cottage Inn *142*
Larkmead *140*
Quail Mountain *147*
Cambria
The Beach House *62*
The Blue Whale Inn *52*
J. Patrick House *65*
Olallieberry Inn *67*
Pickford House *68*
The Squibb House *68*
Camino
Camino Hotel *187*
Capitola by the Sea
Inn at Depot Hill *78*
Carlsbad
Pelican Cove Inn *15*
Carmel
Happy Landing Inn *88*
Sandpiper Inn *89*
Sea View Inn *89*
Stonehouse Inn *90*
Carmel Valley
Stonepine *84*
Cazadero
Timberhill Ranch *159*
Chico
Johnson's Country Inn *173*
Clio
White Sulphur Springs *206*
Coloma
The Coloma Country Inn *183*
Columbia
City Hotel *182*
Fallon Hotel *190*
Crowley Lake
Rainbow Tarns *212*

D

Dana Point
Blue Lantern Inn *34*
Dulzura
Brookside Farm *7*

E

Elk
Harbor House *156*
Eureka
Carter House *161*
"An Elegant Victorian Mansion" *161*

F

Fawnskin
The Inn at Fawnskin *25*
Ferndale
Gingerbread Mansion *155*
The Shaw House Inn *164*
Fort Bragg
Grey Whale Inn *162*

G

Gardnerville
Nenzel Mansion *211*
Genoa
Genoa House Inn *209*
Geyserville
Campbell Ranch Inn *143*
Hope-Merrill House *146*
Glen Ellen
Beltane Ranch *142*
The Gaige House *144*
Gold Hill
Gold Hill Hotel *210*
Groveland
Groveland Hotel *185*

Gualala
St. Orres *158*
The Whale Watch Inn
   by the Sea *160*

H

Half Moon Bay
The Mill Rose Inn *120*
Old Thyme Inn *127*
Healdsburg
Camellia Inn *137*
Healdsburg Inn on the
   Plaza *145*
Madrona Manor *141*
Homewood
Rockwood Lodge *212*
Hope Valley
Sorensen's *205*

I

Incline Village
Haus Bavaria *210*
Inverness
Ten Inverness Way *128*
Inverness Park
Blackthorne Inn *123*
Ione
The Heirloom *192*

J

Jackson
The Court Street Inn
   189
Julian
Julian Hotel *13*
Orchard Hill Country
   Inn *14*

K

Kenwood
Kenwood Inn *139*

L

La Jolla
Bed and Breakfast Inn
   at La Jolla *12*
Scripps Inn *15*

Laguna Beach
Carriage House *42*
Eiler's Inn *43*
Inn at Laguna Beach *43*
Lake Arrowhead
The Carriage House *24*
Chateau Du Lac *23*
The Romantique
   Lakeview Lodge *26*
Lodi
Wine & Roses Country
   Inn *174*
Long Beach
Lord Mayor's Inn *39*
Los Alamos
Union Hotel/Victorian
   Mansion *60*
Los Angeles
Inn at 657 *44*
Salisbury House *46*
Los Olivos
Los Olivos Grand Hotel
   55
Loyalton
Clover Valley Mill
   House *208*

M

Malibu
Maliibu Beach Inn *40*
Mammoth Lakes
White Horse Inn *213*
Marina del Rey
Mansion Inn *44*
Mendocino
The Headlands Inn *162*
Joshua Grindle Inn *157*
Rachel's Inn *163*
The Stanford Inn by
   the Sea *164*
Mill Valley
Mill Valley Inn *126*
Mountain Home Inn
   126
Montecito
Montecito Inn *66*
San Ysidro Ranch *58*
Monterey
The Jabberwock *79*
Old Monterey Inn *82*
Muir Beach
The Pelican Inn *121*

Murphys
Dunbar House, 1880
   189

N

Nevada City
Flume's End *190*
Grandmère's *191*
Red Castle Inn *186*
Newcastle
Victorian Manor *176*
Newport Beach
Portofino Beach Hotel
   45

O

Olema
Roundstone Farm *128*

P

Pacific Grove
Gatehouse Inn *87*
Gosby House *88*
Green Gables Inn *77*
Martine Inn *81*
Seven Gables Inn *90*
Palm Desert
Tres Palmas Bed and
   Breakfast *16*
Palm Springs
Ingleside Inn *13*
Korakia Pensione *14*
Villa Royale *16*
Palo Alto
Cowper Inn *124*
Philo
Highland Ranch *138*
Placerville
The Chichester-McKee
   House *187*
Combellack-Blair
   House *188*
Plymouth
Indian Creek *193*
Pocket Canyon
Applewood *154*
Point Richmond
East Brother Light
   Station *124*

Princeton-by-the-Sea
Pillar Point Inn *127*

Q

Quincy
The Feather Bed *202*
New England Ranch *204*

R

Rancho Cucamonga
Christmas House *37*
Rancho Santa Fe
Rancho Valencia
  Resort *11*
Rutherford
Auberge du Soleil *135*
Inn at Rancho Santa Fe *9*

S

Sacramento
Abigail's *170*
Amber House *171*
Hartley House *172*
The Sterling Hotel *176*
St. Helena
Harvest Inn *145*
San Clemente
Casa Tropicana *35*
San Diego
The Cottage *12*
Heritage Park Bed &
  Breakfast Inn *8*
San Francisco
The Alamo Square Inn *105*
Albion House Inn *105*
Archbishops Mansion *96*
The Bed and Breakfast
  Inn *106*
Bock's Bed and
  Breakfast *106*
Chateau Tivoli *97*
Golden Gate Hotel *107*
Hotel Griffon *107*
Hotel Triton *98*

Inn at the Opera *99*
Inn San Francisco *108*
Inn at Union Square *108*
Jackson Court *109*
James Court Hotel *109*
The Mansions Hotel *100*
The Monte Cristo *110*
Petite Auberge *110*
The Queene Anne *101*
Savoy Hotel *111*
The Sherman House *102*
Spencer House *111*
Union Street Inn *112*
White Swan Inn *104*
San Jose
The Hensley House *125*
San Luis Obispo
Garden Street Inn *64*
San Martin
Country Rose Inn *87*
Santa Barbara
Bath Street Inn *61*
Bayberry Inn *62*
Blue Quail Inn *51*
The Cheshire Cat *53*
The Eagle Inn *63*
El Encanto *54*
Glenborough Inn *64*
Old Yacht Club Inn *56*
The Olive House *67*
The Parsonage *57*
Simpson House Inn *59*
Tiffany Inn *69*
The Upham *70*
Victorian Inn on the
  Park *103*
Villa Rosa *70*
Washington Square Inn *112*
Santa Cruz
Babbling Brook Inn *76*
The Centrella *86*
Cliff Crest Bed and
  Breakfast Inn *86*
Santa Monica
Channel Road Inn *36*
Santa Rosa
Vintners Inn *148*

Sausalito
Casa Madrona Hotel *119*
Scotia
Scotia Inn *163*
Seal Beach
Seal Beach Inn and
  Gardens *41*
Sierra City
Busch and Heringlake
  Country Inn *207*
High Country Inn *203*
Sonoma
El Dorado Hotel *144*
Sonoma Hotel *147*
Thistle Dew Inn *148*
Sonora
The Ryan House *194*
Serenity, A Bed &
  Breakfast Inn *194*
Soquel
Blue Spruce Inn *85*
Stinson Beach
Casa del Mar *118*
Summerland
Inn at Summer Hill *65*
Summerland Inn *69*
Sutter Creek
The Foxes Bed and
  Breakfast Inn *184*
Grey Gables *191*

T

Tahoma
The Alpenhaus *207*
Temecula
Loma Vista Bed and
  Breakfast *10*

V

Venice
Venice Beach House *46*
Ventura
Bella Maggiore Inn *63*
La Mer *66*

W

Washoe Valley
Deer Run Ranch *209*

Y

Yosemite
The Yosemite
  Peregrine *213*

Yountville
Cross Roads Inn *143*
Maison Fleurie *146*
Yuba City
Harkey House *175*

Join us in updating the next edition of your Fodor's guide

Title of Guide:

1 Hotel ☐ Restaurant ☐ *(check one)*

Name

Number/Street

City/State/Country

Comments

2 Hotel ☐ Restaurant ☐ *(check one)*

Name

Number/Street

City/State/Country

Comments

3 Hotel ☐ Restaurant ☐ *(check one)*

Name

Number/Street

City/State/Country

Comments

Your Name *(optional)*

Address

General Comments

Fodor's Travel Guides

Available at bookstores everywhere, or call 1–800–533–6478, 24 hours a day.

U.S. Guides

Alaska

Arizona

Boston

California

Cape Cod, Martha's Vineyard, Nantucket

The Carolinas & the Georgia Coast

Chicago

Colorado

Florida

Hawaii

Las Vegas, Reno, Tahoe

Los Angeles

Maine, Vermont, New Hampshire

Maui

Miami & the Keys

New England

New Orleans

New York City

Pacific North Coast

Philadelphia & the Pennsylvania Dutch Country

The Rockies

San Diego

San Francisco

Santa Fe, Taos, Albuquerque

Seattle & Vancouver

The South

The U.S. & British Virgin Islands

USA

The Upper Great Lakes Region

Virginia & Maryland

Waikiki

Walt Disney World and the Orlando Area

Washington, D.C.

Foreign Guides

Acapulco, Ixtapa, Zihuatanejo

Australia & New Zealand

Austria

The Bahamas

Baja & Mexico's Pacific Coast Resorts

Barbados

Berlin

Bermuda

Brittany & Normandy

Budapest

Canada

Cancún, Cozumel, Yucatán Peninsula

Caribbean

China

Costa Rica, Belize, Guatemala

The Czech Republic & Slovakia

Eastern Europe

Egypt

Euro Disney

Europe

Florence, Tuscany & Umbria

France

Germany

Great Britain

Greece

Hong Kong

India

Ireland

Israel

Italy

Japan

Kenya & Tanzania

Korea

London

Madrid & Barcelona

Mexico

Montréal & Québec City

Morocco

Moscow & St. Petersburg

The Netherlands, Belgium & Luxembourg

New Zealand

Norway

Nova Scotia, Prince Edward Island & New Brunswick

Paris

Portugal

Provence & the Riviera

Rome

Russia & the Baltic Countries

Scandinavia

Scotland

Singapore

South America

Southeast Asia

Spain

Sweden

Switzerland

Thailand

Tokyo

Toronto

Turkey

Vienna & the Danube Valley